Paul's Travail

Tim Gallant

Draft Reviewers

DR MATTHEW COLVIN
Missionary, Philippines

DR JOHN FRAME
Professor of Systematic Theology and Philosophy
Reformed Theological Seminary

DR DON GARLINGTON
Former Adjunct Professor of New Testament
Tyndale Seminary

"A GREAT DEAL OF FRESH AND USEFUL WORK...."

DR NELSON KLOOSTERMAN
Director, Christian Worldview International

"ACCESSIBLE AND HELPFUL...."

Other Pactum Books by Tim Gallant

Feed My Lambs: Why the Lord's Table Should Be Restored to Covenant Children (2002)

These Are Two Covenants: A Reconsideration of Paul on the Mosaic Law (2012)

Sermons on Galatians (2012)

Paul's Travail

A REINTRODUCTION TO GALATIANS

Tim Gallant

A PACTUM NOVUM COMMENTARY

Pactum Reformanda Publishing

Tim Gallant, *Paul's Travail: A Reintroduction to Galatians*

Typesetting and cover design by Tim Gallant Creative (timgallantcreative.com).

Typeset in InDesign with Minion Pro and Poetica Std.

Published by: Pactum Reformanda Publishing (pactumbooks.com)

Cataloguing Data

Gallant, Tim, 1965–
Paul's travail: a reintroduction to Galatians (Pactum Novum Commentary)
Includes bibliographical references and index.
ISBN 978-0-9730119-7-5
1. Bible N.T. Galatians—Commentaries. I. Title

Contents

Introduction

THE DUTY OF A BIBLICAL COMMENTATOR is to wrestle with the text until he dances with it, and to dance with it until he surrenders to it. I am gifted neither as a wrestler nor as a dancer, but I have endeavoured, at least, to surrender to the letter of Paul to the Galatians.

Yet, even wrestling, dancing, and surrendering provide insufficient excuse to deepen the commentary pool. There are luminaries ancient, modern and in between, who have shed their learning and erudition upon the work of biblical interpretation, and Galatians has been given its share of attention.[1]

A commentator therefore needs some sort of justification to add to the literature. One should seek to advance our collective understanding of Scripture in some way, whether through a freshness of statement, an additional insight into pastoral application, or through at least incremental advance in exegetical understanding. I do not claim the former for myself, and consider my abilities rather indifferent as to the second. I am thus primarily attempting to provide something of the latter, the success of which will remain to the reader to assess.

The incremental advance which I principally hope to offer is an effort at a more coherent global reading of the letter than is usually attempted. More specifically, this general effort will key on several areas toward that end:

1 To my knowledge, this is the first commentary to employ the general thesis of Joseph P. Braswell regarding Gal 3:10, and work out its implications for the global interpretation of the

1 In this light, I would be remiss if I failed to salute, in particular, the works of the Golden Mouth (John Chrysostom) among the ancients, and that of Ben Witherington among the moderns—there are profound similarities in my reading to both, and I am indebted to both, as well as to a host of others, not least Richard Hays, whose seminal work regarding the faith of Christ bears fruit on page after page of this commentary.

letter.[2] In my view, Braswell's argument that *under a curse* does not mean *accursed*, but rather something along the lines of *subject to a curse-bearing oath*, is not merely intriguing; it helps resolve rather insuperable difficulties in the near context, and provides a way forward to a more natural and coherent reading of Paul's overall narrative flow. For more on that subject, be sure not only to study the relevant section in the Exposition, but also Appendix 1, "The Reverse of Ebal in Gal 3:10–14."

2 I have sought to provide an admittedly brief and tendential outline of certain aspects of how I believe Paul was handling the Old Testament Scriptures hermeneutically. While I am far from claiming the last word on these points, I believe my initial reflections will aid us in understanding what Paul is doing with the ancient texts in various places in the letter.

3 In my view, Paul's statement regarding crucifixion with the Messiah and living because the Messiah lives in him (2:20) is more programmatic than is generally recognized, and even since the work of Hays,[3] the role of the "faith of Christ" (*pistis Christou*) in connection with the present life of the believer is insufficiently appreciated. I believe the perspective of this verse—entailing a belief in an ongoing life-receiving relationship with the resurrected Jesus—pervades the letter, and recognition of this will further assist in a coherent reading.

4 Even by Paul's standards, Galatians is a special letter. Nowhere does the apostle propound abstract, dispassionate dogma. He argues with reason, but he is emotionally bound up in his subject matter. But the passion in his prose is nowhere more fiery than in this missive to the Galatians. Integrating the letter with the evidence of Acts, I have sought to work with chronological matters to show, not only why Paul is so desperate here, but

---

2 Joseph P. Braswell, "'The Blessing of Abraham' Versus 'The Curse of the Law': Another Look at Gal 3:10–13" (*WTJ*, 53 [1991]), 73–91.

3 Richard B. Hays, *The Faith of Jesus Christ: The Narrative Substructure of Galatians 3:1–4:11*, Second Edition (Grand Rapids: Eerdmans, 2002 [1983]).

also why the Galatians had arrived at this precipice to begin with.

There are other smaller ways I have tried to push the Galatians conversation forward, and doubtless some areas which I suppose are insights will turn out to be nothing more than my own idiosyncrasies. I beg the reader's forgiveness in advance. The Holy Spirit has gifted us with a perfect book, but the Church has not been granted similarly perfect interpreters, no matter how diligent.

I have made no attempt to accomplish everything. *Paul's Travail* does not, for instance, imitate Bruce's magisterial interaction with the literature,[4] nor Witherington's exhaustive analysis of rhetorical devices,[5] nor Burton's painstaking dissection of Greek.[6] I have simply sought to write a work which will present the reader with a coherent interpretation of the letter, and assist him or her in following the direction Paul's train of thought travels on its own terms.

It is my hope that you will enjoy the journey, and see the terrain through new eyes.

4 F. F. Bruce, *The Epistle to the Galatians, The New International Greek Testament Commentary* (Grand Rapids: Eerdmans, 1982).

5 Ben Witherington III, *Grace In Galatia: A Commentary on Paul's Letter to the Galatians* (Grand Rapids: Eerdmans, 1998).

6 Ernest De Witt Burton, *A Critical and Exegetical Commentary on the Epistle to the Galatians* (Edinburgh: T&T Clark, 1920).

Galatians as Biography

Galatians is pastoral pathos—the gut-level response of a mother's desperate love (to borrow from Paul himself in Galatians 4) to an existential threat to her children.

Seduced by a slaveholder's grip, the Galatian churches are not merely weighing religious options. In Paul's view, they stand upon the precipice of a black hole that would suck them into a whole different world.

That world is the old creation, a world they had left behind—nay, more: a world from which they had been divinely delivered by a daring and dramatic rescue, involving nothing short of the loving enfleshment and staggering death of God Himself.[1]

Galatians is the account of how the apostle to the Gentiles attempts to wrestle these, his children in faith, away from that precipice. If at times the letter seems overly forceful—or even, perhaps, manic—it is because the stakes are so high.

◆ ◆ ◆ ◆ ◆

So who are these children standing at the threshold of an abyss?

Reflection on the biblical evidence leads me to the position that Paul's addressees are a number of churches from his first missionary journey—the scattered churches of the regions of Pisidia and its neighbouring territories, where Paul and his partners preached and planted churches in Acts 13–14: Pisidian Antioch, Iconium, Lystra, and Derbe.[2]

---

1 We of course distinguish between the subject and object of death here. God is the active and acting subject in this death, even though the eternal God who is Life itself cannot be subject *to* death.

2 At the time, these regions were encompassed within the Roman province of Galatia (which later was reduced to the more ethnic "Gallican" area further to the north). Although some quarrel that these peoples would have objected to being called "Galatians" (as Paul does in 3:1), the fact remains that no other single term would have identified all of them. In any case, Paul is not above giving offense—in 3:1, the accompanying adjective, after all, is "foolish."

These were largely Gentile churches born in the fiery matrix of opposition and persecution, beginning in Pisidian Antioch. Paul's fellow Jews were jealous of his successful appeal to Gentiles (Acts 13:44–45). In the fallout to their opposition, Paul turned to preaching to the Gentiles, virtually exclusively (Acts 13:46–47). Unbelieving Jews then stirred up persecution, beyond Antioch itself. In Iconium, Paul and company faced stern opposition from both Jews and Gentiles, including the city's rulers. Even in Lystra, where for a time Paul and Barnabas were very nearly worshiped, Jews from Pisidian Antioch and Iconium succeeded in stirring up the crowds to stone Paul.

It is thus as the survivor of rocks thrown before their eyes that Paul can say to these disciples things such as, "I bear in my body the marks of the Lord Jesus" (Gal 6:17). They have seen firsthand how the apostle has entered into the Messiah's sufferings.

Onlookers thought Paul was killed by that stoning (Acts 14:19). But like his Master, Paul arose from the dead and carried on, making many disciples in one further city, Derbe.

At that point, Paul and his companions circled back to confirm the assemblies in the cities where they had already experienced such suffering, danger, and hardship—that is, Lystra, Iconium, and Antioch (Acts 14:21). On this return swing, they ordained local leadership in each of the churches (Acts 14:23).

Paul and his companions then left Galatia, preaching in Perga *en route* to Attalia, and from there sailed back to Syrian Antioch, their home base (Acts 14:24–26). There they stayed for an extended period of time (Acts 14:28).

♦ ♦ ♦ ♦ ♦

It is no accident that the next major event in the book of Acts is the so-called "Jerusalem council"—a meeting that takes place because men had arrived in Antioch from Judea and told the thriving Gentile Christian community that they could not be "saved" without being circumcised in terms of the Mosaic law (Acts 15:1).

What Acts does not tell us is that at the time of the arrival of these Judeans, Peter himself happened to be in Antioch. Moreover, these newcomers were not as "fringe" as we may be tempted to suppose; they are most likely to be identified with the associates of Jacob ("James") whom Paul mentions in Gal 2:11.[3]

As if the arrival of this circumcision party in Antioch were not disruptive enough, at this point the apostle Peter himself—and perhaps even more astonishing, for a time, Paul's closest co-worker, Barnabas—failed in courage and left off eating with Gentiles.[4] The implicit but strong message this communicated was that Christian Gentiles would not be in full fellowship with believing Jews unless and until they adopted Jewish customs, starting with circumcision.

It is precisely in the midst of this unexpected melee and confusion in his own home church that Paul must have received word that a very similar teaching had arisen among the freshly-planted Galatian churches—and they were showing every sign of wholesale capitulation.

Had the Galatians heard of the situation in Antioch with Peter and the "men from James"? It seems likely that they had; indeed, surely it was precisely this which had provided sufficient weight to the teachers' message in Galatia that the churches were now teetering on adopting circumcision *en masse*.[5]

Set within the context of this live grenade battle going on right on Paul's doorstep at that very moment, it should scarcely surprise us if Paul's reaction to the news from Galatia is impassioned, desperate, and indicative of alarm.

Indeed, were his reaction *not* characterized by such things—now,

---

3 We could nearly infer as much from Acts: the letter from Jerusalem which culminates the work of the "council" acknowledges that the troublers in Antioch "have gone out from us and troubled you with words" (Acts 15:24). James was not party to their purpose, still less behind it, as the Acts 15 letter makes clear. The point, however, is that the advocates of Gentile circumcision in Acts 15:1 were at that time fully identified with the Jerusalem church.

4 Barnabas' failure of nerve was surely very short, as we find him standing firm beside Paul in the disputes with the circumcision party as indicated by Acts 15:2.

5 See below. It is hard to imagine Paul would bring up such a damaging scenario as the one he depicts in Gal 2:11ff had not the Galatians already been aware of it. It also explains why the Galatian Gentiles, many of whom had probably been God-fearers in the local synagogues and yet had not been persuaded to be circumcised, would now suddenly think the proposition so compelling: the rite is (apparently) required by the chief Jerusalem apostle himself.

that would be remarkable for a pastoral heart such as Paul's.

◆ ◆ ◆ ◆ ◆

The reader may have noticed certain assumptions regarding my chronology above.[6] I do not, as many do, see an identification between the meeting of Acts 15 and that of Galatians 2:1–10. There are numerous reasons for this, at least three of which I find quite decisive.

1. In Galatians, Paul goes to great lengths to demonstrate, not only the divine origin of his gospel ("good news"), but also his independence from the other apostles. Surely even Paul would have preferred to appeal (also) to the unanswerable argument that all the apostles stood officially and definitively with him on the matter of circumcision—were the Acts 15 decision and letter available to him. But to the contrary, in my view, Paul writes Galatians at the one time when he would be fully justified to think he does indeed stand alone: no such public decision has been made; Peter has collapsed; and the disturbers who have arrived in Antioch are associates of Jacob, arguably the most influential man in the Jerusalem church. If we can put ourselves within Paul's viewpoint, it appears that even the pillars are crumbling. The fact is, the failure to mention the Acts 15 letter in Galatians is a *valid* argument from silence—Sherlock Holmes's quintessential "dog that did not bark."
2. The depiction of the meeting in Galatians 2 and that in Acts 15 differ in significant, and indeed *incompatible* ways, even though the matter of circumcision comes up on both occasions. The meeting mentioned in Galatians 2 is explicitly identified as a *private* encounter with the three Jerusalem pillars (2:2) and in response to a revelation (more on that below), whereas the Acts 15 meeting involves the whole body of elders of the Jerusalem church (probably dozens of men) and indeed the general congregation (note the distinction between the assembly, the apostles, and the elders in Acts 15:4), so that

6 For a more visual representation of the chronology, see Appendix 2.

numerous Christ-believers of the Pharisees were present (15:5). Moreover, unlike Gal 2, the occasion of the Acts 15 meeting is not in response to a revelation, but in response to conflict in Antioch between a circumcision party from Judea, on one hand, and Paul and Barnabas, on the other (15:1–2).

3 Equally critically, the force of Paul's argument for apostolic independence rests upon how often he has been to Jerusalem since his capture by the Messiah. Otherwise, his argument that his teaching is not dependent upon consultation with Jerusalem would be in jeopardy. Paul is very emphatic that following his conversion, at the time of writing, he has made but *two* visits to Jerusalem: those mentioned in 1:18–19, and in 2:1–10. This is decisive, because in Acts, there are clearly two visits by Paul to Jerusalem prior to Acts 15: (1) in Acts 9:26–30, when the believers were still afraid of him until Barnabas stepped in;[7] and (2) in 11:30, when Barnabas and Saul were sent from Antioch to Jerusalem with the material relief for the poor Judean Christians. This second trip was prompted by a prophecy by Agabus of impending famine (11:27–28; cf 12:25). This explains why Paul says that the second trip was "because of a revelation" (Gal 2:2)—that is, the prophecy of Agabus. It further explains that apparently random request by the pillars in 2:10, that Paul remember the poor. Peter, James, and John were not merely asking Paul to keep benevolence on his ministry agenda. Rather, in view of the agreement just made, that Paul's primary mission field was Gentiles, they requested that nonetheless he continue to provide poor relief for the believers in Jerusalem and Judea, *just as he had done on this very trip*, again in response to the Agabus prophecy.

Given these factors, it should be clear that the meeting Paul mentions in Galatians 2 is not the meeting described in Acts 15. Although

7 Note that although "the apostles" are mentioned, none are named. Most were doubtless elsewhere preaching. From Gal 1:18–19, we learn that at the time, Paul met only Peter and Jacob (usually rendered by English Bibles as *James*) the Lord's brother.

Paul had a private agreement with the Jerusalem pillars in this meeting prior to his first missionary journey, at the time he writes Galatians, what he sees out of Jerusalem (and Peter, in particular) is worrisome at best.

◆ ◆ ◆ ◆ ◆

Galatians is not a dogmatic treatise about faith and works, written within the vacuum of an academic's ivory tower. It is the fire-breathing response of a man under attack, defending his children who are equally under attack. And the attack has a specific form: the requirement is being pressed upon Messiah-believing Gentiles to become circumcised according to the terms of the Mosaic law.

Galatians as Hermeneutics

My starting point is that Galatians is divinely-inspired literature—that the ultimate Author who stands behind it is God—the divine Father who breathes out the divine Word by the divine Spirit.

Yet it is wrong to infer from this that Galatians (or any other biblical book) floats above the earth as if it were not *human* literature. We have already seen that the letter's character derives in large part from the current situation both in Galatia and in Paul's personal history and present experience. Both the content and "emotional flavour" bear the marks of that. Inspiration does not make the human writer a mere QWERTY keyboard upon which the Spirit administers His typing skills. Paul's letters commence in his *own* name; and rightly so, for he truly still is the *writer*.

The Spirit works through real active human persons, and who they are provides shape to what is written. The sovereign act of God is seen, not only in the periodic act of inspiration, but also in preparing *this* writer to pen *this* letter in *this* way—through all that has shaped his experiences, thinking, and reactions. Indeed, this is why the styles of different biblical writers are so different.

If we have much to learn about the letter to the Galatians in connection with Paul's experiences (some of which I have attempted to outline, however roughly, in "Galatians as Biography," above), to an even greater degree, we must recognize the place of the Hebrew Scriptures (the "Old Testament") in the letter. Galatians is what it is, not only because Paul is undergoing turmoil at a particular point, but also because Genesis and Leviticus and Isaiah and other Scriptures are what they are, and also, again, due to what Paul's understanding of them is.

It would be scarcely possible to unpack the whole biblical background to Galatians, since we would be in danger of requiring ourselves to expound the entire Hebrew canon. But at the risk of being reductionistic, I want to key on three particular biblical factors that carry decisive significance for what may be called Paul's "worldview" or "theological stance" articulated in Galatians:

1 The respective roles of Israel and the Gentiles, particularly in the foundational promise-narratives connected to Abraham;
2 The signals which the Mosaic law (Torah) gives concerning the human condition in its own era, especially its theme of "flesh";
3 The eschatological and covenantal significance of the advent of the promised Messiah, especially in the prospect of Isaiah.

It must be emphasized that Paul approached none of these as if it were a settled self-contained text or set of texts. Nor did he come as a blank slate. This observation is *apropos,* not merely because he (as all of us) necessarily had particular concerns and perceptions, nor even because he had been instructed by the influential teacher Gamaliel I (cf Acts 22:3).

As important as those things are, the greatest weight must be placed upon the dramatic reordering of Paul's world that occurred when the resurrected and ascended Messiah appeared to him at the very time when he was engaged in a most zealous prosecution of the law.

That event led to a massive Spirit-led seismic shift in Paul's thought, and of necessity, he came to read the ancient texts in a fundamentally new way. Both zeal and wisdom were now to be defined by Jesus, the crucified and resurrected Messiah, rather than by Torah.

"Salvation is of the Jews"

Before we get to the meat of Paul's own worldview shift, however, we would do well to recall that Paul's are not the only hermeneutics at play in Galatians. He is counteracting teachers who have their own reading of the Hebrew Scriptures.

We are not told much directly concerning these teachers. We know with certainty virtually nothing beyond the fundamental fact that they were calling upon Gentile Christians to become circumcised. We presume that their message coincided with that of the circumcision party from Jerusalem that made waves in Antioch, but we do not know if there was a formal relationship.

In truth, it has been suggested that these so-called "Judaizers"[1] may not have been ethnic Jews themselves. This thought arises from the present passive participle in Gal 6:13 (which could be translated something like "those who are being circumcised").[2] This possibility may impact a couple of things Paul says in the letter, but alters little so far as the main lines of interpretation are concerned.

The position of the Jerusalem "circumcision party" was that apart from circumcision, the Gentiles could not be "saved" (Acts 15:1). That invariably sounds like unadorned "works righteousness" to Protestant ears, and perhaps something of that was lurking, but we must be careful with our assumptions. Tying salvation to a ritual is not necessarily evidence of "merit theology" or "works righteousness." The apostles themselves had no qualms about associating salvation with another ritual: water baptism. Indeed, Paul himself in this very letter says that in baptism, one puts on the Messiah Himself (Gal 3:27), and in context, this is directly related to sonship to God, which is at least one perspective on salvation (Gal 3:26).

Similarly, see Peter's response to the question, "What must we do?" In his answer, he ties repentance and baptism in the name of Jesus the Messiah to the forgiveness of sins and the gift of the Spirit (Acts 2:37–38). This too was all in connection to salvation (see especially Acts 2:40–41), and on this point Peter is consistent both in his preaching in Acts and in his writing (1 Pet 3:21).

Moreover, Jesus Himself told the Samaritan woman, "Salvation is of the Jews" (John 4:22), and presumably that "of-ness" had to do with a whole complex of things which marked out who Jews were as God's people.

Now, of course, Jesus never implied that Gentiles could not be right

1 The traditional term is a bit of a misnomer. The Greek word *to Judaize* means *to adopt Jewish customs*, whereas "Judaizer" has usually been employed to refer to someone who was *compelling others* to adopt Jewish customs. The term, however, has stuck, although I generally try to reference the group as "the false teachers" or simply "the teachers."

2 Note that the Byzantine text tradition has a perfect participle, so does not lend itself to this view.

with God apart from circumcision. That was in fact not a requirement even during the period of the old covenant.[3] Circumcision was a covenant sign for Abraham's seed, and although Gentiles were permitted to join Israel by means of that sign (see e.g. Ex 12:48–49), over the course of history there clearly were many worshipers of the true God, who neither were circumcised nor were called upon to do so. (Compare, for example, Elisha's instructions to Naaman, or the form of the repentance of the Ninevites responding to Jonah's preaching.)

Jesus' own statement that salvation is of the Jews, therefore, did not imply that salvation is exclusively *for* the Jews, and first century Jewish notions[4] that Gentiles must be circumcised was in fact an innovation. In the view of the old covenant—and this is reflected in the context of John 4, as well—salvation is *through* Israel. It is in openness to the divine revelation safeguarded by God's covenant people that the *goyim* were to exercise saving faith.[5]

So then, how did the circumcision party arrive at the notion that Gentiles needed to be circumcised in order to be saved? Although there were some non-Christian Jews who were teaching that, the idea was not universal. Why did this thought take such deep hold within the early Christian Church?

It seems likely that the answer lies in the circumcision party's hermeneutical approach to the Hebrew Scriptures.

Circumcision was introduced in Genesis 17, in the story of Abraham. When God gave the rite to Abraham, He called it "My covenant," and identified it as a practice to be kept "throughout your generations."

---

3 A point concerning which Wright is somewhat misleading when he writes, "What Paul was objecting to was the imposition upon his converts of practices which are mandatory in scripture itself" ("4QMMT" 110). Circumcision and Torah were not binding upon *goyim*, even if they embraced Israel's God, unless they wanted to participate in Passover and similar temple-based activities.

4 Which were widespread, but not universal.

5 Cf Rom 3:1–2: One of the chief privileges of "the Jew" was that to them "the oracles of God" were entrusted. In the context of Rom 1:1–3, this was probably primarily a reference to the Messianic prophecies, but (as Jesus' sermon to the travelers to Emmaus shows) the entirety of the Hebrew Scriptures bore witness to Him and to God's saving purposes.

It seems likely that the Christian circumcision party understood that the relationship between the Messiah and the Church is a covenantal one, and given the language of permanence associated with the Abrahamic covenant, made a connection. This is particularly likely, given that God had earlier promised Abraham that all the families of the earth would be blessed in him (Gen 12:3).

Given this, it is to be expected that the advent of the Messiah implied a change in relationship with Gentiles. Apparently, the circumcision party took this change to mean: since Gentiles are now to be saved covenantally, rather than as outsiders, they must become children of Abraham through circumcision. No longer could believing Gentiles pretty well do what was right in their own eyes as "uncovenanted believers";[6] they now must be joined to the seed of Abraham.

Whether this is precisely the rationale behind the Judaizers' program, their hermeneutic was surely something along these lines. It looked like a biblical hermeneutic, with apparent loyalty both to the heritage of the Abrahamic promises and to the advent of Jesus the Messiah.

But Paul called it "another gospel." We need to see why.

Jews, Gentiles and Abraham

Undeniably, the story of Abraham plays a leading role in the pages of Galatians. As we have just seen, this was necessary due to the very nature of the controversy: circumcision was given to Abraham as a covenant sign (Gen 17). It is highly likely that the teachers influencing the Galatians were making a lot of hay with the Abraham story.

Still, this insight does not satisfactorily account for the full extent of the patriarch's place in the letter. For, whatever prompted Paul to write about Abraham here, there is no denying that in the discourse, the discussion of Abraham becomes, not merely an apologetic accounting for circumcision in the Genesis narratives, but a thoroughgoing *architecture* within which Paul defines Christian identity and explains the

6 *Uncovenanted* is perhaps a bit too strong of language. Many first-century Jews would have recognized the authority of the Noachic covenant over Gentiles, although the focus appears to have been primarily upon the commandments provided Noah, rather than a vital covenantal relationship.

relationship between new and old.[7]

Much could be said of Paul's use of the Abraham story—indeed, much *will* be said when we get to the textual analysis. But I am particularly interested here in taking initial note of how Paul deals with the interrelationship of Abraham's offspring and "the nations."

On the face of it, this relationship appears to be primarily one of contrast: the "covenant" is to be established with Abraham's "seed" (variously rendered as "descendants" or "offspring" in the modern English translations), and there is a biological dimension to this ("in *Isaac* your *seed* shall be called"). Even the promise that Abraham would be "father of *many nations*" would appear to have ethnic orientation, given that descendants such as Ishmael, Esau, and Midian became nations in their own right.[8]

But Paul recognizes something more fundamental. Even before God had commanded circumcision and changed Abram's name to "father of a multitude," He had promised the patriarch, "*In* you all the families of the earth shall be blessed" (Gen 12:3).[9]

That, for Paul, means that the Gentiles must be incorporated into Abraham (or is it, rather, that they must be incorporated into *Abram?*). At first glance, that datum may not appear to provide Paul's argument much support: there was already a way for a Gentile to be grafted into Israel—the very rite of circumcision which he was opposing.

But Paul insists on another implication of the "nations" terminology of Genesis. The term "nations" is *goyim*—"Gentiles." Paul's insight is that if the way into Abraham is *via* circumcision, there are, by definition, no more *goyim* in the picture. *To be circumcised is to be no longer Gentile.* And therefore, if the promise is to be fulfilled as given, the way for Gentiles to be "in Abraham" ultimately must not be the way of circumcision.

---

7 This architecture is reflected in Romans, as well, most notably in Rom 4, but also Rom 9, 11 and elsewhere throughout the letter.

8 On Midian, cf Gen 25:2.

9 It is to be noted while the Hebrew could be translated, "*by means of you* all the families of the earth will be blessed," that is not how Paul takes it. Similar to his frequent "in Christ" (ἐν Χριστῷ) language, Paul sees believers to be "in Abraham." He is interested in *incorporation,* not merely *instrumentality.*

Some of the prophetic writings support Paul here. There are eschatological passages which portray a time of allied friendship and common worship between Israel and other nations.[10] In other words, the eschatological vision is not merely that of Gentiles being merged into Israel by way of circumcision. When the nations worship alongside Israel, it is *as Gentiles,* not as circumcised Israelites.[11]

Taken together, the two aspects—blessing *in Abraham*, and blessing *as goyim, Gentiles,* distinct from Israel—require something for which Torah had no provision. This eschatological hope, in other words, is something the law could not do (cf Rom 8:3).

Flesh, Circumcision and Torah

Speaking of what the law could not do raises further issues regarding the human condition. One of the terms which dominates when Paul is speaking of that condition—particularly, in its weakness and/or sinfulness—is *flesh* (σάρξ).

This is not a technical term invented by Paul out of thin air. It is an applied usage of the Hebrew term בָּשָׂר (*bsr*), a word that dots the Old Testament but is particularly clustered in the pages of Leviticus devoted to matters of cleanness and uncleanness.

One of the earliest appearances of the term is Gen 2:21: when Adam falls into "deep sleep" (*tardemah*), God opens him up, removes a rib, and then closes up its place with "flesh." The story depicts a typological death, and corresponding to later death–resurrection themes, Eve is created as a sort of glorified version of man.[12]

At any rate, flesh is related to mortality. Man was not created *to* die, perhaps, but he was created such that he *could* die. (Something somewhat similar can be observed regarding sin.) Thus even apart from sin, *flesh is a first creation condition.* Sin then exacerbates the weakness of flesh.

Circumcision, of course, has to do with flesh. It is a "covenant in the

---

10 See e.g. Isa 19:23–25; see also below on Isa 42 and 49.

11 That this is significant in Paul's theology is amply demonstrated from Rom 15:8–12, in particular.

12 Cf 1 Cor 11:7—the woman is the "glory of the man."

flesh;" it involves cutting the flesh of the foreskin. As such, circumcision is a "first creation act" (that is, *flesh* and *new creation* do not belong together; cf 1 Cor 15:50), and not so surprisingly, in Paul's reading, it is tied to weakness and mortality.[13]

This meshes well with the fact that in Leviticus, the whole discussion of flesh in connection with cleanness and uncleanness is framed in terms of circumcision. It is the law of circumcision in Lev 12 which initiates the detailed instructions regarding flesh and cleanness and uncleanness running through Lev 13–15.

In Leviticus 13, "leprosy" is primarily exposure of "flesh," as the skin fails in its task. Similarly, the uncleanness laws of Lev 15 have to do with bodily discharges that come from within and pass through the flesh into the outer world.

This, it would appear, helps explain the rationale of Lev 12 itself: the newborn child is discharged from within and passes through the woman's flesh into the outer world. Thus both woman and child are unclean, a situation ceremonially resolved in different ways for male children and female.[14]

These uncleannesses prohibit those affected by them from entering God's presence at the tabernacle; they must be kept separate. There must be cleansing; this is resolved initially for the male child by way of circumcision, which introduces a clean state that will be maintained or regained throughout his life by way of offerings and washings (*baptisms;* cf Heb 9:10's βαπτισμοῖς); see especially the cleansing laws of Lev 14.

The relationship of flesh to uncleanness and to death suggests a triangle; this is further supported by passages such as Num 19:11ff, where we learn that touching a dead body causes uncleanness. The implication of the triangle is that wherever there is flesh, there is uncleanness and

13 Jordan, "Ishmael," Pt 1, thus states things too strongly when he suggests that Ishmael was "not 'of the flesh,' for his flesh was cut off." Circumcision was *in your flesh,* not a wholesale cutting off of the flesh so that one was no longer "of the flesh."

14 In the case of a male child, he is circumcised on the eighth day (intended as a reference to new creation), while his mother has 33 more days of purification. In the case of a female child, there is no circumcision, so the mother's purification is doubled (i.e. her purification covers herself and her daughter).

death.[15] Death is the triumph of flesh.

While circumcision was aimed to deal with "uncleanness," Paul's insight is that it does not do so at a fundamental level. Circumcision cuts away flesh, but it is *in* the flesh and presupposes the continuing existence of flesh. Wherever there is circumcision, flesh retains hegemony; life is dictated by its terms.

Nonetheless, Paul does see some continuity between Torah's regulations and the new creation: Christian baptism picks up on the cleansing washings of the law. However, the key thing here is that in baptism, one is not merely personally washed (and thus remaining what he was, with the implication there would need to be repeated washings), but is rather clothed with the Messiah (Gal 3:27). The Messiah of course is the One who has been raised from death (Gal 1:1)—has gone past flesh into glorified life. And thus this baptismal act is so flesh-transcending, Paul adds in Gal 3:28, that there is no Jew–Greek or slave–free or even male–female distinction involved in baptism (as of course there was with circumcision).

Although the foregoing is neither a thorough exposition of the laws of uncleanness nor of circumcision—and certainly Paul had more thoughts on these matters—I think what we have seen does help to account for some of the things we find in Galatians. Paul is not merely flying by the seat of his pants, stretching for *anything* that can help him in his argument. He is working from hermeneutical principles that are in fact quite coherent. Becoming circumcised requires keeping the whole Torah (Gal 5:3) because it ties one to flesh, and at least one implication of that is that one is then bound to Torah's provisions of dealing with fleshly uncleanness.

Moreover, Paul's focused discussion of flesh in chapter 5 ties σάρξ not only to circumcision, but also to Sin, over against the fruit of the Spirit. Those who belong to the Messiah rather than to Torah have *crucified the flesh* with its passions and desires (5:24)—this is not possible for anyone defined by Torah. Torah is limited, circumscribed by flesh,

15 On these themes, see especially the work of James B. Jordan, who has investigated them at considerable length. See especially "The Meaning of Clean and Unclean," as well as "Rite Reasons No. 60," *passim*, and *Through New Eyes*, 100–102.

and cannot go beyond it (cf Rom 8:3). But this new once-for-all baptism, baptism into the Messiah, is a baptism into His death (cf Rom 6:3), and when He died under the verdict of Torah, He representatively died for all flesh. When one comes out the other side of that baptismal death, circumcision can no longer matter, because the Messiah is the Head of new creation (cf Gal 6:15). Whereas connection to flesh before meant connection to death and *vice versa,* connection to Christ's death and participation in His flesh now means connection to His resurrection and life.[16]

Eschatology and Covenant

Paul's fundamental assumption is that Torah is a structured relationship, an administrative covenant—an insight that has frequently been lost by later interpreters, and at other times radically confused by a notion that it is a so-called "covenant of works" offering life on strict legalistic terms.

"Covenant" in Scripture can have various senses. It can simply mean something like "promise," and at that level, it is easy to speak of numerous "covenants." Paul may be using the term this way in Romans 9:4.

There is a more comprehensive use, however, which, for our purposes, is most significant in Galatians 4:24, where Paul contrasts two mutually-exclusive covenants, one of which is based upon freedom and the other of which engenders slavery.[17] In the context of the latter part of Galatians 3, in particular, we can see that Paul characterizes Torah this way. This is not because he thinks the Mosaic law is evil, nor yet because he construes it as a legalistic arrangement that is impossible to keep, holding out a sort of false promise of unattainable life. Rather, it is because he sees it as a temporary restrictive arrangement suitable for a particular period in history. That period he characterizes as Israel's childhood; the law, for its part, is a *paidagogos*—a slave (generally) who acted as a child custodian during the child's minority.

Thus, Paul's fundamental position is no longer that of his fellow Jews, many of whom thought that Torah was eternal, an articulation

16 A point Jesus Himself makes in John 6; Paul speaks in similar terms in Rom 6.

17 See my book, *These Are Two Covenants: Reconsidering Paul on the Mosaic Law.*

of Yahweh's unchangeable character. Although they would agree that Torah is comprehensive—a covenantal *administration*, an arrangement to govern life, they thought this arrangement was indissoluble.

For Paul, however, Torah is temporary: it enters at a given point in time, and was intended to be "put out of gear" at a later point in time (see, particularly, Gal 3:19's terminology of "added," coupled with the *terminus*, "until").

This conviction is indeed unusual for a first century Jew. But it is not merely an idiosyncratic invention of Paul's. He is apparently drawing insight from the Hebrew Scriptures.

In particular, we should take note of the prophecy of Isaiah.

Regarding the law, this book does indeed speak of "the everlasting covenant" (LXX: διαθήκην αἰώνιον; Heb *berith 'olam*, Isa 24:5), although the terminology does not necessarily mean "eternity." (Indeed, in context, it likely means something more like "ancient.")

But Isaiah also speaks of something new. Addressing the Servant, Yahweh says, "I am Yahweh; I have called you in righteousness; and I will grasp you by the hand and guard you; and I will *give you as a covenant for the people*, a light for the nations" (Isa 42:6). The term for "people" is עָם (*'am*) and probably refers to Israel; the term translated "nations" is *goyim*—the common term for Gentiles.

Isaiah 49 confirms this reading. In 49:5, we learn that the Servant has been formed in order to restore Jacob and regather Israel to Yahweh. But that is "too light a thing"—the Servant will not only "raise up the tribes of Jacob" and bring back the diaspora (LXX) of Israel. Yahweh "will give you as a light for the Gentiles, to become My salvation as far as the end of the earth" (49:6). And again in 49:8, Yahweh repeats that He will "guard you and give you as a covenant to the people." (In the LXX, the "covenant" language also appears in 49:6: "Behold, I will set you as a covenant of the people, as a light of the Gentiles, to be salvation unto the end of the earth.")

Thus, Isaiah explicitly identifies the Servant as a covenant to be given for Israel, and this covenant-gift for Israel is parallel to the Servant being given as a light for the Gentiles. Indeed, the Servant is to become "My salvation" as far as the end of the earth. All of this suggests that the

Servant will also be a covenant both for Israel and for the Gentiles.

Because Torah was Gentile-exclusive, it is understandable that Paul takes these promises of Servant-as-new-covenant to imply that the Messiah becomes a new covenantal administration who supplants the covenantal administration of Torah.

It is not sufficient to object that Paul never explicitly calls Jesus "the covenant." He repeatedly uses covenantal terms and concepts to refer to the Messiah, not least with his distinctive "in the Messiah" (ἐν Χριστῷ) language, which identifies Christ as a covenantal sphere corresponding to Torah, under which and within which Jews lived. Paul uses the parallel ἐν νόμῳ—*in Torah*—construction explicitly in Rom 2:12; 3:19 and, here in Galatians, 3:11 (cf 5:4), to refer to those living within the covenantal polity of the Mosaic law.[18] Moreover, for Paul, the Messiah Himself is the τέλος (*telos, goal*) of Torah (Rom 10:4), which likewise probably has covenantal overtones.

There is more. Paul's statement regarding what the Messiah has "become" for us, *wisdom and righteousness and sanctification and redemption* (1 Cor 1:30), in part at least is surely intended as a way of saying how the Messiah has gloriously supplanted Torah. In Deut 4:6, it is *Torah* which is "your *wisdom*." In Deut 6:25, "it will be *righteousness* for us," if we carefully follow Torah.[19]

Paul's strongest statement in this regard, however, may be in 1 Corinthians. In speaking of living among Jews "as though" he were under Torah, and among Gentiles as though he were without Torah, Paul says that he is in fact not ἄνομος (*without nomos, law*) with reference

---

18 These *in Torah* phrases are unfortunately obscured somewhat by English renderings such as "under the law"—a phrase (ὑπὸ νόμον), to be sure, that Paul is also capable of using elsewhere, e.g. Rom 6:14–15, where the parallel is with *grace* (of which, of course, Jesus is the embodiment; cf Jn 1:17). But Paul's point with this particular phrase is more explicitly covenantal: the juxtaposition is between being *in Torah* or *in the Messiah*.

19 The other terms in 1 Cor 1:30, while not specifically echoing earlier biblical language regarding Torah, fit well into the overall theme. *Redemption* was a predominant metaphor for the exodus, although ἀπολύτρωσις is not used in the LXX for that purpose. Similarly, the rabbis stressed the role of Torah as a means of *sanctification* (see e.g. the opposition between "the evil impulse" and Torah in *Kiddushin* 30b of the Talmud).

to God, but rather is ἔννομος Χριστοῦ,[20] in-lawed to the Messiah, as it were (1 Cor 9:21). In short: *he is covenanted to the Messiah rather than to Torah.*

This viewpoint bears directly upon the letter to the Galatians. For Paul, Abraham is the repository of promise and is in that sense *the* covenantal man; the nations will be blessed *in him* (Gal 3:8).[21] When the time fully comes (cf 4:4), that Abrahamic blessing then devolves upon the Messiah as the Seed concerning whom the promise speaks (3:16).

During their days under the law, Israel was called upon to interpret all things in light of Torah. But for Paul that time is past. The Messianic Servant is the new administration and administrator who serves as the key to all things ("in Him all things hold together," Paul writes later, in Col 1:17). It is now, with the revelation of the Messiah, the Son of God, crucified and resurrected, that the inscrutabilities of the ancient promises can come to light and find their resolution. All the things written in the law, the prophets, and the writings are exegeted in Him.

20 Or, as the Byz text has it, ἔννομος Χριστῷ (dative).

21 Or rather, Abraham is the *proto*-covenant man; the gospel is "pre-preached" to him. He receives the promise only as eschatological word; Jesus receives the promises in person, receiving both Gentiles and Jews into Himself.

Overview of Galatians

We now have a bit of information in mind to help us view the sweep of Paul's letter from the inside. While the body of the commentary will undertake the task of examining the letter verse by verse, it will be helpful for us to indicate in advance the overall approach that (in my judgment) makes the best sense of Paul's train of thought in the letter.

The first two chapters of Galatians, in particular, are biographical in character, especially with reference to Paul (a bit of Galatian biography pops up in 3:1–5 as well as in chapter 4 and, to a lesser degree, chapter 5). Conversely, it is particularly in chapters 3–4 that Paul's biblical hermeneutic comes to the fore.

Chapter 1 in Brief

The apostle expresses astonishment at the quickness of the Galatians' "desertion" of the call of God in the Messiah (Gal 1:6)—again, supportive of the view that these critical events are timed in the period immediately following the planting of the churches in Lystra and the other cities.

Paul's first line of defense regarding what he had preached in Galatia (i.e. a good news of the Messiah, absent any requirement of Gentile circumcision) is that he had obtained his message through direct divine revelation. This is aimed to undercut any possible weight the Galatians may put upon what they had surely heard: that Peter and Jacob at least think that something is lacking if Gentiles are not circumcised. This explains why Paul resorts to the "angel from heaven" language (Gal 1:8)—he is responding, not merely to the influence of some unknown locals, but to that (ostensibly) of fellow leaders in the global Church.

Paul did not derive his authority or message from the Jerusalem apostles, spending only fifteen days with Peter some three years following his conversion. The implication is that Paul's gospel had already taken shape by then, and fifteen days could scarcely have been considered sufficient to be catechized as a disciple, even if it is not credible to suppose the pair did not talk about Jesus.

Chapter 2 in Brief

Then further, Paul goes on in chapter 2:1–10, these same Jerusalem leaders had affirmed him as apostle to the Gentiles when he finally returned fourteen years later—implying that at least at one point they themselves had recognized that his message was appropriate for Gentiles.

Paul then rehearses Peter's conduct in Antioch, along with his own response (2:11–21).

As we have suggested, this surely arises because word of Peter's conduct has reached Galatia and has helped provide the false teachers impetus in pushing the Gentile churches toward circumcision. It makes little sense to suppose that Paul introduces Peter's ambiguity (at best) regarding uncircumcised Gentiles unless the Galatians were already aware of the event; by itself, the knowledge would hinder rather than support Paul's struggle to free them from circumcision tyranny. In contrast to the authority Peter implicitly grants Torah, Paul says he has died, and the full power of his life derives from the Messiah Himself.

Chapter 3 in Brief

In 3:1–5, Paul appeals to the Galatians' own experience, not only of the clarity of his own preaching that made the Messiah crucified the decisive touchstone, but also the gift of the Holy Spirit—evidence of their full acceptance by God altogether apart from the circumcision agenda.

The autobiographical element of the letter now recedes for the moment into the background. What follows is usually treated as an "appeal to Scripture"—which it is, but is much more than a simple account of God's promises to Abraham and rationale why the law could not negatively impact the promise of free grace.

In 3:6–9, Paul draws from the Abrahamic narrative the thought that the promises themselves implied salvation of Gentiles as *Gentiles* (i.e. uncircumcised).

Even more, the ultimate blessing is tied to *not* being under the law. The law is not a complement to the promise but rather an oath-bound covenant that stands in the way of Israel herself until God does something further: send His Son to die the death due to covenant-breakers, so that Israel can move forward into the realization of the new creation. Just as the Galatian Gentiles needed to be "delivered from this present evil age" (1:4), Israel had need of redemption from the law, as they were held fast by an oath hanging overhead (3:10).

The Abrahamic promise was primarily, or at least, climactically, reserved for the Messiah (3:16). Thus the law was not a helpful codicil to aid the people on to reception of the promises; to the contrary, it was given in order to increase transgression, hemming Israel into a semi-permanent status of childhood until the Messiah (the mature Son) should come (3:15–24). After His arrival, both Jews and Gentiles gain full sonship status by being clothed with the mature Son (3:25–29).

Chapter 4 in Brief

Over the course of this argument, Paul has identified the law as a "child custodian" (*paidagogos*)—a slave who ruled the heirs in their minority, to the degree that their own position was slavelike. The *terminus* to this condition was not in this case some automatic "coming of age"; it was the advent of the Messiah, "born under Torah in order to redeem those who were under Torah" (4:4–5). That is, deliverance from the *paidagogos* required the redeeming death of the Messiah. As a result of this rescue from the old creation, the new creation Spirit has been given, and Jew and Gentile are now sons, fully qualified to inherit the promises (4:1–7).

Prior to their own deliverance, the Galatian Gentiles too had been enslaved—not to Torah, to be sure, but to false gods. And now, having been known by God as sons, they seek to return to the constitutive elements of the old world (4:8–11).

The gist of much of 3:6–4:11 is thus that the old creation was a prison, not only for unbelieving and idolatrous Gentiles, but also for Israel, and that the death of the Messiah was the effective release agent for both. For Gentiles to become circumcised and embrace Torah would not be an advancement forward in Christian maturity, but rather a decisive spiral out of the new creation back into the old.

Paul thus urges these Gentiles as one who has himself been rescued from Torah ("I also have become as you are," 4:12), to become resettled in this new creation status as they once were. He depicts the rival teachers in Galatia as young men with evil intent attempting to seduce daughters from the influence of their parents. Paul in his mothering instincts sees the image of the Messiah being lost—that is, they are losing their identity as new covenant persons (4:12–20).

In carrying forward the slave child–free child theme, Paul refers again to the Abrahamic narrative: Ishmael was not a son of a free wife, nor the child of promise, and therefore could not inherit. That privilege was Isaac's alone. So similarly, the law-oriented teachers are identified with Torah-slavery and cannot inherit with the free children that have been born through Paul's ministry (4:21–31).

Chapter 5 in Brief

Over the course of chapters 3–4, Paul has been painting a sort of global portrait of old creation and new creation and their fundamental mutual exclusivity. In the fifth chapter, he proceeds to unpack more specifically the implications of the direction the Galatians are headed. Circumcision means the loss of the Messiah and His benefits. Not simply observance of formal markers such as feast days and Sabbath (cf 4:8–11), an embrace of Torah is of necessity wholesale, including, for example, performance of the "sacrificial" rituals superseded by the Messiah's cross. Circumcision is thus severance from the Messiah and His whole significance (5:1–4).

The genuine journey of faith is a Spirit-enabled pursuit of the hope of vindication to be found in Jesus the Messiah, a journey characterized by love and one where circumcision and uncircumcision are irrelevant (5:5–6). But in pursuing circumcision, the Galatians are in fact removing the offense of the cross by placing significance in the old creation which has met its judgment there (5:7–12).

Freedom is liberation for faith to serve in partnership with the Messiah, who loved us and gave His life up for us (cf 2:20). In such free service the law is not "observed" but "fulfilled"—*filled up* by a glorious transformation, as the new covenant Spirit leads one not into and under

Torah, but into a full-bodied resemblance of the Messiah. Indeed, living by the Spirit is living in union with the Messiah, and in the Messiah the old creation flesh has been crucified (5:13–26).

Chapter 6 in Brief

A particular aspect of this Messiah-likeness is central in Paul's mind. The self-giving love which bears the burdens of others *fulfills* the law of the Messiah (6:2)—that is, it fills in what is lacking. Christian faith is not simply assent to "doctrines" regarding Christ, but an entering into His practical self-giving for others. This is a "sowing to the Spirit" which will reap the harvest of eternal life.

In the final analysis, circumcision is an old creation activity, and therefore sowing to the old creation flesh, the old world to which the believer has been crucified. It can count for nothing; what matters is the new creation.

Translation[1]

1:1–5

Paul, an apostle not from men nor through man but through Jesus the Messiah, and God the Father who raised Him from the dead, and all the brothers with me, to the churches of the Galatians:

Grace to you and peace from God our Father, and the Lord Jesus the Messiah, who gave Himself for our sins, so that He might deliver us from this present evil age, according to the will of our God and Father—to whom be glory unto the ages of the ages, amen.

1:6–10

I am amazed that so quickly you are deserting from the One who called you in the grace of the Messiah unto another "good news"—which is not another, except certain ones are troubling you and wishing to pervert the good news of the Messiah.

But even if we, or an angel from heaven, make proclamation to you alongside of what we proclaimed to you—let him be anathema. As we said beforehand, also now again I say: if anyone makes proclamation to you alongside of what you received—let him be anathema.

For now—do I persuade *men*—or *God?* or do I seek to please men? If I yet pleased men, I would not be the slave of the Messiah.

1:11–14

Now I make known to you, brothers, the good news which I proclaimed, that it is not according to man. For neither did I myself receive it from man, nor was I taught, but through the revelation of Jesus the Messiah.

1 The translation here is primarily simply the rendering to be found in the Exposition, but occasionally slightly reworded to facilitate somewhat smoother English.

For you heard [about] my conduct, when I was in Judaism, that I went to extremes, persecuting the church of God, and tried to destroy it, and was advancing in Judaism above many contemporaries among my kinsmen, being excessively zealous regarding the traditions of my fathers.

1:15–24

But when God pleased—the One who separated me from my mother's womb and called [me] through His grace—to reveal His Son in me, in order to proclaim Him among the Gentiles, immediately I did not consult with flesh and blood, nor did I go up unto Jerusalem to those who were apostles before me, but departed into Arabia and again returned unto Damascus.

Then, after three years, I went up unto Jerusalem to visit Cephas, and remained with him fifteen days. But other of the apostles I did not see, except Jacob the brother of the Lord. (Now the things I write to you, behold, before God—I am not lying.)

Then I went into the regions of Syria and Cilicia. But I was unknown by face to the churches of Judea in the Messiah. Only, they were hearing, "The one who once persecuted us now proclaims the faith he once was trying to destroy." And they were glorifying God in/because of me.

2:1–10

After fourteen years, again I went up unto Jerusalem with Barnabas, taking along Titus also. Now I went up according to a revelation, and placed before them the good news which I proclaim among the Gentiles—but privately, to those who were reputed, lest somehow I run, or had run, in vain.

But not even Titus, who was with me, though a Greek, was forced to become circumcised.

But [this was] on account of smuggled-in false brothers, who slipped in to spy out our freedom which we have in the Messiah Jesus, so that they might enslave us—to whom not even for an hour we yielded subjection, so that the truth of the good news might remain with you.

But from those who were reputed as something—whatever once

they were, it makes no difference to me: God does not receive the face of a man—for those who were reputed contributed nothing to me. But contrariwise, seeing that I had been entrusted the good news of the uncircumcision, just as Peter of the circumcision—for the One working in Peter as the apostle of the circumcision worked also in me unto the Gentiles—and recognizing the grace given to me, Jacob and Cephas and John, the ones reputed to be pillars, gave to me and to Barnabas the right hand of partnership, so that we [should go] unto the Gentiles, but they unto the circumcision. Only the poor, [they wished] that we might remember, which also [was] the same thing I was eager to do.

2:11–21

But when Cephas came unto Antioch, I opposed him against his face, because he was condemned. For before certain ones came from Jacob, he was eating with Gentiles; but when they came, he withdrew and separated himself, fearing those from the circumcision. And the rest of the Jews joined in hypocrisy with him, so that even Barnabas was carried away with them in the hypocrisy.

But when I saw that they did not walk straightly along the path of the truth of the good news, I said to Cephas before [them] all,

"If you, being a Jew, live 'Gentilely' and not 'Jewishly,' how do you compel the Gentiles to live Jewishly? We who are by-nature-Jews and not sinners from the Gentiles, knowing that a man is not justified from the works of Torah, but rather through the faith of Jesus the Messiah—even we in the Messiah Jesus have believed, so that we may be justified from the faith of the Messiah and not from the works of Torah; because from works of Torah all flesh shall not be justified.

"Now if seeking to be justified in the Messiah, we are found also sinners ourselves—is the Messiah then a servant of sin? Impossible! For I constitute myself a transgressor if I build up again the things I destroyed. For through Torah, to Torah I died, so that I might live to God. With the Messiah I have been crucified; now I live no longer, but the Messiah lives in me: But what life I now live in the flesh, I live in faith—the faith of the Son of God Himself, who loved me and gave Himself for me. I do not invalidate the grace of God: for if righteousness is through

Torah, indeed the Messiah died for nothing."

3:1–5

O foolish Galatians, who has bewitched you with an evil eye—before whose eyes Jesus the Messiah was placarded crucified [that you should not obey the truth]? This only I wish to learn from you: Did you receive the Spirit from works of Torah, or from the message of faith?

Are you so foolish? Having begun in the Spirit, are you now being completed in the flesh? Did you experience so much in vain?—if indeed yet [it was] in vain.... He therefore who supplies the Spirit to you and works power-works among you, [does He do so] from works of Torah, or from the message of faith?

3:6–9

Just as Abraham believed God, and it was accounted to him unto righteousness, you know, then, that those from faith, these are the sons of Abraham.

Now the Scripture, foreseeing that God would justify the Gentiles from faith, preached beforehand to Abraham, "In you will all the Gentiles be blessed"—so that those from faith are blessed with the faithful Abraham.

3:10–14

For as many as are from works of Torah, are under a curse: for it is written, "Cursed is everyone who does not remain in all the things written in the book of Torah, to do them."

Now that in/by Torah no one is justified before God is evident, since "The just one from faith shall live." But Torah is not from faith, but: "The one doing them shall live in them."

Christ redeemed us from the curse of Torah, becoming a curse for us, because it is written, "Cursed is everyone who hangs upon a tree"—in order that unto the Gentiles the blessing of Abraham might come in the Messiah Jesus, in order that the promise of the Spirit we might receive through the faith.

3:15–18

Brothers, according to man I speak: Although merely a covenant of man, if it has been ratified, no one invalidates it or adds conditions.

Now to Abraham the promises were spoken, and to his seed. It does not say, "and to seeds," as upon many, but as upon one, "and to your seed," which is the Messiah.

Now this I say: A covenant earlier ratified by God, the after-430-years-coming Torah does not revoke it, so as to nullify the promise. For if the inheritance is from Torah, it is no longer from [the] promise: but God has given [the inheritance] to Abraham through promise.

3:19–24

Why Torah, then? It was added for the sake of transgressions, until the time should arrive when the seed should come to whom [it] was promised, and it was ordained through angels by the instrumentality of a mediator. Now he is not the mediator of [that] one, but God is one.

Is Torah, then, against the promises of God? Impossible! For if Torah was given as able to give life, truly righteousness would have resulted from Torah.

But the Scripture has imprisoned all things under sin, so that the promise might be given from the faith of Jesus the Messiah to those who believe. Now before the faith came, we were confined under Torah, because we were imprisoned until the revelation of the impending faith, so that Torah became our custodian until the Messiah, that we might be justified from faith.

3:25–29

But because the faith has come, we are no longer under a custodian. For you are all sons of God through the faith, in the Messiah Jesus. For as many of you as into the Messiah were baptized, are clothed with the Messiah; there is neither Jew nor Greek, neither slave nor free, there is not male and female: for you are all one [Man] in the Messiah Jesus.

Now if you are the Messiah's, indeed you are the seed of Abraham, and heirs according to [the] promise.

4:1–7

Now, I say, as long as the heir is a child, he differs nothing from a slave, despite being master of all, but rather is under guardians and managers until the set time of the father. Thus also we, when we were children, we had been enslaved under the elements of the world.

But when the fullness of time came, God sent forth His Son, born from a woman, born under Torah, in order that He might redeem those under Torah, in order that we might receive the adoption.

Now because you are sons, God sent forth the Spirit of His Son into our hearts, crying out, "Abba, Father." So that no longer are you a slave, but a son; but if a son, also an heir through God.

4:8–20

But then indeed, while not knowing God, you were enslaved to those which by nature are not gods.

But now, knowing God, or rather, having been known by God, how do you return again upon the weak and poor elements to which again you wish to be enslaved? You are observing days, and months and seasons and years. I am afraid of you, lest somehow I have laboured among you in vain!

Become as I am—for I also became as you—brothers, I beg you—you have not harmed me at all.

Now you know that because of weakness of the flesh I proclaimed the gospel to you at the first; and you did not despise nor disdain your/my trial in my flesh, but as an angel of God you received me—as the Messiah, Jesus [Himself].

Therefore, where is your blessing? For I bear witness to you that if possible, you would have gouged your eyes out and given [them] to me.

Therefore, have I become your enemy, by telling truth to you?

They are zealously courting you in a manner not good, but they wish to exclude you, so that you may zealously court them. But it is good to be zealously courted in good always, and not only in my presence with you, my children, whom again I am birthing with travail, until the Messiah may be formed in you.

But I wish to be present with you now, and alter my voice, because I am uncertain concerning you.

4:21–5:1

Tell me, the ones wishing to be under Torah: do you not hear Torah? For it is written, Abraham had two sons, one from the slave woman, and one from the free woman. But the one indeed from the slave woman was born according to [the] flesh, but the one from the free woman, [was born] through [the] promise; which things are an allegory: for these are two covenants—one from Mount Sinai which bears children into slavery, which is Hagar.

Now this Hagar is mount Sinai in Arabia: now it corresponds to the present Jerusalem, for it is enslaved with her children. But the above-Jerusalem is free, which is our mother [Byz: *which is the mother of all of us*]. For it is written, "Rejoice, barren woman who does not bear; break forth and shout, one who does not suffer birth-pains, because more are the children of the wilderness than of the one having a husband." Now, you [Byz *we*], brothers, corresponding to Isaac, are the children of promise.

But just as then the one born according to [the] flesh persecuted the one [born] according to [the] Spirit, so also now. But what does the Scripture say? "Cast out the slave woman and her son, for the son of the slave woman shall not inherit with the son of the free woman."

Therefore, brothers, you are not children of the slave woman, but of the free woman. For the freedom, the Messiah has freed you: stand firm therefore and do not again be subject to the yoke of slavery.

5:2–6

Look! I Paul say to you that if you become circumcised, the Messiah will benefit you nothing.

Now I bear witness again to every man becoming circumcised, that he is under obligation to do the entire law. You are severed from the Messiah, whoever is justified in Torah; you have fallen away from the grace.

For in the Spirit, from faith, we anticipate the hope of righteousness. For in the Messiah Jesus neither circumcision is effectual for anything, nor uncircumcision, but faith working through love.

5:7–12

You were running well—who impeded you, to not follow the truth? This persuasion is not from the One calling you.

A little leaven leavens the whole lump. I am persuaded concerning you in the Lord, that you will not be otherwise minded; but the one troubling you will bear the judgment, whoever he may be.

Now I, brothers, if I still preach circumcision, why am I yet persecuted? then the scandal of the cross has been nullified.

Would that those disturbing you would also castrate themselves!

5:13–15

For you were called on the basis of freedom, brothers: only not the [sort of] freedom [serving] as an occasion to/for the flesh, but through the love serve one another. For the whole law is fulfilled in one word—in this: Love your neighbour as yourself.

Now if you bite and prey upon one another, beware lest you are consumed by one another.

5:16–18

Now I say, walk in the Spirit, and you will not carry to completion the longing of the flesh. For the flesh longs against the Spirit, but the Spirit against the flesh, for these oppose one another, so that you may not do the things you might desire.

Now if you are led by the Spirit, you are not under Torah.

5:19-21

Now the works of the flesh are evident, whatever is [Byz *adultery,*] fornication, uncleanness, sensuality, idolatry, sorcery, hostilities, strifes, zealotry, wraths, rivalries, divisions, factions, envies, [Byz *murders*], drunkennesses, carousing, and things similar to these—which things

I forewarn you, just as I did forewarn you, that the ones doing such things will not inherit the kingdom of God.

5:22–26

But the fruit of the Spirit is love, joy, peace, longsuffering, kindness, goodness, faith/faithfulness, meekness, self-control: against such people there is no Torah.

Now those of the Messiah [Jesus] have crucified the flesh with the passions and the lusts. Since we live in the Spirit, let us also walk in the Spirit. Let us not become conceited, provoking one another, envying one another.

6:1–5

Brothers, if a man is taken in any trespass, you spiritual ones restore such a one in the spirit of gentleness, watching yourself, lest you also be tempted. Bear the burdens of one another, and thus fulfill the law of the Messiah.

For if anyone thinks himself to be something, being nothing, fools himself.

Now let each prove his own work, and then he will have the boast concerning himself alone, and not concerning the other. For each shall bear his own cargo.

6:6–10

Now let the one being taught the word be a partner to the one teaching in all good things.

Do not be deceived; God is not mocked: for whatever a man sows, this also he shall reap. Because the one sowing into his own flesh, from the flesh shall reap corruption, but the one sowing into the Spirit, from the Spirit shall reap life eternal.

But let us not become discouraged, those doing the good, for in its own time we shall reap if we do not give up.

Therefore, as we have occasion, let us do the good to all, but especially to the household members of the faith.

6:11–18

See, how large letters I have written to you by my own hand!

As many as wish to make a good showing in the flesh, these are compelling you to be circumcised, only in order that for the cross of the Messiah, they may not be persecuted. For neither do the ones being circumcised themselves keep the law, but they wish you to be circumcised, so that they may boast in your flesh.

But it is impossible for me to boast, except in the cross of our Lord Jesus the Messiah, through which the world has been crucified to me, and I to the world. For [in the Messiah Jesus] neither circumcision is [Byz *effectual for*] anything, nor uncircumcision, but [a] new creation.

And as many as walk by this rule, peace upon them, and mercy—and upon the Israel of God.

From now on, let no one cause me trouble: for I myself bear the identifying scars of [the Lord] Jesus in my body.

The grace of our Lord Jesus the Messiah [be] with your spirit, brothers.

Amen.

Paul, Apostle from God

THE ACCENT IN THE OPENING SECTIONS OF THE LETTER is that Paul is a representative sent from Jesus the Messiah, not from men or through men. The Messiah's commission has met, challenged and overcome Paul's own inclinations and training, and that commission is in no way inferior to the apostolic commission given to other apostles such as Peter.

The result of this calling from Jesus is that Paul's gospel for the Gentiles is not of mere human origin, but of divine authority.

Greeting for Troubled Churches (1:1–5)

As so often is the case with Paul's letters, the burden of Galatians can be found in seed form in the opening words. The narrative is an unfolding of the things we find here: God, who is already Father not only to Jesus but also the Galatian believers; the Messiah, who has given Himself up to death, achieving forgiveness of sins for us, in order to carry out a rescue from the present evil order of things; and Paul, the emissary of both. This salvation-historical and eschatological reality grounds Paul's rationale for the Galatian Gentiles to stand firm in not becoming circumcised and coming under the domain of Torah.

Paul, an apostle not from men nor through man but through Jesus the Messiah, and God the Father who raised Him from the dead. 1:1

The apostle identifies himself as ***Paul.*** While Saul was his "closest" name—he being a Jew and identified as Saul when we first meet him in Acts 7:58—the apostle always identifies himself as "Paul" in his letters. Why? Not because the name (which means something like "little") represents a change in his character; he likely had this as his Roman name from birth, since he was born a citizen (Acts 22:25–29). Most likely, the choice of using this name is rooted in his Gentile mission. Rather than presenting himself by his Israelite name, he chooses to identify himself by his Greco-Roman name.

Longenecker observes that Paul never provides his other two Roman names,[1] which means his self-identification is status-neutral. If so, this arises out of Paul's conviction (expressed in 3:28) that in the Messiah, worldly status has no bearing upon one's standing in the new order of things in the Messiah, Jesus. However, it is not clear that Paul would necessarily have had any other Roman names.

Paul is ***an apostle not from men nor through man but through Jesus the Messiah***. The term *apostle* is perhaps a Greek equivalent of the Jewish *shaliach*. Both words refer to one sent with representative authority; to receive or reject the apostle is to do the same to the sender who appointed him.

Paul is therefore asserting that he has not been sent by the Jerusalem church nor other merely human institutions. He has been sent by Jesus the Messiah and God the Father Himself.

The Christological dimension here should also be noted. The verse implies that Jesus is not *merely* a man—otherwise there would scarcely be a contrast between *from men/through man* and *through Jesus the Messiah*. The Messiah, as it turns out, is more than a man.

God the Father is preeminently the One ***who raised Him from the dead***. Paul is the emissary of the life-giving Father, who has inaugurated the new age, the new creation, through the resurrection of Jesus the Messiah.

Although Paul does not again speak directly of the resurrection, this event provides the basis of the whole salvation-historical framework[2] that runs throughout the letter, and is the baseline and foundation of the new creation theme which drives the argument (see especially 6:15 for the importance of new creation in Paul's view).

1 Richard Longenecker, *Galatians* (WBC 41; Waco, TX: Word, 1990), 2.

2 I am not using "salvation-historical" in the technical sense sometimes contrasted with "apocalyptic" (which I largely consider a false dichotomy). My usage instead intends more generally to underscore that there is a *fundamental historical sequence* underlying and pervading Paul's argument rather than simply or primarily an abstract doctrinal or religious "system."

And all the brothers with me, to the churches of the Galatians. 1:2

Although Paul appears to stand like Athanasius, *contra mundum*, with even Peter and Jacob coming into question at this particular juncture, yet he can still speak of ***all the brothers with me***, assuring the Galatians that he is not in fact alone. While Barnabas at this point has probably not recovered (cf 2:13), the other brothers in Antioch (and, probably, Titus; cf 2:1) do stand with him and share in his vision and concern for ***the churches of the Galatians***.[3]

Grace to you and peace from God our Father, and the Lord Jesus the Messiah. 1:3

The opening benediction consists of the familiar duo of ***grace to you and peace***. While *peace* (εἰρήνη) is an LXX equivalent for the Hebrew *shalom*, the LXX does not often—if at all—use *grace* (χάρις) in the manner Paul does. It is very reasonable to suggest that what Paul means by grace is essentially equivalent to the Hebrew term *chesed*, which the LXX translates using a number of different terms. The likelihood of this is perhaps fortified by the fact that in the Old Testament, *chesed* and *ʿemeth* (*faithfulness, truth*) are frequently paired (e.g. Ps 85:10)—similar to the link Paul himself frequently makes between *grace* and *faith*.

Peace in the Old Testament frequently takes on eschatological overtones, speaking of a time when God grants Israel prosperity and wholeness (see e.g. Isa 9:6–7; 32:17).

In addition, the Levitical offering which the worshiper shared with God was *the peace offering* (which, interestingly, the LXX translates as "the sacrifice of salvation," θυσία σωτηρίου; see e.g. Lev 3:1, 3, 6, 9).[4]

---

3 While Paul later had numerous other assistants, given the chronology we have adopted, beyond Titus it is not clear who else would have been considered his companions at this point. Arguably, Acts 13:13–14 implies Paul and Barnabas may have had additional company beyond John Mark (who at that point returned home).

4 Note that in Acts 15:1, the circumcision party was insisting that Gentiles could not be "saved" unless they were circumcised according to the custom of Moses. This language may be rooted in part in the LXX's salvation language in connection with the peace offering, a form of which the early Church considered the Lord's Supper (see Collins, "The Eucharist as Christian Sacrifice").

Given that in part this letter concerns eating together (Peter's stumble consists of a withdrawal from table fellowship with Gentiles, for instance), the extension of peace from God as the One who shares His table with His people may bear some significance.

God is not merely the Father of Jesus the Messiah (v 1); He is ***God our Father***. This by itself is an understated refutation of the Judaizers' position. The greeting must be understood in connection with 3:26–29: *the as yet uncircumcised Galatians are already heirs;* God is their Father, even now, apart from entrance into Israel *via* circumcision.

The grace and peace of which Paul speaks are provided by ***the Lord Jesus the Messiah***. He is the One who "published peace," bringing the happy proclamation of salvation rooted in the reign of God (Isa 52:7).

The relationship between verse 1 and verse 3 is not to be missed. It is the same God the Father and Lord Jesus the Messiah who commissioned Paul in his apostleship who also grant grace and peace. Put another way, grace and peace are found in connection with the particular happy proclamation which Paul has been commissioned to bring.

1:4 *Who gave Himself for our sins, so that He might deliver us from this present evil age, according to the will of our God and Father.*

In describing aspects of the Messiah's work, Paul notes as of first importance that He ***gave Himself for our sins*** (cf 1 Cor 15:3), and the purpose was eschatological: ***so that He might deliver us from this present evil age***.

As the rest of the New Testament teaches, the Messiah is not a passive victim; as Paul expands in 2:20, He *loved* me and gave Himself for me. Reminiscent of the Servant in Isa 53:5–6, 12, Messiah makes it His task to make Himself an offering for sin.

This characterization of *the Messiah* and of His *purpose* should not be separated. The Messiah's self-giving for sin is aimed, not merely at the resolution of a personal guilt complex or even an objectively real guilt. It accomplishes that, of course; but it does even more. The Messiah's death is eschatological in its focus and character; it aims to bring liberation from the old *aeon*, the first creation world serving under various forms of slavery. Cf Col 1:13–14: the Messiah brings liberation from the power of darkness, as God conveys us into the kingdom of the Son of His love, "in whom we have redemption through His blood, the forgiveness of sins" (cf also Eph 1:7).

While forgiveness of sins is not necessarily as pervasive a theme in Galatians as in some other Pauline contexts, it is nonetheless foundational to the entire argument. Apart from forgiveness of sins, there is no sonship to God, and no messianic community within which Jews and Gentiles may share equally. There is simply slavery to the flesh and attendant eschatological judgment (cf 6:8).

Paul's mention of the Messiah's sin-bearing death here immediately moves to its *purpose*—the *so that*. Forgiveness of sins is not viewed in isolation (as a personal "fire escape," if you will) or as an end in itself, but as a necessary and crucial precondition for removal from *this present evil age*, and correspondent arrival in the new creation. Reconciliation is in service of God's plan of new creation. The problem of sin (or Sin) must be seen more globally than as something whose consequences make life miserable; more fundamentally, Sin is a roadblock against God's good (new) creational purposes.

The term I have rendered as *deliver* (ἐξαιρέω) is used nowhere else by Paul, but some parallel can be found in Paul's *redemption* language of 3:13 and 4:5. He uses the term, not merely with regard to rescue from sin, narrowly, but to rescue from the *age* in which Sin is master. Hence the point in 3:13 and 4:5 includes not only forgiveness, but redemption from the hegemony of Torah (see also 4:21–5:1, which speaks of Torah as a slavemaster; for more on this theme, see the Exposition on the relevant passages, as well as Appendix 1).

The word is found elsewhere in the NT only in Matthew and Acts (Matt 5:29; 18:9; Acts 7:10, 34; 12:11; 23:27; 26:17). In Acts 7, the term is used to refer first to Joseph's deliverance from his troubles, and then for the rescue from Egypt. The other Acts references also carry the meaning of *rescue* or *deliverance*. In Matthew, the meaning is *cast out;* this negative meaning provides an interesting counterpoint to the command to cast out the son of the bondwoman here in 4:30.

This new creation-inaugurating work of the cross is thus ***according***

to the will of our God and Father. Martyn rightly stresses that the self-giving death of Jesus was God's own act. "The cross … is fundamentally God's act, and as such the inversion of the sacrificial system."[5]

Note the contrast between τοῦ αἰῶνος τοῦ ἐνεστῶτος πονηροῦ ("this present evil age") in this verse and εἰς τοὺς αἰῶνας τῶν αἰώνων ("ages of ages") in the next. The old *kosmos* has fallen away from the ability to glorify the true God, which can only be done by faith in the God of resurrection (cf Rom 1:21–23; 4:20–25).

1:5 *To whom be glory unto the ages of the ages, amen.*

It is the Father ***to whom be glory***, echoing passages such as Isa 45:25: "In Yahweh, all the seed of Israel shall be justified and shall glory." *Glory* has fundamental connotations of *weight* (one Hebrew word serves for both); God is the weighty one, and the future He is shaping is likewise weighty.

God's glory is ***unto the ages of the ages***. The eschatological and eternal glory of God is set over against "this present evil age." The rescue from the old *kosmos* brings about a new participation in the eschatological glory of God.

Paul gives his ***amen*** without offering the sort of thanksgiving customary to his other letters—arguably a sign of his distress regarding the condition of these churches.[6]

The Happy Proclamation Perverted (1:6–10)

1:6 *I am amazed that so quickly you are deserting from the One who called you*
in the grace of the Messiah unto another "good news."

Instead of his more usual "I give thanks," Paul says, ***I am amazed***. The situation is not appropriate for thanksgiving, but for shock. There is

5 J. Louis Martyn, *Galatians* (Anchor Bible Commentary; Yale, 1997), 91.

6 Compare Rom 1:8; 1 Cor 1:4–8; Eph 1:15–16; Phi 1:3; Col 1:3; 1 Thess 1:2–3; 2 Thess 1:3 etc. I say "arguably," because this may well be Paul's earliest letter, and he has not necessarily fully established his epistolary pattern at this point.

a time for peace, but this is a time for war.

Paul is amazed that ***so quickly you are deserting***. Longenecker aptly suggests an echo of the Golden Calf incident: "They have turned quickly from the way that you commanded them" (Exod 32:8 LXX; cf Deut 9:16; Judg 2:17 LXX).

Both verbal and noun forms of the term for *deserting* (μετατίθημι) are by and large used for references to *transfers* rather than to indicate internal change (see e.g. Acts 7:16; Heb 7:12; 11:5; 12:27). There is, to be sure, a change of mind involved on the issues in question (circumcision and Torah). But this is not merely a doctrinal shift; it entails and effects an altered relationship to the Messiah rather than simply a private shift in viewpoint (see 5:4).

This is a *personal* apostasy, not simply a theological declension. It is desertion ***from the One who called you***—truly ironic, since the contemplation of circumcision is motivated by a hope to gain full membership in the covenant family. Paul says the opposite is true: this is desertion of God and His family.

The Galatians were originally called ***in the grace of the Messiah***. Cf John 1:17: "the law was given through Moses—the grace and truth came through Jesus the Messiah." *Chesed* and *'emeth* are embodied in the Messiah.

In the meat of the letter, Paul will speak of how the Messiah has taken upon Himself the consequences of desertion from Torah (3:10–13), so that Israel may move from old covenant to new.[7] Here Paul implies consequences of desertion from the Messiah Himself, which he will address further in chapter 5 (cf 5:4, where he says that those who would be justified through Torah have "fallen from grace").

The Galatians are embracing ***another "good news."*** The *good news* ("gospel")—a "happy proclamation"—is an allusion to the announcement of the Messiah's triumphant and saving rule which Paul had preached among the Galatians, who are now deserting the original form of the proclamation in favour of a substitute.

7 See on 3:10–14, as well as Appendix 1.

1:7 *Which is not another, except certain ones are troubling you and wishing to pervert the good news of the Messiah.*

Paul speaks of another good news, ***which is*** in fact ***not another***. Many commentators make a great deal of hay out of the different Greek words Paul uses in vv 6–7. Their point is that this is not "another of the same kind," but a completely *different kind* of news.

While that may be true, I find it to be a strain upon Paul's purpose here. Rather, as he says, the teachers are ***wishing to pervert the good news of the Messiah***. The teachers have not come with a whole different message, but have perverted the one true existing proclamation. So it is not really "another" good news, but a perversion of what the Galatians have already heard. Perhaps we could say that it is an "un-gooding" of the good news, with a dash of the "news" itself removed, to boot.

Certain ones are troubling you, says Paul: these new messengers are "you-troublers"—Paul uses an article to define them by their troublesomeness. These teachers are thus classed with their apparent allies who were making difficulty in Antioch; as the subsequent letter from the Jerusalem Council states, "we have heard that some who went out from us have *troubled* (ταράσσω) you" (Acts 15:24).

Longenecker suggests a possible allusion to Achan, "the troubler of Israel" (1 Chr 2:7). This connection does seem likely, given the LXX's use of ἀνάθεμα in that verse—a term Paul uses twice in the succeeding verses here. This, however, raises the question of what these "Achans" had laid their hands upon. Achan had troubled Israel by stealing that which was devoted to Yahweh. Because he had taken that which was ἀνάθεμα, he himself became ἀνάθεμα. It is possible that Paul has in mind the Galatians themselves as utterly holy and set apart to the Lord, but the prominence of the *evangel* in the context suggests that he may be thinking of the gospel itself.

Another "troubler of Israel" was Ahab, who made the same charge against Elijah, only to have it reversed upon himself (1 Kgs 18:17–18). Elijah identified him as such because he had abandoned Yahweh's commandments and followed the Baals. Paul perhaps can relate to the feelings of the prophet, who repeatedly complained, "I alone am left." While

Paul clearly has supporters in Antioch, the troubles in Galatia along with the capitulation of both Peter and Barnabas (see on 2:11ff, below) surely made his plight seem similar to Elijah's.

> *But even if we, or an angel from heaven, make proclamation to you along-* 1:8
> *side of what we proclaimed to you—let him be anathema.*

Paul is so certain of the unalterable truth of his gospel that he denies that anyone could have authority to change it: ***even if we, or an angel from heaven*** speak otherwise. Paul did not of course expect an angel from heaven to be instructing the Galatians, but he resorts to exaggerated language to counter the then-prevalent assumption that the apostle Peter himself was requiring circumcision.

The fact that Paul includes himself in this malediction indicates that the issue is not simply one of his personal authority over against that of Peter or the other apostles; it is not his interest to seek supremacy for himself. Rather, it is *the divine authority and character of the message* which counts.

While the mention of angels is primarily deployed as a rhetorical extreme to undercut the authority even of apostles to alter the received message, yet of itself it is *apropos*, because angels had a role in the mediation of the law (see 3:19–20; cf Deut 33:2 LXX; Acts 7:53; Heb 2:1), as Garlington points out.[8] The good news of Jesus the Messiah trumps Torah and its associated authority figures, even angels.

Paul fiercely stands against any who would ***make proclamation to you alongside of what we proclaimed to you***. The term "make proclamation" is the verbal form of "good news" or "happy proclamation" (gospel). Where I have "alongside of," many translations have something like "contrary to" or "in contradiction to." That, however, may in fact be too strong; the Greek term παρά with the accusative may simply be translated "alongside of" or "beyond." Just as Paul will say in chapter 3 that Torah may not be taken as a codicil which amends the promises to Abraham, so he requires that the happy proclamation of the Messiah

8 Don Garlington, *Exposition of Galatians* (Wipf and Stock, 2003), 44.

stand in self-sufficiency, without amendment. Additional news is bad news.

If anyone, therefore, however great, should proclaim a news that competes with or adds to the gospel as Paul has preached it, ***let him be anathema***. See the notes on verse 7, above. Whoever so seeks to destroy the ineffably holy Word of the gospel, let him be devoted to utter destruction, just as Achan was, who laid hands on that which belonged to God alone.

1:9 *As we said beforehand, also now again I say: if anyone makes proclamation to you alongside of what you received—let him be anathema.*

When Paul refers to something ***we said beforehand,*** and ***also now again I say,*** most commentators (with Bruce as a notable exception) take Paul to be referring to something he said in his earlier time in Galatia.

That is possible, but I find it more likely to refer simply to the previous verse. Paul elsewhere repeats himself in this fashion, and draws attention to the fact that he is doing so (see especially Phil 4:4).

As may be supposed, ***if anyone makes proclamation to you alongside of what you received—let him be anathema*** is largely a repetition of verse 8. It is nonetheless significant, underscoring that Paul is not merely resorting to hyperbole with his *anathema* language.

1:10 *For now do I persuade men—or God? or do I seek to please men? If I yet pleased men, I would not be the slave of the Messiah.*

Paul is likely setting forth, not one, but two sets of contrasts: ***For now do I persuade men—or God? or do I seek to please men?***

Most obvious is the contrast between men and God, but the point also seems to be the difference between persuading and pleasing. Yes, Paul *does indeed* seek to persuade men (which he does effectively with Jews and Greeks in Acts 18:4). See especially 2 Cor 5:11: "knowing, therefore, the fear of the Lord, we persuade men; but we are evident to God, and I also trust are evident to your consciences." God, however, is impossible to persuade and His truth is unalterable.

If, on the other hand, ***I yet pleased men, I would not be the slave of the Messiah***. If he should seek to *please* men, Paul would be treating God as a mere man. Pleasing God means holding His Word inviolate, even in the face of opposition.

Paul here introduces the notion of slavery to the Messiah, but as he progresses through the letter, he will show that service to Christ is the only true freedom, and the alternative is slavery under the elements of the world, such as Torah.

Meanwhile, surely Paul's implication here is that the circumcision teaching is in fact man-pleasing. As he later suggests, the teachers promote circumcision in order to minimize persecution (6:12; cf 5:11).

For his part, however, Paul's insistence on being the Messiah's servant rather than men's is—counterintuitively, perhaps—an insistence that is in service to men. For it is only by being faithful to the sure liberating word of God that Paul communicates to the Galatians what they truly need to hear. His unswerving and uncompromising faithfulness is for their salvation.

Paul's Persecuting Past (1:11–14)

Verses 11, 12, and 16 of chapter 1 together assert that flesh and blood did not teach Paul his gospel, but it was given as a revelation of Jesus the Messiah.

This should be understood against the backdrop of the Apostle Peter's confession of Jesus as "the Messiah, the Son of the Living God" in Matt 16:16, where Jesus in response calls him blessed and declares, "Flesh and blood has not revealed this to you, but my Father who is in heaven." Appropriately, it is in this context that Jesus says the Church will be built upon Peter (and implicitly, the other apostles; cf Eph 2:20). Paul is claiming no less for the significance of the revelation and corresponding authority given to himself as the apostle to the Gentiles.

This assertion stands over against Paul's past. He was sold out to life as a Torah-observant Jew, conducting himself with a zeal that outshone most of his own contemporaries. That zeal took the form of attempting to destroy the church of Jesus. Paul's personal history was such that he would require, not further instruction, but divine intervention, in order to move from persecutor to proclaimer of the divine news.

1:11 *Now I make known to you, brothers, the good news which was proclaimed by me, that it is not according to man.*

Now I make known to you. There is a text-critical question whether the conjunction is γὰρ (*for*) or δέ (and, *now*). Not a whole lot rides on the question. The latter is simpler; if the former, the connection to the preceding may be that in his accounting of himself which follows, Paul is expanding on the fact that he is the Messiah's slave.

Although Paul is calling everything into question regarding the Galatians, he nonetheless calls them ***brothers***. It is noteworthy that despite the fact that they are in the process of capitulation, Paul still distinguishes between them and the false teachers. This perhaps hints (as is likely in any case) that the teachers are not indigenous. Crucially, simply by way of this title of *brothers*, Paul is preaching the gospel to the Galatians, since they have lost the sense that they are already children of God, apart from the circumcision they are contemplating (cf 3:21–26).

As hinted earlier, Paul's earlier assertion of the divine character of his apostleship is not about personal authority (see on verse 8); it is in service to the *message:* ***the good news which was proclaimed by me … is not according to man***. One further thing that *not according to man* means is that, by human standards, what is proclaimed is *unexpected*. As Paul writes in 1 Cor 1, the happy proclamation of Jesus is foolishness to the Greeks who seek after wisdom, as well as a stumblingblock to the Jews who seek after a sign. In the Messiah, God has acted in a way that defied human logic and expectation.

1:12 *For neither did I myself receive it from man, nor was I taught, but through the revelation of Jesus the Messiah.*

Paul's claim, demonstrated in what follows, is that ***neither did I myself receive*** [my gospel] ***from man, nor was I taught***. Paul's proclamation is not due to reception of a tradition or teaching; it was given him *via* an apocalypse, a revelation.

It should be underscored that Paul is not denigrating teaching. In fact, he has just stressed what the Galatians *received from him through his preaching and teaching* (1:8–9). As Martyn observes, "the gospel is both divine apocalypse (v 12) and after that tradition (v 9)."[9] Thus, Paul does not discredit a pattern of teaching (διδαχή), but what he has preached was not arrived at in that manner. It is a revelation divine in character (cf 2:2), above human knowledge. He did not receive catechesis, even from the other apostles, as he will show presently (cf vv 16–19).

Regarding Paul's reception of his proclamation ***through the revelation of Jesus the Messiah***, Martyn is also probably right in wishing to go beyond the general idea of "revelation."[10] In 3:23 and context, Paul speaks of a *coming*, a new event, not simply the unveiling of existing realities.

However, we must not confuse God's invasion of history in Christ with how Paul as an individual and an apostle was introduced to that decisive divine action. The *coming* of 3:23 is a reference to the advent on earth of Jesus, with His ensuing ministry, death, and resurrection, and it is fair to call Paul's reception of it a "revelation," so long as we retain its divine character and guard against depersonalizing it. It is *the revelation of Jesus the Messiah* Himself, not simply the communication of doctrines or even events. On this point, Martyn is on target: "God is the subject of the verb ἀποκαλύψαι [in v 16], being the actor who carried out the invasive revealing. The Messiah is the object of God's revelatory act."[11]

In all of this, there is an emphatic *I, I myself.* Certainly, this is not a contrast to the other apostles, who also received the gospel directly from Jesus (if not necessarily in as full a nature regarding Gentiles, since that was not the primary target of their ministries).

There likely is a contrast, however, to the false teachers: *their* message does not come from the Messiah.

As with Paul's apostleship in 1:1, so here with his proclamation: the

9 Martyn, 150.

10 See *ibid,* 99.

11 *Ibid,* 144.

denial and corresponding affirmation contains an implicit claim that Jesus the Messiah is no mere human being. He has full divine authority.

1:13 *For you heard [about] my conduct, when I was in Judaism, that I went to extremes, persecuting the church of God, and tried to destroy it.*

The Galatians themselves have already ***heard about my conduct, when I was in Judaism***. Paul's previous behaviour was based on διδαχή similar in some respects to that of the false teachers. Noteworthy here is that Paul focuses upon *conduct*, and Dunn suggests that it was his conduct rather than his beliefs which were most "relevant to the Galatian crisis."[12] I think Witherington offers a stronger, more balanced statement; Galatians:

> ... is not about getting in, or staying in, but about the right and wrong ways of going on.... One's way of life involves beliefs, behavior, and social interaction. It involves certain rites of passage and not others, certain beliefs about salvation and not others, certain forms of behavior and not others among Christians.[13]

This conduct was sincere and wholehearted: ***I went to extremes, persecuting the church of God, and tried to destroy it***. The verbs are imperfect, indicating actions prolonged over an extended period of time.

Paul here is anticipating the *zeal* language he will employ in the following verse. He also speaks elsewhere of how his persecution of the church demonstrated the zeal of his former devotion to Torah (Phil 3:6).

Notice the charge regarding Stephen—in whose stoning Paul was involved. He had spoken against the holy place and the law, claiming that Jesus would "change the customs which Moses delivered to us" (Acts 6:13–14). This underscores the fact that Paul's persecution of the church was, in his own mind, a defense of Torah. Given this, when he was converted, Paul was not likely simply to attempt a synthesis between

12 James D. G. Dunn, *Galatians* (BNTC; Hendrickson, 1993), 55.

13 Witherington, 99–100.

the Messiah and Torah; he recognized that they were in some sense antithetical.

This conduct was a destructive opposition to God's own assembly. Dunn 58 notes the irony: "The very actions aimed at preserving the purity of the assembly of Israel … had actually been directed against that assembly itself!"

Paul's former persecution of the church is in implicit parallel to the present circumcision party, who likewise are trying to destroy the church as the Messiah has founded it.

Note the ***for***. Beyond the implicit comparison above, Paul here is putting forward his own history as proof that his gospel was not to be attributed to men. Why? Because it shows that he had not been a proper subject for "teaching." Had it not been for dramatic divine revelation, he would have remained on his destructive course.

Excursus: Jacob and Paul

There are numerous threads which connect the story of Jacob and that of Paul. When Esau was breathing out threats and slaughter against Jacob (Gen 27:41), Jacob fled to the land of the Arameans in Paddan-aram (Gen 28:2ff). *En route,* he had a vision of God, who reaffirmed the Abrahamic promises to him. In response, Jacob erected a pillar to mark God's house (Gen 28:10–22).

Jacob remained in Paddan-aram some twenty years (Gen 31:28), but the more prominent number was the 14 years he served for Laban's daughters (cf Gen 29:20, 27, 30). Following his return, the first story recorded in Genesis is that of Shechem, who along with his townsmen was compelled to be circumcised—and was then slaughtered by Simeon and Levi for defiling Jacob's daughter Dinah (Gen 34).

The Paul story reflects somewhat of a reversal of the Genesis narrative. Paul implicitly begins as an Esau, breathing out threats and slaughter against the people of God (Acts 9:1). In the context of that, he heads north to the land of the Arameans in Damascus (Acts 9:2ff). *En route,* he has a vision of the Lord, who commissions him and gives him promises (compare Acts 9:3ff; 22:6ff; and especially Acts 26:12–18). Paul then stays in Damascus, and returns briefly to Jerusalem after three years

(Gal 1:18), but more notably after fourteen years (2:1).

The parallels, however, go deeper and further. The primary conflicts of Paul's ministry, not least in this letter, center around circumcision of the Gentiles; and indeed one of the principal surface adversaries in Galatians appears to be *Jacob* (usually translated as *James* in English versions, which of course obscures the connections). Indeed, Jacob along with Simon (Simeon!) Peter and John are described as *pillars* (Gal 2:9).

Paul's closing benediction in Galatians is a pronouncement of peace and mercy upon all those who follow the new creation, "and upon the Israel *of God*" (Gal 6:16).

Just as there is a conflict between "Ishmael" and "Isaac" at the forefront in chapter 4, the above observations would seem to indicate that the letter likewise has a Jacob (and Esau) subtext providing underlying support. (Intriguingly, Esau married a daughter of Ishmael when Jacob left to find a wife in Paddan-aram; see Gen 28:6–9.)

Paul is concerned with the eschatological justification of the Gentiles apart from circumcision (overturning the Shechem event, if you will); and more than that, he wishes to identify the Israel of God as those who, like himself, walk by this rule of the new creation rather than judging Gentiles by the norms of Torah. Those who would truly be pillars in this new house of God must be shaped by new creation realities rather than by the dividing characteristics of the law. (For similar sentiments in Paul, but with some aspects developed much more explicitly, see Eph 2:11–22.)

1:14 *And was advancing in Judaism above many contemporaries among my kinsmen, being excessively zealous of the traditions of my fathers.*

Having been trained by Gamaliel I, Paul became a star pupil by his devoted activity, ***advancing in Judaism above many contemporaries among my kinsmen***. I am not inclined to think this is primarily academic advancement;[14] the context here seems to do with a later period—i.e. what was happening in Paul's life at the time God laid hold

14 As Witherington 101 suggests.

of him (note that Paul's record of the latter event follows immediately upon this verse).

The advancement here therefore would appear to be connected to Paul's vigorous defense of Torah: he was becoming increasingly influential in upholding the law. This was reflected, for example, by the responsibility entrusted to him in the very trip to Damascus which ultimately changed his course.

Either way, however, whether tied to academic excellence or later growing influence, the statement reveals a portrait of success within the context of Paul's heritage. "As a Jew he had no reason to leave Judaism."[15]

Paul was not merely a stolid supporter of the party line; he was ***excessively zealous of the traditions of my fathers.*** The teachers in Galatia (and the corresponding Jerusalem circumcision party even now troubling Antioch) have nothing on Paul—he had overflowed with zeal. No doubt styling himself after Phinehas (see Num 25), who saved Israel from catastrophe by means of his spear, or after the Maccabees, who violently opposed the disrespect of their Syrian overlords toward Torah, Paul is attempting to rescue Israel's purity by the sword. As N. T. Wright likes to put it, as often as not, zeal in his context was something you did with a knife.

We see that Paul was not sitting around with a guilty conscience wondering how to relieve it, nor engaging in theological investigations, trying to discern whether someone had developed a superior dogmatics to that of Gamaliel. He was not a failure full of self-doubt; he was a paragon of religious success, certain that what he was doing was service to God Himself.

There is some question regarding the referent of *the traditions of my fathers.* Does this refer to Torah, or to the oral teaching of the Pharisaic teachers influential in Paul's circle? A number of commentators suggest the latter, but in truth it was probably both. Citing Acts 22:3, Witherington judiciously writes, "The phrase 'ancestral traditions' to [the Galatian Gentiles] would have surely connoted the Mosaic law, and perhaps also any oral extrapolations, but in any case would not have

15 Betz, 68.

excluded the Law itself."[16]

In any case, *the traditions of my fathers* stand in contrast to the gospel, which Paul has in no way received from men—the very word *tradition* has the idea of passing down. Thus there is an implicit claim regarding the superiority of the apocalyptic gospel which Paul now preaches, over against the way of life he once defended with such zeal. Garlington puts it this way:

> In a manner remarkably dissimilar to his training as a young rabbinical student, whereby he was taught both Torah and the interpretive tradition "line upon line and precept upon precept," his proclamation and mission to the nations came "straight down from above" by virtue of his vision of the risen Christ on the Damascus Road.[17]

An Apostle is Born (1:15–24)

And now begins the contrast. In the following verses, we learn that, upon the revelation of Christ to him and in him, Paul and his zeal defected to the Messiah in place of Torah, whereas the circumcision party is attempting to combine the two.

1:15 *But when God pleased—the One who separated me from my mother's womb and called [me] through His grace.*

Paul has been speaking of how effective his own zeal apparently was, but now he turns to what happened ***when God pleased***.

Paul's persecuting past was part of God's purpose, who in fact had ***separated me from my mother's womb***. This echoes the language of the prophets, who frequently are spoken of as separated from birth for their role (see e.g. Jer 1:5). It is also an echo of Isaiah's language regarding the Servant (Isa 49:1).

Paul's earlier self-identification of himself as the δοῦλος of Jesus

16 Witherington, *Grace*, 104.

17 Don Garlington, *Exposition*, 50.

(1:10) is also connected to this. In Isa 49:5–6, Yahweh has formed the speaker from the womb to be His Servant (LXX δοῦλος). The purpose is not only to bring Jacob back to Himself, which is "too small a thing"; "I will also give You as a light to the Gentiles."

This is a succinct outline of Paul's ministry. To be sure, it may seem strange for us to make that connection, since the Servant is generally (and rightly) understood to be the Messiah Himself. But in his apostolic calling, Paul was an emissary who stood in for the Messiah and acted on His behalf.

There may also be a bit of a pun with Paul's use of the term *separated* here, which was generally linked to the idea of the *Pharisees* as the separated ones. Saul was a Pharisee, but even before that, God had already "phariseed" him from the womb for His own purpose.

How could Paul be *separated from his mother's womb,* since he did not serve in this role from the beginning, and in fact opposed the Messiah most vigorously? Burton 52 clarifies that the verb does not mean "to remove from a place," but "to mark off from something else," "to separate or set apart from others." Paul may have spent his early life opposing Christ, but God already had other purposes for him.

Paul says that ***God called me through His grace***, and the clause is particularly poignant in the context. If ever God's favour has been given as a gift in the face of ill-desert, it is in the case of Paul, who was attempting to destroy God's own community.

To reveal His Son in me, in order to proclaim Him among the Gentiles, immediately I did not consult with flesh and blood. 1:16

Paul says that God pleased ***to reveal His Son in me***. Commentators and translators usually take *en* here in the sense of "to me," but note 2:20, where the Messiah is "living in me," as well as 4:19, where Paul longs to see the Messiah formed in the Galatians again. (Cf too 4:6, where the Spirit of the Son resides in our hearts.) This holds true with what Paul says elsewhere about his apostolic commission: God "has *shone in our hearts* with the light of *the knowledge of the glory of God in the face of the Messiah*" (2 Cor 4:6).

Thus although the revelation is objective, it is also existential and internal. Just as God had promised that at the advent of the new covenant, He would put "the law" within His people and write it upon their hearts (Jer 31:33), this finds its fulfillment in the Messiah being revealed within Paul and his converts.[18] Paul has been transferred into the new creation, and the new creation has come to life in Paul in the person of Jesus the Messiah.

It is also interesting to note the correspondence between Jesus' self-revelation to Stephen—whom Paul had persecuted—and to Paul himself. (Stephen's testimony of his vision of Christ in Acts 7:55–56 sounds remarkably similar to 2 Cor 4:6; cf Acts 9:3; 26:13).

This revelation was not simply for Paul's own benefit; it is immediately and preeminently *vocational*. The revelation of the Son in Paul was ***in order to proclaim Him among the Gentiles*** (see again Isa 49:5–6).

This of course is in line with the from-the-womb prophetic callings mentioned above. Men were not ordained to be prophets in order to have private assurance regarding themselves or their thoughts; they were commissioned for the sake of others.

But in particular, God chose Paul to take up the Servant's calling connected to the other nations. Such is the irony of God's ways that He chooses the purist of the purists, the persecuting Pharisee who breathed out threatenings and slaughter against what he saw as (at best) the Hellenizing influence of the Jesus message—and He makes *this* one the missionary to the Gentiles.

There is no need to get caught up in the "call vs. conversion" dichotomy. While it is true that Paul did not see himself as changing from one religion to another—and indeed his own testimony in Acts would lead us to believe that he worshiped "the God of our fathers" both before and after the Damascus road encounter (cf Acts 22:3; 24:14, 16)—in the biblical sense, conversion involves a turnaround, which Paul certainly experienced. He was transferred from darkness to light. Indeed, he was transferred from one creation to another—if that is not "conversion," certainly nothing is! Nonetheless, the purpose of this conversion was

18 On this matter of the Messiah coming in place of and in fulfillment of Torah, see my expanded treatment in *These Are Two Covenants*, as well as pp 20–23 above.

vocational (cf the purpose of Abraham's call in Gen 18:19).

Paul says that ***immediately I did not consult with flesh and blood;*** he is likely intending a contrast to ὁ θεὸς in v 15. God Himself has revealed His Son to and in Paul, an event that does not require conferral with flesh and blood. What would normally be sane, wise, and judicious has been trumped: the living God has spoken. Having conferred with Him, man can add nothing.

Nor did I go up unto Jerusalem to those who were apostles before me, but 1:17
departed into Arabia and again returned unto Damascus.

When Paul says ***nor did I go up unto Jerusalem to those who were apostles before me***, he is reinforcing the contextual point regarding the (humanly speaking) independence of his message: he did not receive his gospel from the Jerusalem apostles.

Instead, Paul ***departed into Arabia and again returned unto Damascus***. Perhaps this implies a Moses/Elijah theme, but geographically we should keep in mind that Arabia would refer to the Nabatean kingdom, which extended to the walls of Damascus. Thus, departing into Arabia would not necessarily have required a lengthy journey, and it should be no surprise that Luke does not mention such a journey in Acts.

Although some see this departure into Arabia as a solitary meditative excursion into the desert, it is more plausible that Paul immediately begins his response to the call to spread the Messiah-proclamation to the nations, especially since Aretas is seeking his arrest after his return to Damascus (2 Cor 11:32). This makes best sense of the context: before he has any conferral of any sort with the Jerusalem apostles, Paul begins to obey the command to preach Jesus the Messiah. Meditating quietly on the back side of the desert does not spark persecution from kings and rulers. Without any input from the Twelve, Paul already had a message to proclaim, and he was proclaiming it.

The Moses–Elijah theme nonetheless is probable, especially given the fact that *Arabia* appears only here and in 4:25 (where it refers to Sinai) in the entire NT. Second Corinthians 3 demonstrates well enough that Paul is comfortable making a contrast between his own ministry and that of Moses. Elijah too went to Horeb (Sinai), and then returned to Damascus—in a context that mentions *zeal*, no less (1 Kgs 19:8, 14–15).

Given this backdrop, Paul is likely making the implicit claim that, just as Moses received his commission directly from God at Horeb in Arabia (Exod 3:1ff), where he also was given direct revelation of the law later, and likewise as God spoke to Elijah in Arabia, so too Paul's own encounter of commissioning and revelation has not been with mere men but with God Himself.[19] If he will later suggest the teachers should hack their privates to pieces (cf 5:12), he at least has authority similar to Elijah, who destroyed the prophets of Baal.

1:18 *Then, after three years, I went up unto Jerusalem to visit Cephas, and remained with him fifteen days.*

It is only ***then, after three years, I went up unto Jerusalem***. This implies that up to this point, Paul had made no visits to Jerusalem since his conversion. This visit is therefore the one mentioned in Acts 9:26–29. Paul is establishing his "alibi"—at the writing of this letter, he had only been in Jerusalem twice since his conversion (the visit mentioned here, and that discussed in 2:1–10), and neither time for the purpose of receiving his message from the hand of men.

This particular journey was ***to visit Cephas***, and Paul ***remained with him fifteen days***. Consistent with the issue at hand, the terminology is one of *getting to know* Cephas, rather than being instructed by him. This is not to say that Peter would not have passed on what he had witnessed regarding the life and teaching of Jesus, which was to be expected (cf 1 Cor 15:1–7). At any rate, the *fifteen days* was scarcely long enough for Peter or any of the other Jerusalem leaders to disciple or catechize Paul—particularly when we learn from Acts that during this time, the latter was busy "going in and out," preaching boldly in the

19 Wright, in "Paul, Arabia, and Elijah" 683–687, makes a fascinating connection between how in his *zeal* Elijah had executed the prophets of Baal just prior to his trip to Arabia, while in his zeal Paul had been persecuting the Church before his own trip there.

name of Jesus (Acts 9:28). Both Paul and Peter were far too busy with public proclamation to set aside two weeks of private time.

Interestingly, it was precisely the men mentioned in vv 18–19, Peter and Jacob, whom Paul saw during the first visit to Jerusalem following his conversion. The very figures of authority around whom the present controversy swirls are in fact the men in the Jerusalem church whom Paul knows best.

But other of the apostles I did not see, except Jacob the brother of the Lord. 1:19

With this statement, Paul is placing a limitation upon what we read in Acts 9:27, where we learn that Barnabas brought him to "the apostles." Here we learn that this was not the whole number of the twelve, but only Peter and Jacob.

While some may think it problematic to identify Jacob as an apostle, he arguably met the qualifications as implied in 1 Cor 15:7ff. In any case, in Acts, Luke uses the term in a broader sense, identifying Barnabas himself as such later (Acts 14:14). Paul's own grammar here sounds like he intends to identify Jacob as an apostle, anyway.

Still, it must be acknowledged that this is not entirely satisfactory. Luke surely refers to Barnabas as an apostle due to his being sent out by the church in Antioch (Acts 13:1–3). Barnabas is thus not an apostle in the same sense Paul claims for himself—namely, as a direct representative of Jesus Himself. If Paul does not grant that sort of apostleship to Jacob, the question then remains: who *was* his sender? And of course, if he *does* grant that sort of apostleship to Jacob,[20] how does this apostolate relate to that of the Twelve?

Fung sidesteps the difficulty by suggesting that the "except" refers back to the entire preceding clause and should be understood in the sense of "I did not see any other apostle, but I saw only…."[21] This expedient is apparently possible, although arguably not probable.

20 Which, given the context of Paul's statement about him in 1 Cor 15:7, would appear to be a possibility.

21 Ronald Y. K. Fung, *Galatians* (NICNT, 1988), 77–78.

1:20 *Now the things I write to you, behold, before God—I am not lying.*

The expression, ***behold, before God—I am not lying*** is a form of oath, which Paul takes up regarding ***the things I write to you***. While we can expect Paul to speak the truth regardless, this emphatically underscores his own record: up to the time of writing, he has made only two visits to Jerusalem since his conversion, and they were not for the purpose of being catechized by the Jerusalem apostles.

The fact that he swears upon this point reinforces the importance that the Galatians pay attention to the chronological matters he is providing. That chronology is also crucial for our own understanding of the letter.

1:21 *Then I went into the regions of Syria and Cilicia.*

Not having to do with Jerusalem, these are apparently not listed strictly chronologically here. We learn from Acts that Paul ***went into the regions of Syria and Cilicia*** in the reverse order. When he fled Jerusalem at the end of his first visit, he headed for the regions of his birthplace (Tarsus was in Cilicia).

In the meantime, believing Jews who had fled Judea during the persecution had been spreading the new faith in Syrian Antioch (the fourth largest city of the Empire), and in their zeal some of them had begun to preach to Gentiles. The response was so great that Jerusalem sent Barnabas to help lead the new church there. He in turn, having had previous connection with Paul, and doubtless already being aware of the latter's particular calling to Gentiles, fetched him from Tarsus (on all this, see Acts 9:30; 11:19–26).

1:22 *But I was unknown by face to the churches of Judea in the Messiah.*

Even after visiting Jerusalem, Paul was ***unknown by face to the churches of Judea***. Why is this important to Paul's argument? Again, in context, Paul is arguing for his independence from the Jerusalem apostles. It would hardly do for him to claim that he did not settle in

Jerusalem, if in fact he had worked in Judea, which was their field of labour. Had he done so, he could easily have been instructed by them wherever he happened to be.

Moreover, Fung 82–83 suggests that were Paul dependent upon the Jerusalem authorities, they presumably would have commissioned him to work in Judea; in that case, his field of labour itself could be evidence of his independence.

Paul adds his characteristic phrase, ***in the Messiah***—it is the assemblies ἐν Χριστῷ of whom he speaks.

Only, they were hearing, "The one who persecuted us once now proclaims the faith he once was trying to destroy." 1:23

While they did not get a chance to see him face to face, ***they were hearing*** about his about-face and corresponding calling: ***"The one who persecuted us once now proclaims the faith he once was trying to destroy."***

Here πίστιν (*faith*) appears to take on something of an "objective" sense. Given the early date of this letter, incidentally, Paul's use here demonstrates that the thought of a notion of a "received body of belief" being a late development is wrongheaded. The apostolic preaching from the beginning had a recognizable core of teachings.

In this connection, Hays aptly writes that this faith

> ... is not just a matter of inward attitudes of the heart; it alludes to the substantive content of Christian preaching, as summarized in kerygmatic formulas such as Gal 1:3–4 and 1 Cor 15:3–5.... [it] can function for Paul as a synonym for "the gospel."[22]

The statement is important: what Paul proclaims is *the same faith* he once was destroying. He has not been preaching some aberrant variant on the real Christian message. Contrary to the implied viewpoint of the

22 Hays, *Galatians*, 217.

false teachers, it is Paul who proclaims the catholic message. His message may indeed have been received independently of the other apostles, by direct revelation, but it is nonetheless the same message of the Messiah believed by the churches of Judea.

Thus, if there is now some question regarding Peter or Jacob, let it not be said that it is Paul who has moved.

1:24 *And they were glorifying God in me.*

Here again there is overlap and interchange with the Isaianic Servant: ***they were glorifying God in me*** is an echo of Isa 49:3: "You are my Servant, Israel, in whom I will be glorified." Because the Son/Servant is revealed *in* Paul (1:16), God the Father likewise receives glory in and through him.

Although some controversy within the Jerusalem church regarding Paul can be detected later (as referred to by Jacob himself in Acts 21:20–21), this passage provides testimony that there is no general long-standing rift between Paul and the Jewish churches (*contra* a number of critical scholars). Despite Peter's present collapse (see the "Galatians as Biography" chapter, as well as the Exposition on 2:11–21) and questions about Jacob, there is a history of shared purpose in the gospel of Jesus the Messiah.

Paul and the Pillars in Partnership (2:1–10)

Here Paul recounts his second visit to Jerusalem after his encounter with Jesus. This visit again keys on Peter and Jacob, this time along with John, the other stalwart pillar of the Jerusalem church. Unlike the council of Acts 15, this meeting occurs in private.

Paul explains that even though he met with these leaders to ensure that they would not be working counter to his message, they had nothing to add to his approach to proclamation. Rather, they were pleased to form a working partnership, which recognized Paul's primary field as the Gentiles, while they continued to work primarily among their kinsmen and those who had previously converted to the Jewish faith *via* circumcision.

After fourteen years, again I went up unto Jerusalem with Barnabas, taking 2:1
along Titus also.

The ***fourteen years*** which intervened prior to his next visit indicates that Paul had no anxiety regarding his own position or that of his message; nor did he expect opposition from the other apostles.

When ***again I went up unto Jerusalem with Barnabas***, this was for the famine relief visit recorded in Acts 11:30. (See the "Galatians as Biography" for more details on the chronology.)

Paul and Barnabas made this visit, ***taking along Titus also***. Titus is first mentioned here; Luke never mentions him in Acts. This is not surprising; the only men named in Acts 11 are Paul and Barnabas, who were responsible for delivering the famine relief collection. Not having been made a partner in the public task in view, Titus is not referenced by Luke. Paul will reference him later as his own partner in the gospel (2 Cor 8:23). Given the casual mention here, it seems likely that Titus had accompanied Paul and Barnabas on the earlier missionary journey to Galatia.

Now I went up according to a revelation, and placed before them the good 2:2
news which I proclaim among the Gentiles—but privately, to those who were
reputed, lest somehow in vain I run or had run.

Paul ***went up according to a revelation***, namely, the prophecy of famine made by Agabus (Acts 11:28), in response to which the Antioch church sent a collection for the poor in Judea (Acts 11:29). This fundamental purpose of the visit explains the presence of the concern for the poor mentioned in v 10 here.

Paul took advantage of the visit, ***and placed before them the good news which I proclaim among the Gentiles***. This should not be thought of as a request for permission to continue to preach, nor as a request for validation. Had Paul required either of those, he would have sought them long before.

Rather, he does this ***privately, to those who were reputed, lest somehow in vain I run or had run***. Paul's efforts for a unified church of Jew and Gentile, based on equal, common footing in Jesus the Messiah, would have been threatened if the Jerusalem leadership was actively working in a different direction. There would be the danger that two churches would arise, one Jew and the other Gentile.

The centrality of this concern shows the wrongheadedness of "separate but equal churches" for various ethnicities. That is not what Paul laboured so hard for, at such great cost. His vision was for full-orbed *koinonia*, where all peoples share the same table.

So Paul reports to these "certain men" in Jerusalem the shape of his Torah-free proclamation to ensure that there will be common purpose. As Burton writes, "disapproval of his work by the leading apostles in Jerusalem would seriously interfere with [Paul's] work and to a serious degree render it ineffectual."[23] The Galatians' own response to hearing of Peter's actions in Antioch serves as eloquent testimony to this observation.[24]

Paul retains the present tense: this is the good news which he *presently* proclaims; he has not altered it since meeting with these pillars.

The fact that this meeting is carried out *privately* underscores that Paul is not speaking of the council in Acts 15. The visit by Paul and Barnabas on that occasion was commissioned by an apparent official action of the Antioch church (Acts 15:2b), and the conciliar meeting itself was not "private." The fact that Luke does not mention this meeting in Acts 11 is explicable from the very fact that it was indeed *private.*[25]

2:3 ***But not even Titus, who was with me, though a Greek, was forced to become circumcised.*** Paul will shortly say that the pillars contributed nothing to him or his proclamation; in line with that, they had nothing to add to Titus either. Titus therefore became living and lasting demonstration of the unity between Paul and the Jerusalem pillars regarding the appropriateness of his Torah-free message for Gentiles. Assuming

23 Burton, *Galatians*, 72–73.

24 On the *in vain* terminology, cf also 3:4 and 4:11. With reference to the Galatians themselves, the initial success of the gospel would be in vain if the Galatians were to embrace circumcision and Torah.

25 For more demonstration that Gal 2:1–10 and Acts 15 refer to different events, see the introductory section above, "Galatians as Biography."

therefore that he had accompanied Paul and Barnabas in Galatia (cf on v 1 above), Titus has already become an embodied witness among Paul's readers to this earlier agreement not to trouble the Gentiles with circumcision and Torah.

But on account of smuggled-in false brothers, who slipped in to spy out our freedom which we have in the Messiah Jesus, so that they might enslave us. 2:4

This is a broken sentence … what exactly happened ***on account of smuggled-in false brothers***, and how is it that they ***slipped in to spy out our freedom which we have in the Messiah Jesus, so that they might enslave us***?

One view is that false brothers were present for the meeting between Paul, Barnabas, and the "pillars." It seems highly doubtful, however, that other people could have been smuggled into such a small, private meeting.

The best explanation of the text is that the aorist in 2:4 (παρεισῆλθον, *had slipped in*) is functioning in the sense of a grammatical perfect, and referring to some prior situation. The *false brothers* had come, not to the private meeting, but to Antioch, to spy out the liberty of the largely Gentile church there. Thus what likely occurred on a larger, more open scale in the leadup to Acts 15 (of which 2:11ff here forms a partial account) had already been foreshadowed in Antioch once before.

In view of this (then) smaller-scale trouble in Antioch, Paul and Barnabas decided to take Titus with them during their famine relief visit, as a sort of test case. (Note that if this is the case, the private meeting recorded makes the later events even more inexcusable on the part of Peter.)

This reading of course does assume that the *you* in v 5 is a general "you," as in *you Gentiles* (which would appear to fit with how Paul generally seems to use the second person plural in most of the letter)—at the time of the meeting in question, Paul had not yet made his first missionary journey, and so the Galatians were not yet converted.

I thus take the broken sentence to be due to the parenthetical nature of the remark, referring to the precipitating event which led to the inclusion of Titus in the trip to Jerusalem and the private meeting that ensued.

Paul mentions *false brothers* also in 2 Cor 11:26, where he speaks of the perils they bring. What is the sense of *false?* The prefix ψευδ- is used to modify terms such as prophets (*false prophets*), apostles (*false apostles*) and testimony (*false witness*). It could apparently mean something like *counterfeit,* although at least in some instances, something like *deceitful, unfaithful, untrue* would be more appropriate.

At any rate, these "brothers" give the lie to their genuine brotherhood by their attempt to bring slavery; at the very least they are being *untrue* to their brotherhood. They were false brothers, because they refused to be brethren to Gentiles as Gentiles.

While elsewhere in the letter, *we* generally seems to refer to "we believing Jews," in referring to "the freedom which we have," in the present case Paul is probably using the first-person plural in connection with his "home church" in Antioch. In any case, note that this is freedom for both Gentile *and* Jew, together. They are free to worship God in the Messiah together, on the same footing, as fellow-heirs.

So that they might enslave us introduces the slavery theme which dominates much of Galatians, especially chapters 3–5. Torah is itself a *paidagogos* (3:24ff)—a slave who served as a child custodian—and those under its care likewise must differ nothing from a slave even if they are heirs (4:1). Subjection to Torah's calendar is slavery (4:10); the slave-woman and her son must be cast out, for the slave-son will not inherit with the free (4:30); the Galatians must stand fast in the freedom gained by the Messiah, and not come under slavery's yoke (5:1).

This story is a poignant reminder that the "conservatives," the "strict party," are not always the good guys. They may in fact be enforcing rules which are not in accord with Scripture, and in that case even the gospel itself can be in danger.

2:5 *To whom not even for an hour we yielded subjection, so that the truth of the good news might remain with you.*

Paul shows how resolutely he has remained opposed to slavery: ***to***

whom not even for an hour we yielded subjection—in order words, he gave no quarter for submission to enslavement. There are times to listen patiently and carefully; there are also times to stand firm without budging.

This steadfast defense was ***so that the truth of the good news might remain with you.*** Again, this is not specifically a reference to the freedom of the Galatian churches in particular (which did not yet exist at the time of the event recorded in 2:1–10), but to that of "all you Gentile believers" (see above on the previous verse).

The *truth of the good news* is here implicitly contrasted with the *falsity* of the "brothers." God's good news is faithful, even if men are not always so.

> *But from those who were reputed as something—whatever once they were, it* 2:6
> *makes no difference to me: God does not receive the face of a man—for those*
> *who were reputed contributed nothing to me.*

Referring back to what he had started to say in v 2, Paul adds that ***from those who were reputed as something*** he received no additional instruction. When Paul says that the pillars ***contributed nothing to me***, this coordinates with his earlier curse against anyone who would dare *add* anything alongside the gospel he had preached (1:8–9). Even though the false brothers had been attempting to add circumcision to the gospel to the Gentiles (cf vv 3–5), the pillars made no such addition to Paul's message.[26]

In the course of this, though, he adds, ***whatever they once were, it makes no difference to me: God does not receive the face of a man***, i.e. is not a respecter of persons, is not partial. I have retained the literal idiom, because it carries an important contrast to Paul's claims that his message and apostleship were not derived *from men* nor *through man.* Paul sounds a great deal like a *dis*respecter of persons here, but that is not the point. If neither he nor an angel from heaven was qualified to alter the message he had preached, then the same could be said for

26 On the various options for understanding προσανέθεντο, see especially Burton, 89–91, who adopts a similar position to mine.

the Jerusalem leadership. In that sense, Paul does not care about their standing.

While Paul elsewhere is the first to grant genuine authority to the Messiah's Church and her leaders, here it becomes clear that all of them stand under the judging authority of the Word of the gospel (see also 1:8–9). Neither Peter as an individual, nor all of Jerusalem's pillars together, can be taken as the Messiah's absolute vicar upon the earth.

The addition of *once* likely reflects Paul's current uncertainty with regard to those who seemed to be "something" (i.e. *pillars;* see v 9). If, as it appears from Peter's actions in Antioch (vv 11ff), they have capitulated to the circumcision party, Paul no longer views them as genuine pillars in God's new temple, a temple made up of Jew and Gentile together (Eph 2:11–22).

2:7 *But contrariwise, seeing that I had been entrusted the good news of the uncircumcision, just as Peter of the circumcision.*

At the time of the meeting in view, however, the pillars themselves were ***seeing that I had been entrusted the good news of the uncircumcision.*** Doubtless this commission was observed particularly through the open doors which God had granted to Paul's ministry, as well as through the pillars' knowledge of his initial call.

The implication of ***just as Peter [was entrusted the good news] of the uncircumcision*** is not that there are two distinct ways of salvation, one for Jews and one for Gentiles, but rather that the proclamation deals with the status of Gentiles in relationship to circumcision and Torah. Since Jews were already circumcised, the issue for them did not have the same sort of acuteness. The "good news of the uncircumcision" is thus enfleshed a bit differently from that to the circumcision (pardon the pun). The former is the happy announcement that Gentiles do not need to become circumcised and keep Torah in order to become full members of the people of God; the latter is the happy proclamation that the Messiah has come and fulfilled Torah and received the promises.

In both cases, the gospel is the proclamation of the new age enacted by the Messiah's victory and has identical content. But the gospel is good news for Gentiles in a different way than for Jews, since it comes to them as those who were (and are) outside Torah and its polity (cf Rom 2:6–12).

(For the One working in Peter as the apostle of the circumcision worked also 2:8
in me unto the Gentiles.)

Paul reminds his hearers again that what he is about is not merely human; and despite his protests against dependence upon Jerusalem, he is the first to speak of ***the One working in Peter as the apostle of the circumcision***.

It is important to note, both that Peter's own ministry is attributed to the power and calling of God, and that Peter's field of calling among the circumcised is assumed as legitimate. It is nonsense to call Paul "anti-Semitic" (as some have done); he retained a great love for his kinsmen throughout his ministry, and delighted in the fact that God had called fellow labourers into that field. What he did not countenance was Jewishness trumping the new creation in the Messiah.

This acting God who worked among the circumcision through the agency of Peter ***worked also in me unto the Gentiles***. The fact that God is the same One working in both implies that at base Peter and Paul were united in a common purpose and common message. Whatever confusion there may be now, it is not because these are simply two men who have gone each to their own way. At any rate, this verse in context makes it clear that the pillars recognized the apostleship of Paul, just as Peter's own was unquestioned.

And recognizing the grace given to me, Jacob and Cephas and John, the ones 2:9
reputed to be pillars, gave to me and to Barnabas the right hand of partner-
ship, so that we [should go] unto the Gentiles, but they unto the circumcision.

It is only here that Paul at last explicitly names those who were ***reputed to be pillars***. The term is fertile, suggesting an allusion to the temple pillars; Paul says elsewhere that the church is the new temple, built upon the foundation of the apostles and prophets (Eph 2:20).

It is easy to see why, independent as the source of his gospel may have been, Paul was eager to partner explicitly with them. There is *one* new temple in the Messiah, and there needed to be mutuality between the Judean and largely Gentile international churches.

So who are they? Along with Cephas (Peter) are Jacob (James) and John.

If our timeline is correct (identifying this visit with the one recorded in Acts 11), the Jacob in question could theoretically be James the son of Zebedee (since he was not martyred until Acts 12, although the "about that time" in Acts 12:1 could possibly precede the just-mentioned visit).

However, Paul has already identified Jacob the Lord's brother in 1:19, which by itself suggests this is the same individual. Moreover, were this Jacob the son of Zebedee, we would expect his name to be paired together with that of John, but instead the name of Cephas intervenes. Additionally, Jacob the son of Zebedee was already martyred by the time the Galatians were evangelized. I think we can be safe in saying that Paul would have clarified were this Jacob John's brother.

Thus, as it turns out, two of these pillars are (wittingly or not) figures in the present controversy. But at the time of the meeting, all of these men ***recognized the grace given to me*** and ***gave to me and to Barnabas the right hand of partnership***. The term is κοινωνίας, frequently translated *fellowship* or *communion*, depending on context. The basic idea is partnership, commonality in identity and task. Paul and the pillars have a brotherly cooperative agreement that presupposes the commonality of their task and calling.

This partnership is ***so that we should go unto the Gentiles, but they unto the circumcision***. What was already the case became an explicit partnership. It should not be thought that these spheres were mutually-sealed, so that Paul could not preach to Jews nor the pillars to Gentiles. There is no thought here of some sort of "separate but equal" institution, after all; in all of Paul's letters, his manifest purpose is to plant churches where there is no Jew nor Greek, barbarian, Scythian, bond nor free, but all are one in the Messiah Jesus. Thus, Witherington 141 aptly writes, "We are speaking of the major focus and purpose of their respective ministries."

Only the poor, in order that we might remember, which [was] also the same thing I was eager to do. 2:10

While there is calling to different primary fields, the pillars bring up ***the poor, in order that we might remember***. This can scarcely be a general concern that Paul think about benevolence, not just proclamation. There is no reason to think that Paul himself would not have been already committed to a "deeds" ministry.

Rather, we learned above that this visit was "in response to a revelation" (2:2), which apparently was Agabus' prophecy of impending famine (Acts 11:28), which prompted the collection in Antioch and led to this visit to Jerusalem to begin with.

In this light, it is only natural that this hope is expressed by the pillars here. They understand that Paul will go farther and farther afield in his task among the Gentiles, but in the meantime they do not want him to forget the abject poverty of the believers in Judea (who at the best of times were in general much closer to subsistence level than the average Gentile).

This remembrance was ***also the same thing I was eager to do***. In other words, all along Paul had it in mind that this was not to be a one-off sending of aid. His claimed eagerness is no vain boast; Jerusalem support is mentioned in many of his letters, and is clearly one of his ongoing central concerns (1 Cor 16; 2 Cor 9; Rom 15).

A possible eschatological cast should be considered here. As Witherington 145 notes, in Rom 15:25–29, the collection is described as "part of the eschatological action of God where Gentiles will go up to Zion and contribute to what is going on there with Jews, having shared in the spiritual blessings offered to them." The treasures of the Gentiles were to come in to the new temple (cf Hag 2:7; Zech 14:14).

It should be noted that it is not only the historical context behind this passage that prepares us for this verse. The term *koinonia* itself, just used in v 9, frequently referred to financial partnership (in this letter, see Gal 6:6; cf Rom 12:13; 15:26; 2 Cor 8:4; 9:13; 1 Tim 6:18). Thus the *partnership* is not limited to field of labour; there is sharing of material things, as well.

All of this is a reminder that we are our brothers' keepers. Just as the churches of Judea did not know Paul by face following his conversion, certainly the Gentile congregations did not know the Judean churches by face either. But they expressed full solidarity with their brothers and sisters, providing relief, sharing with them their own material things, just as they had received the spiritual gifts from the Jews through Paul (Rom 15:27).

Apostles in Conflict

NOTWITHSTANDING THE PRIVATE AGREEMENT made between Paul and Barnabas, on the one hand, and Jacob, Peter, and John, on the other, the partnership was challenged by both the passage of time and a particular form of public pressure. Following the famine relief visit just recounted in 2:1–10, Paul and Barnabas had engaged in a massive missionary tour of southern Asia, focusing especially upon the south Galatian cities of Pisidian Antioch, Lystra, Iconium and Derbe. After a long double tour of these cities, they had returned to home base in Syrian Antioch.

During this long "furlough," the critical events recorded in 2:11–21 transpired. These events included not only pressure from the Jerusalem circumcision party which arrived in Antioch, but also the capitulation of Peter, who happened to be present, as well.

Paul and Peter stand in stark contrast to one another regarding their respective responses to others. Peter altered his actions out of fear of other circumcised believers. Paul, on the other hand, did not hesitate to challenge, not merely that circumcision party, but Peter himself. In his public response, he takes Peter to task for his inconstancy, and in so doing outlines many of the basic issues that would soon be at play in Galatia.

Peter's Collapse (2:11–13)

> *But when Cephas came unto Antioch, against his face I opposed him, be-* 2:11
> *cause he was condemned.*

That ***Cephas came unto Antioch*** illustrates well enough that the division of labour established in v 9 was not hard and fast; the large Jewish population in Antioch, as well as its proximity to Judea, apparently provided particular motivation for the pillars to labour there, even if the division of the task was primarily geographical.

Paul says that ***against his face I opposed him***. Witherington 151 notes the risk involved in this: had Peter not backed down, Paul could have been seen as discredited. But the defense of the happy proclamation of the Messiah at times requires taking risks.

The phrase *against his face* echoes v 6, where the literal idiom is that God *does not look at any man's face*. There is thus likely a subtle allusion to the fact that here Paul is on God's side. Whatever Peter legitimately was, it made no difference to Paul when it came to defending the truth of the gospel. Paul is demonstrating practically that his words in v 6 were not empty.

Paul's opposition to Peter was ***because he was condemned***. This is a translation that neither the versions nor the commentators are generally willing to follow. Invariably, they opt for something much weaker, such as *he was to be blamed*. The term (καταγινώσκω), however, does mean *condemn*, and given the courtroom terminology of *justification* which will arise in Paul's corresponding speech (see esp vv 16, 18), it seems best to understand it in its natural meaning. Instances of usage show that the term can mean that one is condemned by virtue of one's own actions. Paul is not merely concerned that Peter has demonstrated himself blameworthy in some general sense; he wishes to show Peter that his actions in fact constitute him as a transgressor (see v 18).

Beyond the sense of guilt described in v 18, we can also say that Peter's actions render him guilty with regard to the κοινωνία (*partnership*) established in the earlier meeting in Jerusalem (see v 9). His withdrawal from the Gentiles in Antioch implicitly charges Paul's circumcision-free and Torah-free gospel with deficiency, in contradiction to the partnership and agreement between Paul and the pillars. In the terms of the partnership, therefore, Peter is unrighteous.

2:12 *For before certain ones came from Jacob, he was eating with Gentiles; but when they came, he withdrew and separated himself, fearing those from the circumcision.*

The ***certain ones*** who ***came from Jacob*** were surely the men mentioned in Acts 15:1, who came to Antioch from Judea, and were teaching the Gentile Christians there, "Unless you are circumcised according to the custom of Moses, you are unable to be saved."

Just as had been the case some years earlier, prior to the famine relief visit, so again representatives from the circumcision party are attempting to interfere in Paul's home church, laying further requirements alongside his Torah-free message and that of his fellow teachers there.

In what sense was this party *from Jacob* ("James")? In the ensuing letter from the Jerusalem council (Acts 15:24), it appears that Jacob grants an association (the visiting party consisted of τινὲς ἐξ ἡμῶν, *certain ones from us*), and that these men unsettled the Gentiles' lives by troubling them with their words (ἐτάραξαν ὑμᾶς λόγοις ἀνασκευάζοντες τὰς ψυχὰς ὑμῶν). But the letter denies that this was according to "our" instructions (οἷς οὐ διεστειλάμεθα). The latter phrase by itself could indicate that the circumcision group which came to Antioch from Jerusalem had no instructions at all from Jacob; given Paul's language, however, it is more likely that Jacob had made some sort of request of them. Perhaps he sent them as a support team for Peter's ministry. At any rate, he apparently did not give them warrant to challenge the Torah-free gospel which shaped life in the Antioch church. But that is what they in fact did.

Paul says that Peter ***was eating with Gentiles;*** the imperfect tense indicates that this was ongoing or customary. He apparently ate with the Gentiles, not once, but over a period of time. The meals in question were not solely or even primarily the Lord's Supper, although that would also likely be implicated. The eucharist apparently was ordinarily conducted within the context of a communal meal (cf 1 Cor 11), and thus eucharistic participation would have had a broader eating together as its corollary.

With the arrival of the circumcision party, Peter ***withdrew and separated himself, fearing those from the circumcision***. Why would Peter feel this pressure? Torah itself did not prohibit one from eating with Gentiles. Nonetheless, Peter had a history of struggling with that very pressure (see Acts 10:28), and devout first-century Jews in general were disinclined to eat with non-kosher Gentiles. (There may also have been eschatological rationale behind some of the circumcision party's thinking; see the introductory section, "Galatians as Hermeneutics," above.)

This fear of the circumcision party stands in contrast to Paul's own claim in 1:10, that he was not seeking men's approval. Peter was collapsing under the opinions of mere men, rather than standing fast in the truth of the good news of the Messiah.

It would be interesting to pursue the resonances between this event and the Joseph story, where it was Joseph who withdrew and ate with the Gentiles when his brothers came from their father *Jacob*. In that light, Peter would appear to be putting the wrong people to the test. Rather than in effect tempting the Gentiles to Judaize, it would have been more appropriate for Peter to test the circumcision party to see where their true loyalties belonged. In Paul's view, casting Torah down from the throne rightly belonging to Jesus (and thus entering full communion with believing Gentiles) is a key component of Jewish repentance.[1]

2:13 *And the rest of the Jews joined in hypocrisy with him, so that even Barnabas was carried away with them in the hypocrisy.*

When Paul adds, ***the rest of the Jews joined in hypocrisy with him***, he is saying that Peter's own action was hypocrisy, i.e. *pretense, acting*.

This implies that Peter was wanting the circumcision party to believe that he lived in the same manner in which they did, whereas in reality he did not. (See v 14 on Peter's living "Gentilely.") This charge of Paul thus informs the Galatians that, while they have doubtless heard this story, there is more back of it than Peter implicitly agreeing with the circumcision party. Namely, Peter himself has habitually lived in a way that contradicts the message of the circumcision party (cf Acts 11:3 in context); he is not in fact a slave to Torah by habit.

The powerful pull of this collapse is illustrated by the fact ***that even Barnabas was carried away with them in the hypocrisy***. The

1 Note also that in Gen 42:24, Joseph imprisoned *Simeon* (of which Peter's other name, *Simon,* is a variant), which has some analogy to Paul's charge of guilt against Peter.

construction suggests Paul's shock that his colleague in the Gentile mission could fall for this.

Witherington 194 (footnote 150) reminds us that Barnabas was a Levite (Acts 4:36), and speculates that perhaps he could be appealed to somewhat more readily regarding "the importance of Jewish Christians following Jewish food laws and customs." Be that as it may, Barnabas's co-labour with Paul made him an unlikely person to fall into Peter's error, and no doubt this too was made much of among the Galatian churches. "Even Barnabas, who helped in the planting of your churches, agrees with Peter and with us." But Paul here too restates that this is hypocrisy.

The collapse was not simply that of Peter and Barnabas; *the rest of the Jews joined in*. Who were these Jews? Possibly, Jews who accompanied Peter, but that seems unlikely, since the verse connects Barnabas to this group. It would seem therefore that (at least) a significant number of the believing Jews in Antioch joined with Peter in withdrawing from table fellowship with their brothers and sisters among the Gentiles. In other words, Peter's action triggered a serious schism in Paul's own home church.

Paul's Response to Peter (2:14–21)

Although most commentators think that very little of what follows was actually part of Paul's rejoinder to Peter, I see little reason for this. Given the way speeches were then recorded, there seems little reason to discount the whole as a general summation of what he said on that occasion. (In truth, one wonders if Acts 15:10–11 is something of Peter's personalized appropriation of what Paul says in 2:14–16 here.)

Paul's charge is essentially twofold: (1) Peter's action is hypocritical, since he himself was not strictly Torah-observant; and (2) Peter's action places him under a twofold judicial censure: By reattributing authority to Torah, Peter is constituting himself a transgressor against it, because he has been living according to new covenant norms rather than by strict law observance; and meanwhile, by reattributing authority to Torah and withdrawing from full table fellowship with Gentiles, Peter is transgressing against the new norms of the Messiah.

2:14 *But when I saw that they did not walk straightly along the path of the truth of the good news, I said to Cephas before [them] all, "If you, being a Jew, live 'Gentilely' and not 'Jewishly,' how do you compel the Gentiles to live Jewishly?"*

Paul here introduces a new metaphor: ***when I saw that they did not walk straightly along the path of the truth of the good news.*** In ch 5, he will speak extensively of *walking in the Spirit* as well as refer to how the Galatians previously *were running well* until someone impeded them.

This is the second time that Paul has referred to *the truth of the good news* (see v 5). This "truth" has to do with the veracity of the proclamation of the Messiah in connection with the relationship between Jews and Gentiles. Back of that, it may well also have overtones of the veracity, faithfulness and righteousness of God—terms Paul ties together in Rom 3:1–7—concerning His promises to Abraham (see below on 3:8).

Paul said this ***before them all***, in public, and likely in front of the circumcision party which so intimidated Peter. Clearly, they did not intimidate Paul. He knew their type from the inside out.

While it is always appropriate to correct private sins privately at the outset, often severe public failure requires a bold public response for the sake of others, particularly if it is the sort of sin that will exert public influence. That is what Paul provides here.

In his response to Peter, Paul states explicitly what he had implied in the previous verse: ***"If you, being a Jew, live 'Gentilely' and not 'Jewishly,' how do you compel the Gentiles to live Jewishly?"***

By becoming a genuine disciple of the Messiah, and also by his own practice at least since the conversion of Cornelius, Peter has found a new identity in the Messiah which has reshaped his lifestyle in a practical way, to the degree that it is no longer defined by Torah or Jewishness but by the good news of the new creation. Wright (*Justification* 115) correctly notes specifically how Peter could be said to be living "Gentilely":

> Peter was by now well and truly used to eating with Gentile Christians, and to making no difference between himself and them. That, after all, is what Acts says Peter had learnt in the house of Cornelius.

It being the case that Peter himself is (has been) "living like a Gentile," Paul presses the point: If this is your own practice, even though you yourself are a Jew, how can you, by your actions, put pressure upon believing Gentiles to live under the Torah-identity that you have abandoned?

It is crucial to note that the matter here is not a theological proclamation of what later came to be called "works righteousness." Peter certainly gave no indication of making an error such as that. The error he made, rather, was that by his actions he implicitly demanded that Gentiles should live as Jews, i.e. be circumcised and keep Torah. It is absurd to suppose that Paul thought Peter's action taught a system of merit. But it did teach that the *modus vivendi* (way of life) for Christian Gentiles should be according to Torah, and therefore that circumcision needed to be added to baptism as a rite of entry into full membership in the people of God.[2]

We who are by-nature-Jews and not sinners from the Gentiles. 2:15

Paul self-identifies with Peter: ***We by-nature-Jews and not sinners from the Gentiles***. This is similar in thought to Rom 11, where Paul speaks of the "natural" and "unnatural" branches who are united to the common covenant root. Notwithstanding his emphasis on equal participation in the Messiah, Paul maintains the distinction—which is necessary in terms of the promises as given to Abraham and repeated and expanded upon through the prophets.

The contrast must be correctly understood. Paul adopts the general terminology of his contemporary kinsmen in identifying Gentiles as *sinners*. Paul is not implying that unlike Gentiles, Jews are not sinful by nature (he too confessed Ps 51). Rather, the Jews had received by heritage marks such as circumcision and Torah which distinguished them covenantally from the nations. Paul is arguing from this point of view

2 Of course, the scope of this passage and of Galatians as a whole does not determine the scope of other writings. Romans, for example, while consistent with Galatians, has a different set of interlocuters and more "layers" of concern, and must be addressed on its own terms.

which he shared with Peter toward a conclusion that stands wholly in opposition to what Peter has just done.

2:16 *Knowing that a man is not justified from the works of Torah, but rather through the faith of Jesus the Messiah—even we in the Messiah Jesus have believed, so that we may be justified from the faith of the Messiah and not from the works of Torah; because from works of Torah all flesh shall not be justified.*

Paul assumes a common knowledge with Peter, ***that a man is not justified from the works of Torah***—that is, deeds done in response to and in the context of the covenantal polity of the Mosaic law.

This is Paul's first use of *justification* language in the letter.[3] *Justified* (δικαιόω) is a lawcourt term and, as the corresponding verbal form, is directly related to the term usually translated *righteousness* (δικαιοσύνη). It is a rather comprehensive term that addresses the legal judgment ensuing from the judge's decision, including such aspects as *vindication* (declaring one to be righteous, in the right before the court) and *rectification* (setting things right).

Lest we be misled by the way modern courts operate within our own context, this can be compared to the book of *Judges*, where the principal characters do not merely sit making decisions in the abstract, but are primarily men who rectify Israel's situation, and on God's behalf vindicate her over against her enemies. To put it succinctly: *God sent judges in Judges to justify Israel.*

Paul is thus saying that a man is not granted ultimate vindication and rectification by means of Torah. While this is generally taken by Protestant interpreters as an argument on the basis of the incapability of keeping the law perfectly, that is not likely. Torah itself had provisions for restoring the sinner to right standing within its covenantal structure. (It is important to grant, however, that those provisions pointed forward to the ultimate provision for sin made in the Messiah's death and resurrection.)

3 On the significance of the *justification* (and related) terminology arising so far into the letter, see especially T. David Gordon, "The Problem at Galatia."

The point is more likely related to Paul's eschatology: Torah is part of the old creation, and its judgment cannot ultimately satisfy the true rectification for which all the creation groans.

It is my position that treating the genitive ***faith of Jesus the Messiah*** as objective (*faith in Jesus the Messiah*) is misguided and makes the verse considerably more redundant than even Paul is usually given to being.[4]

In my view, the older translation of the genitive with *of* is preferable; the phrase refers to the πίστις of Christ Himself. In the words of Rom 1:17, the righteousness of God is revealed from πίστις (*faith, faithfulness*) unto πίστις. Given the argument as Paul expands it in Rom 3–4, I believe the primary point is that *God's faithfulness* is embodied in Jesus the Messiah, through whom His truth and promises have been kept and enacted (thus, the *from faith* of Rom 1:17), and this faithfulness is to be responded to by a faith which gives glory to God as the One who is faithful and even gives life to the dead and calls that which is nothing into a state of being (thus the *unto faith* of Rom 1:17; cf Rom 4:17, 20).[5]

My total reading here is not dependent upon that subjective genitive interpretation, but I think that the subjective genitive interpretation does make the best sense of a fair bit of the data both here and elsewhere, and lends a great deal of coherence to Paul's narrative. This is the case, not least with v 20: Paul lives by *the life, love, and death of the Son of God,* "who loved me and gave Himself for me." This love which took the Son to self-giving death, resulting in life, can be identified as the core demonstration of the faith(fulness) of the Messiah.

As Hays notes, this also places in parallel v 16 (where righteousness is through the faith of Christ rather than Torah) and v 21 (where righteousness is said to come by Christ's death rather than through Torah).[6]

Note further that in 3:22–24, faith is something that *came*, which is parallel with the fact that *the Messiah* came. Thus the faith in view has an "advent." It is the faith *of* the Messiah.

4 For more on the *pistis Christou* question ("faith *of* Christ" *vs* "faith *in* Christ"), see the Excursus immediately following the exposition of this verse.

5 On this general point, see esp Richard Hays, *The Faith of Jesus Christ, passim*, and *Galatians,* on this verse. Cf Philo *De Abr.* 273, which offers an expression of mutuality between the *pistis* of Abraham and the *pistis* of God; see Hays *Faith* xlv–xlvi.

6 Hays, *Galatians*, 240.

The subjective genitive underscores that our faith, important as it is to the picture, is not self-referential. Faith looks away from *me,* to Jesus the Messiah, who has acted in ultimate faith and faithfulness. (Contrast this to contemporary pseudo-spiritual catchphrases such as "Believe in yourself." The value is not in faith in the abstract; the value is in the Messiah, upon whom faith believes.)

Paul says that together with Peter, having understood that Torah does not bring true vindication and rectification (justification), but rather that such comes only in the faithful person and work of Jesus the Messiah—***even we in the Messiah Jesus have believed, so that we may be justified from the faith of the Messiah and not from works of Torah***.

In other words, Paul and Peter have both abandoned being defined by Torah and have believed in Jesus as the source of justification, as the means by which they will find "righteousness"—vindication, rectification, and of course eschatological forgiveness.

Paul uses the preposition εἰς, which is quite commonly paired with πιστεύω elsewhere in the NT, along with perhaps more obvious prepositions such as ἐπὶ (*upon*) and ἐν (*in*). The present term has a general idea of *motion into;* perhaps it is not unsuitable to say that by genuinely believing upon Jesus the Messiah, one is leaning into Him. The sort of faith of which Paul speaks is not merely an intellectual assent to certain propositions about Jesus, but a placing of one's weight, one's trust, upon Him. Compare Jn 11:48, where the Jewish leaders are threatened by the idea that "everyone will believe in Him" (πάντες πιστεύσουσιν εἰς αὐτόν), because it may result in the Romans coming and abolishing the present political order. Clearly, such a concern is not simply about an abstract mental agreement about Jesus; the point is that if the people *place their trust in Him as the Messiah*—the long-awaited promised King—there will be repercussions.

Here, this faith in Jesus the Messiah is set over against acting out of works of Torah. To be "justified" is by way of the former, rather than the latter.

So far as the total statement goes, we must see how this response arises from Peter's action. It is frequently assumed that Paul here is speaking of the futility of trying to earn one's salvation through doing good works, but such a futile theology was not in any way implied by Peter's action. It simply will not do to say that Peter withdrew because the Gentiles were not sufficiently good morally, and this is *legalism,* "justification by works." For one thing, Peter's rationale for withdrawal was not moral shortcoming on the part of the Gentiles; for another, Paul elsewhere *commands* refusal to eat with so-called believers who do things at fundamental odds with the Messiah's commandments (1 Cor 5). Thus, if Peter is being a "legalist" here, Paul is so at least as much elsewhere—a conclusion which must be rejected.

Paul, however, does use *justification* language appropriately—not because on his view works are optional, but because Peter's action implies that *Torah* is decisive in justification, whereas both Paul and Peter know that the Torah covenant does not rectify, vindicate. Genuine justification is eschatological and outside the scope and ability of Torah.

There is much that could be said here. Certainly, forgiveness of sins was available under Torah, and there is a connection between such forgiveness and Torah's arrangements for atonement. In view of this, it is reasonable to suggest that there is an eschatological cast to Paul's interest in justification. Note in particular Jer 31:34's promise of *a day coming* when God would forgive Israel's sins—such was clearly a promise that went beyond private forgiveness of sins for the individual, which was always available. It had to do with the new covenant.

Similarly, in another eschatological context, God says in Isa 45:25 that Israel will be justified *in Him:* "In YHWH all the descendants of Israel shall be *justified,* and shall glory." That indicates where justification will be found, and also when (in context, at the time when all men would come to YHWH, when every knee would bow to Him and every tongue take an oath.)

Moreover, in Isaiah, justification is something which both happens to the Servant (Isa 50:8), and something which He does, justifying many (Isa 53:11). Because the Servant receives courtroom vindication (justification), He bears iniquity for others and accomplishes courtroom vindication for them as well (cf Rom 4:25, where the vindication of the Messiah in His resurrection is the basis of our justification).

A related dimension to this is the link between righteousness and covenant. In Rom 4:11, the sign of circumcision is a seal of *righteousness;* in Gen 17:11, it is a sign of the *covenant.* It appears that Paul interprets "sign of the covenant" as "sign of righteousness." Righteousness and covenant are bound up with one another.

This being so, one should expect that *a new covenant brings into being a new justification.* Paul is thus talking about the justification that comes only in and with Jesus the Messiah, the Servant who represents Israel. It is the justification of Jesus the Messiah that made possible earlier forgiveness, to be sure—the grace shown to David, Manasseh, and so on. The Messiah's work is the basis of all grace for sinners, both before and after the cross. But the vindication for which Isaiah looked can only come into history when the Servant comes into history. Whatever Torah may have been effective for, it certainly was not effectual for eschatological justification.

Paul does not get into the issue of whether Peter's refusal to eat with Gentiles was mandated by Torah itself. In truth, Torah did *not* enforce strict separation, only that Israelites eat clean food. But Paul is not concerned with Peter's action in the abstract. Rather, he is concerned with its effect: the compulsion of Gentiles to "Judaize" (live as Jews, i.e. come under Torah).

So much for the source of Paul's issue with Peter. Regarding the substance of his argument, what Paul is saying is that he and yes, *Peter,* have traded in Torah in favour of the Messiah and His faithfulness, because only there is vindication to be found. Meanwhile, by his action of separating himself, Peter has made an accusation against the Gentile brothers in Antioch, that they are not in fact the people of God, fully qualified for table fellowship. And the reason they are not qualified is because they are not circumcised and Torah-observant. Peter did not of course literally believe that (and his customary behaviour belied it), but that is what his withdrawal really and truly communicated. It said that circumcision and Torah actually defined whom were to be identified as God's righteous ones, His eschatological people, after all.

Paul's argument, then, is that since Peter has believed in the Messiah and His faithfulness in place of Torah, Peter's withdrawal is a betrayal of his own faith-position, and a betrayal of the "truth of the good news," i.e. steadfast and faithful verity that God has brought eschatological salvation to Gentiles.

Paul seals it all by saying, ***because from the works of Torah all flesh shall not be justified.*** This could be understood as providing another undergirding rationale: in line with Joel 2/Acts 2, "all flesh" is to include all sorts of human beings without distinction, including Jews and Gentiles. Along those lines, Torah could not justify *all flesh,* by the simple nature of the case, since Gentiles are not under Torah. Such an argument would not be unprecedented for Paul; it is implied by e.g. Rom 3:28–29, and fits the larger thought here.

Nonetheless, given the first clause of the verse, where Paul is specifically thinking of individuals like Peter and himself not being justified by Torah, he is likely simply reaffirming something similar here at the end: no one shall be justified by works of Torah. But either way, there is probable eschatological cast to his statement.

Excursus: *The Faith of Jesus Christ*

In this commentary, I have adopted the subjective genitive reading of πίστις Χριστοῦ (*pistis Christou*) and similar phrases in Paul's writings. This phrase has customarily been translated as "faith *in* Christ" for some time.[7] This is the *objective genitive* reading: on this understanding, Christ is being referred to as the *object* of faith. The *subjective* genitive reading, by comparison, takes Christ to be the subject; the faith referred to is *His* faith. Thus: "the faith [or *faithfulness*] *of* Christ." (I briefly comment on that distinction between *faith* and *faithfulness* below.)

Others have already well defended this position far more ably and comprehensively than I can,[8] so I make no pretense to be thoroughgoing or definitive here. Nonetheless, given the importance of the question, on the one hand, and the fact that not everyone necessarily has access to the relevant literature, on the other, I do think it is appropriate

7 This was not the case with the old King James Version, which rendered such phrases "the faith *of* Christ." This does not necessarily imply that the translators held to a subjective genitive reading. "Of" is the most "naked" rendering possible for the genitive, and they simply chose to leave the phrase as underinterpreted as they could.

8 On this, see especially Richard Hays, *The Faith of Jesus Christ,* particularly pp 141–162. Hays ably summarizes much of the relevant scholarship on the question.

to give it at least cursory attention.

Before I do so, however, it is important to clarify precisely what is at stake here.

What is *not* at stake is whether the Bible presents Jesus as the object of the believer's faith. That is certainly the case (certain critical scholars notwithstanding)—but the phrase in question is not necessary to demonstrate that particular point. Indeed, here in Gal 2:16, Paul uses a verbal formula to express exactly that: ἡμεῖς εἰς Χριστὸν Ἰησοῦν ἐπιστεύσαμεν (*we into the Messiah Jesus have believed*). On faith in Jesus using other grammatical forms, see also e.g. Acts 16:31; 19:4; 20:21; 22:19; 24:24; 26:18; Rom 9:33; 10:11, 14; Eph 1:15; Phi 1:29; Col 2:5; Phlm 5; 1 Jn 3:23; 5:10, 13 etc. Note also alternative terminology, such as Eph 1:12's language of *hope* (προελπίζω) in Christ.

Neither is this a matter of a so-called "high" Christology over against a "low" Christology. Affirming the faith of Jesus does not imply that He is a mere man and not also God, any more than affirming the *obedience* of Jesus (as Heb 5:8 does) does so. If anything, the subjective genitive reading guards against the Docetist error of denying full humanity to Jesus—a danger that frankly still raises its head in ostensibly Bible-believing circles.

My concern here, however, is not particularly a dogmatic point, although the subjective genitive reading of *pistis Christou* does have implications for matters relating to the Messiah's *representative* role. What is important to me here is making good exegetical decisions, which in turn bear further fruit as the implications spin outward.

Hays *Faith* 277 helpfully distinguishes between the competing readings as the *anthropological* (objective genitive) and *christological* (subjective) interpretations. This clarifies the matter at hand, which has to do with whether in this particular phrase Paul is concerned with men in general, or with Jesus the Messiah. Without negating the role of the disciple's faith (see above), we should ask: is Paul's primary contrast between Torah (and Sin) on the one side, and our faith, on the other? Or is his solution rather more Christ-centered?

A word should be said about the options. The Greek genitive has a broad variety of uses, and there are indeed other alternatives to the choice between subjective and objective genitive. In Acts 14:9 ("faith to be healed"), for instance, *pistis* + the genitive has the idea of *faith appropriate for healing,* which of course is an instance neither of the subjective nor objective reading.

Our concern here, however, is what is the most likely usage in the case of *pistis* + a *personal* genitive, and in the particular contexts where Paul uses the construction.

Why then should we take *pistis Christou* and related phrases in a subjective genitive sense? Here are a few considerations that I find quite compelling.

1 In Paul's writings, in instances of *pistis* + a *personal* genitive that does not refer to Christ, the meaning is invariably subjective.[9] In fact, only in one passage in the NT (Mk 11:22) is this formula quite clearly intended as an objective genitive.[10] In Paul, consider the following.
In Rom 1:12, πίστεως ὑμῶν τε καὶ ἐμοῦ refers to *your faith and mine,* not *faith in you and me.*
τὴν πίστιν τοῦ θεοῦ in Rom 3:3 clearly refers, not to *faith in God,* but to *the faithfulness of God.*
In Rom 4:5, ἡ πίστις αὐτοῦ refers to the faith *of* the one who believes, not to *faith in* the believer.
In Rom 4:12, πίστεως τοῦ πατρὸς ἡμῶν Ἀβραάμ is Abraham's own faith, not *faith in* our father Abraham. Similarly, in Rom 4:16, τῷ ἐκ πίστεως Ἀβραάμ refers to those who are of Abraham's faith, not to those who believe *in* Abraham.
In 1 Cor 2:5, 15:14, 17, ἡ πίστις ὑμῶν refers to the Corinthians' own faith, not faith *in* the Corinthians. Likewise 2 Cor 10:15; Phi 2:17; Col 1:4; 2:5; 1 Thess 1:8; 3:2, 5, 6, 10; 2 Thess 1:3; Tit 1:1; Phlm 5, 6; cf also 2 Cor 1:24; Eph 1:15; 1 Thess 3:7, 2 Thess 1:4,

9 For *pistis* + *im*personal genitive, an objective meaning appears appropriate at Col 2:12 and 2 Thess 2:13.

10 James 2:1 is likely neither subjective nor objective, but a reference to holding "the Christian faith." An objective usage makes little sense ("do not have faith in our Lord Jesus Christ in partiality"). In any case, it is a minority usage.

which also use *pistis* + the genitive, but in a different order.

2 Numerous places in Paul that look redundant (including 2:16 and 3:22 here in Galatians) become coherent if what is in view is taken as the faithfulness of God in Christ being responded to by the faith of the believer. The programmatic instance of this is Rom 1:17 (albeit without the genitive), where the righteousness of God is revealed ἐκ πίστεως εἰς πίστιν (*from faith unto faith*). Surely it is not the believer's faith which reveals the righteousness of God, but rather the faithfulness of the Messiah Himself. That righteousness is then revealed *unto* faith. Thus, from the faith(fulness) of Christ, God's righteousness is directed toward and draws forth the faith of the believer.

Similarly, the righteousness of God borne witness to by the law and the prophets is spoken of in Rom 3:22 as δικαιοσύνη δὲ θεοῦ διὰ πίστεως Ἰησοῦ Χριστοῦ εἰς πάντας τοὺς πιστεύοντας. It surely seems more comprehensible to say that this is the righteousness of God exhibited through the faithfulness of Jesus the Messiah unto all those who believe than to adopt the usual superfluous rendering: *the righteousness of God through faith in Jesus Christ unto all who believe*. Even Paul is not readily given to that level of redundancy.

3 Further, *the righteousness of God* in Rom 3:22 is tied to the previous verse, with its perfect tense. The righteousness of God *has been made manifest* (δικαιοσύνη θεοῦ πεφανέρωται). This manifestation is not through the believer's faith (which in any case would be untenable, due to the perfect).

How, then, has the righteousness of God been manifested? Through *the faithfulness of Jesus the Messiah,* is Paul's answer in 3:22. The apostle's intended contrast is implicit in 3:21: this manifestation of God's righteousness is apart from Torah (χωρὶς νόμου); rather, it is bound up in the faithfulness of God's own Son, His Messiah.

Three verses later, in Rom 3:25, Paul writes concerning Jesus, ὃν προέθετο ὁ θεὸς ἱλαστήριον διὰ [τῆς] πίστεως ἐν τῷ αὐτοῦ αἵματι εἰς ἔνδειξιν τῆς δικαιοσύνης αὐτοῦ. Here, taking *pistis* to refer to that of the believer would appear to imply that God's setting forth of Jesus as propitiation occurred by way of the believer's faith, which frankly is absurd. The believer's faith indeed *responds* to that setting forth of Jesus as a propitiation for sin—but it is not *instrumental* in the setting forth itself. This problem dissipates if we understand the *pistis* in view to refer to that of Jesus Himself. In this verse, *by His blood* and *through faith* are parallel and mutually interpreting. The faith and faithfulness of Jesus are what brought Him to and through death on behalf of others.

4 The construction of Rom 4:16 (mentioned earlier) which refers to *the faith of Abraham* is in fact a very precise parallel to two key instances of the *pistis Christou* formula in Galatians, which also append *ek* to the beginning of the phrase. Rom 4:16 has ἐκ πίστεως Ἀβραάμ; compare this construction to ἐκ πίστεως Χριστοῦ in Gal 2:16 and to ἐκ πίστεως Ἰησοῦ Χριστοῦ in Gal 3:22. Given the fact that Paul's argument is that new covenant believers are *in Abraham* (see the Exposition below, particularly on 3:6–9) by virtue of being *in Christ* (see e.g. 3:26–29), it is hardly a stretch to suggest that Paul sees some sort of relationship between our being "of the faith of Abraham" and "of the faith of Christ." In view of that, taking both instances as subjective genitives makes good sense. It is precisely by participating directly in the faith of the Messiah that we come to participate indirectly in the faith of Abraham.

5 In Galatians, Paul describes the specific *pistis* in view as something with an advent corresponding to the coming of the Messiah (3:23, 25). This clearly does not refer to the advent of the human characteristic of believing, since there have been believers throughout history (including, quite obviously, Abraham himself). While in this instance *pistis* (which here is independent of the genitive construction) could conceivably refer to the *Christ-oriented faith* of believers, I suggest it more probable that in fact Paul intends the advent of the Messiah

and the advent of faith to be mutually interpreting, and the *pistis* in view is that of the Messiah Himself. This is made even more likely by the fact that in both verses Paul deploys, not a perfect tense (*pistis has come*), but an aorist (*pistis came*).[11] Perhaps even more decisively, in Gal 2:20 Paul says that the life he lives in the flesh is not in fact his own life, but the Messiah lives in him; and ἐν πίστει ζῶ τῇ τοῦ υἱοῦ τοῦ θεοῦ τοῦ ἀγαπήσαντός με καὶ παραδόντος ἑαυτὸν ὑπὲρ ἐμοῦ. Surely the most natural way to read this is to understand that Paul lives in and by the *pistis* of the Son of God Himself, a *pistis* made manifest in His love which led Him to give Himself for us. This further relates to the placarding, in Paul's preaching, of Jesus the Messiah crucified (3:1), which is then described in 3:2 as "the message of *pistis*." It also sounds remarkably similar to Eph 3:17, where Paul speaks of the Messiah dwelling "in your hearts through *pistis*" (κατοικῆσαι τὸν Χριστὸν διὰ τῆς πίστεως ἐν ταῖς καρδίαις ὑμῶν).

6 Continuing in Galatians, Paul says in 3:22 that the promise was *given* (not merely *received*) ἐκ πίστεως Ἰησοῦ Χριστοῦ to those who believe. This, in the context of the Scripture consigning all things under Sin. The most natural reading of this is that the whole old creation was bound in the death and slavery of Sin; God sent His life-giving Messiah as the answer. It is thus by way of the Messiah's *pistis* that God fulfills His promise, which He thus gives to believers.

7 In Phi 3:9, the contrast is between "my own righteousness, which is from Torah," and two parallel phrases: "[the righteousness] which is through the *pistis* of the Messiah" and "the righteousness which is from God by faith." However we understand the final *pistis* in this verse, the correlation between "the *pistis* of the Messiah" and "from God" over against "from Torah" pushes us in the direction of a subjective genitive reading. The righteousness in view is "from God," not

11 As noted by Hays *Faith* 202, although he takes a somewhat different view of *pistis* in 3:23, 25.

so much because it is through faith *in* the Messiah (although that much is true), but because it is through the faithfulness *of* the Messiah, who is sent from the Father and embodies God's righteousness. As in Gal 2:20, the genitival phrase is followed in Phi 3 by a reference to the suffering and death of the Messiah (Phi 3:10) and stresses participation with Him in both His death and His resurrection life.

8 In Heb 12:2, the Messiah is described as τὸν τῆς πίστεως ἀρχηγὸν καὶ τελειωτὴν Ἰησοῦν—*the pioneer* (or *originator*) *and completer/finisher of faith.* (Note that the text does not say "*our* faith.") We need to notice the relationship between this verse and two earlier statement in Hebrews.

Heb 11:39–40 (just two verses earlier) says that the sundry "heroes of faith" listed throughout the chapter all were commended through their faith but did not receive what was promised, because God had provided something better for us, so that apart from us they should not be *made complete.* That Greek term here rendered *made complete* (τελειωθῶσιν) is a form of the same word used to refer to Jesus in 12:2.

Meanwhile, in Heb 5:7–9, the writer says that Jesus *made pleas and petitions to the one able to save Him from death,* and *learned obedience through the things He suffered; and being made complete, He became the source of eternal salvation to all who obey Him.* Here we see that through what Jesus Himself did in His suffering, He "became complete" (τελειωθεὶς ἐγένετο), and in so doing became the source of salvation. This surely shows that the way He became *originator and completer of faith* (Heb 12:2) was by attaining completeness through his own faith and faithfulness. Thus our faith arrives at completion, not independently, but by participating in the *pistis* of Jesus.[12]

Neither should it be overlooked that the writer to the Hebrews

12 Cf also Heb 6:12, which says that the promises are inherited through faith and patience—an apt description of how Jesus' actions and posture are described in Heb 5:7 and 12:2.

> says that without *pistis* it is impossible to please God (Heb 11:6), and meanwhile the same letter everywhere presents Jesus as the one who preeminently pleases the Father. Indeed, He comes specifically to do the ultimate will of the Father, in place of the ascension offerings and sin offerings in which God has taken no pleasure (Heb 10:5–10). Jesus is the one who is "*faithful* (πιστός) to Him who appointed Him" (Heb 3:2) over against those who depart from the living God in unbelief (cf Heb 3:12); and He is the captain of those who enter into God's rest by faith (cf Heb 4:3).
>
> In summary, the argument in Hebrews presupposes and articulates "the faith of Christ."[13]

The further question that needs to be addressed is the actual meaning of *pistis* when we understand our phrase as a subjective genitive. Is it the *faith* of Christ (emphasizing belief, trust), or the *faithfulness* of Christ (emphasizing steadfast fidelity)? The Greek term can mean both.

I suggest that Paul is not choosing between the two; he means both, as well. For his part, Hays *Faith* 295 suggests that such a sharp distinction between *faith* and *faithfulness* is anachronistic, doubting it is "semantically possible in Hellenistic Greek to make such a conceptual distinction."

I am unwilling to go quite so far: after all, Greek knows an active and passive form of the corresponding verb, and the resulting distinction in fact lines up quite precisely with notions of *faith* and *faithfulness*.

Yet with regard to *pistis*, I would want to caution against precipitate dismissal of one connotation or the other. This is because saving *faith*, as biblically conceived, involves the sort of trust that expresses itself in *fidelity* to the promise and to the One who has made it. The Messiah's own perseverance through the suffering of the cross is *fidelity* to His

13 In addition to the NT arguments here, at least one OT Messianic prophecy refers to the faithfulness of the Messiah, and in connection with the righteousness theme, although in this case the LXX does not render the term with *pistis*. Isa 11:5 says: "Righteousness will be the belt of his loins; and the faithfulness (הָאֱמוּנָה) the belt of his waist." The articular form of *faithfulness* is interesting, given Paul's parallel usage in Galatians.

commitment—and at the same time, it is persistent *faith* in the hope set before Him; these are somewhat distinguishable, but it is scarcely conceivable to separate them.

Likewise with regard to believers, Hebrews speaks of holding fast our confidence (Heb 3:6) "firm to the end" (Heb 3:14) in a context which unites and even identifies *belief* and *obedience,* on one side, over against *unbelief* and *sin,* on the other (see especially Heb 3:12–19). In Hebrews 3, at least, faith as belief implies faith as loyalty, i.e. faithfulness.

This mutual relationship between the two sides of *pistis* fits with our present letter, as well. After all, what is the letter to the Galatians itself, but an exhortation to maintain *fidelity* to the promise of God in the Messiah, just as it is an exhortation to *believe* that promise? Else, what do the warnings against deserting God (Gal 1:6), being severed from the Messiah, and falling from grace (5:4) mean? Effectual faith maintains fidelity to the faithful Messiah.

Further then to the matter of the faith(fulness) of the Messiah, in Phi 2:8–11, Paul depicts Jesus humbling Himself to the point of death upon the cross in anticipation of the vindication that awaited Him. This view is made more explicit by the writer to the Hebrews, who says that as the originator and completer of *pistis,* Jesus endured the cross on account of the joy set before Him (Heb 12:2). In such texts, the accent is upon how Jesus placed His hope upon the promise of God, believing that His Father is the One who calls the things that are not into existence and gives life to the dead. This is precisely how Paul describes the faith of Abraham in Rom 4:16–17, which in turn is ultimately tied to the confession that Jesus was "raised because of our justification" in Rom 4:25. The faith of the Messiah and the faith of Abraham thus have fundamental similarities in shape.

At the same time, Rom 3:21–26 quite clearly depicts the *pistis* of Jesus as the embodied manifestation of the righteousness of God, and in describing Him as the One "who loved me and gave Himself for me" in Gal 2:20, Paul would appear to have the matter of the Son's *faithfulness* primarily in view.

It seems fair to say that with reference Jesus' own relationship to the promise of God (think here especially of Gal 3:16, where the Messiah is the particular recipient of the promises to Abraham) as well as His entrusting of Himself to the Father in the face of suffering,[14] the thought of *faith* is more at the forefront. On the other hand, with reference to Jesus' love and commitment to saving us (again, as in 2:20; cf Eph 3:12), the accent is upon the thought of *faithfulness*. In both cases, *pistis* is the faithful and appropriate representative response which God is seeking; and it is undertaken most particularly, poignantly and decisively in the face of the suffering of the cross.[15]

As Paul writes in Rom 1:17, the righteousness of God is revealed *from faith to faith*. The faith of Christ is representative, but far from excluding the necessity of our faith, it elicits and invites it.

2:17 *Now if seeking to be justified in the Messiah, we are found also sinners ourselves—[is] the Messiah [then] a servant of sin? Impossible!*

Working forward from v 16 from the common ground that Paul and Peter both are ***seeking to be justified in the Messiah*** (not merely *by;* Paul uses his familiar phrase ἐν Χριστῷ, *in Christ*), Paul confronts the effect of Peter's action with relationship to Torah itself. The new *habitus* Peter has formed (along with Paul) means that ***we are found also sinners ourselves***, if Torah has the authoritative status that Peter's action implies.

The logic here is quite unfamiliar, but I suggest it goes something like this: If Peter has indeed been living in the Messiah rather than under Torah, and his customary habits are no longer strictly Torah-observant but dictated rather by the new eschatological situation introduced by the Messiah, then a return to placing significance upon Torah in turn constitutes Peter a sinner under Torah's own terms (see too v 18).

Paul here again is using the term *sinner* to refer to those outside of right status under Torah, as he did above with reference to Gentiles in v

14 Outside of the recognized Pauline corpus, this is likely the intent behind the biblical quotation in Heb 2:13, "I will put my trust in Him." Cf Heb 5:7; 1 Pet 2:23, although neither of these texts uses *pistis* terminology. In any case, Heb 5:7 lies in the background of Heb 12:1–2, which enjoins believers to endure difficulty by looking to Jesus as the originator and complete of *pistis,* referring explicitly to His endurance of the cross.

15 On the thought of the Messiah's *faithfulness* elsewhere, see e.g. Heb 3:1–2, 6.

15. If Torah is genuinely the proper authority, the covenantal touchstone, then ***the Messiah*** has made Peter a "sinner," and He is therefore a ***servant of sin***—which is of course ***impossible***.

Paul is thus arguing in a circular manner, based upon the assumption that Peter's previous behaviour was in fact the normative behaviour as far as Christian living was concerned. It was in being faithful to the Messiah that Peter previously ate with Gentiles, and the old way of defining *sinner* according to Torah was rightly set aside.

> *For if the things I destroyed, these things again I build up, I constitute myself a transgressor.* 2:18

Paul then clarifies the unfamiliar logic of the previous verse by referring to ***the things I destroyed***. Paul has not destroyed the requirements of the law *per se*, but he has destroyed his particular relationship to it, by virtue of dying with the Messiah, as he immediately goes on to say in v 19.

Paul says that having destroyed those things, ***if these things again I build up, I constitute myself a transgressor***. Elsewhere, Paul attributes this tearing down and building up to the act of God Himself. In Eph 2:14–16, the Messiah has broken down the dividing wall of Torah; and what is being built up in turn is God's new temple. (See also 1 Cor 3:10–15; 2 Cor 10:4.)

In view of that, if Paul were to draw back from that severed relationship to the law by renewing its authority over him, he would be building up the force of its requirements, and of necessity constitute himself a transgressor of its terms.

To borrow from Paul's metaphor of Rom 7, if a man courts a woman while married to another, that is an adulterous relationship, but if the prior marriage has been ended through death, the new relationship is not adulterous but licit.

But suppose one could reverse the death? Then the other relationship is adulterous. So too here: the way of living mandated by the Messiah differs in an incompatible way with that required by Torah, because the new creation integrates Jew and Gentile into a new *koinonia*, a new partnership that begins at the table. Thus if one follows the Messiah's new way of living and then returns to Torah, he thereby constitutes himself a violator according to Torah's own standards.

However, Paul may well have a double meaning here. Simply by returning to Torah's norms, one also constitutes himself a transgressor against the Messiah's norms. It is surely in this sense that Paul says above that Peter was "condemned" (2:11).

2:19 *For I through Torah, to Torah died, so that to God I might live. With the Messiah I have been crucified.*

Paul's claim is that ***I through Torah, to Torah died***. The parallel with Rom 7:1–6 explains the significance of dying to Torah, and the end of this verse explains that this occurred through union with the Messiah in His death.

What is again cryptic in a passage frequently so is the suggestion that this death to Torah is *through* (διὰ) *Torah*. How did Paul die to Torah *through Torah's own instrumentality* when he died with the Messiah? Presumably, by the fact that Jesus was condemned under Torah, and it was that very death which provided for release from Torah.[16] This will become an important datum when we consider the meaning of 3:13.

Meanwhile, this verse introduces—for a first-century Jew—a stunning wedge between Torah and living unto God: I died to Torah, ***so that to God I might live***. In some way, life under Torah was holding him back from living to God in the way that God intended.

As so often with Paul's cryptic statements, this will be further unpacked later, and we should be careful about what we read into it. Paul is not talking about how he was living under the law as a wage-earner and therefore alienated from God, but that after being united to the Messiah, he was freed from that economic relationship and could now live out of free grace before the face of God. He of course does *not* believe in living before God on the basis of a work-for-wages relationship (as he indeed makes clear in Rom 4), but that is not within his purview here.

16 So too Hays, *Galatians*, 243: "the Law played an active role in the death of Jesus and pronounced a curse upon him (Gal 3:13)."

What concerns Paul now, and as he will explain in detail throughout the last half of ch 3 and into ch 4, is the way in which Torah governed Israel as a child custodian (παιδαγωγός). Paul has now moved out from under that relationship, carried forward by virtue of his connection to the mature Son, who has inducted Paul into an eschatological inheritance. *This* is the sort of *living to God* that the Father was after in sending His Son, although of course bound up in that is the accomplishment of redemption from sin—apart from which no inheritance could be possible.

The statement, ***with the Messiah I have been crucified***, has far-reaching implications. Looking backward in this passage, the primary point is that, with regard to Torah's authority, Paul shares in the Messiah's death. By dying with Christ, he has now passed out from under the old creation and Torah's role in governing it, into the new creation united to his resurrected Lord.

That latter aspect of union with the resurrected Messiah is already looking forward, and ties in to the previous clause. The purpose of dying to Torah is not to become a "free agent," but—again—*so that to God I might live* (compare also to Rom 6:14 in context). Just how this living is to be done is again expanded upon in the next verse, but it is clear enough that union with the Messiah entails union not only with His death, but also with His (new, resurrected) life.[17]

> *Now I live no longer, but the Messiah lives in me: But what I now live in* 2:20
> *the flesh, in the faith I live, that of the Son of God, who loved me and gave*
> *Himself for me.*

The union with the Messiah is all-encompassing; it involves more than a changed relationship to Torah, as central as that is to Paul's

17 Note that contrary to some theological constructions, there is no hint of a reference to the meritorious character of the earthly life of Jesus being transferred to the believer. The "life" of the Son which matters is His *resurrection life* which He now lives within those joined to Him, as is made clear by v 20. Cf Rom 4:25, where Jesus' resurrection grounds "our justification," in turn providing context for understanding what Paul means in the ensuing, particularly Rom 5:10, when he asserts that, having been reconciled to God by the death of His Son, "we shall be saved by His life."

argument: ***Now I live no longer, but the Messiah lives in me.***

Paul of course is not saying that he simply had vapourized. But because he had been united with Jesus in His death and resurrection (cf Rom 6:3ff), a fundamental change had occurred in Paul's identity. He is now defined, not by the natural, fleshly "I" of the old creation, but by the One to whom he is joined in life. Thus, ***what I now live in the flesh, in the faith I live, that of the Son of God.***

Without denying that he lives *in the flesh* in the sense that his "outer man" remains unglorified and corrupt (on this, see 2 Cor 4–5), yet even within that context, Paul is new, because he lives in the Messiah, in the faith of the Son of God. Here too I read this in parallel to the subjective genitive πίστις Ἰησοῦ, *faith of the Messiah,* which the article likely further supports.

Hays *Faith* 291 notes the syntactical relationship between this verse and Rom 5:15, a relationship that underscores the subjective genitive reading of *pistis* here. In Rom 5:15, Paul says that the gift of life is *by the grace of the one man, Jesus the Messiah* (ἐν χάριτι τῇ τοῦ ἑνὸς ἀνθρώπου Ἰησοῦ Χριστοῦ); here, that he *lives by* or *in the faith of the Son of God* (ἐν πίστει ζῶ τῇ τοῦ υἱοῦ τοῦ θεοῦ). This again provides further support for the subjective genitive reading; just as the *grace* of Rom 5:15 is that of the one man, Jesus, so too the *faith(fulness)* of Gal 2:20 is that of the Son of God.

The fact that Paul is speaking of now living *in the flesh* undercuts any notion that living in the faith of the Son of God is some mystical "higher life" that floats above the real world, and indeed, above "this present evil age" (cf 1:4). What we have here is not the evacuation of Paul's personhood in favour of that of Jesus. Rather, *I* now live in the flesh, but I live within the faith(fulness) of the Son of God, within the new possibilities that arise because He has arisen and I am united with Him.

Tying this verse to Heb 12:2, which describes Jesus as the author and finisher of faith, Hays *Faith* xxxii offers key insight here: "We are taken up into his life, including his faithfulness, and that faithfulness therefore imparts to us the shape of our own existence."

Paul then defines the Son of God as the One ***who loved me and gave Himself for me.*** As Hays *Galatians* 244 aptly notes, the verbs are aorists; the love in view is not a mere general warmth, but the practical, bloody, enacted love of suffering upon the cross. (Cf Rom 5:8.)

There is a tendency to reduce this verse to mean merely that Christ's death has provided forgiveness of sins and the resulting justified state provides new motivation for Christian living. But while that is true enough, Paul means considerably more than that, as can be seen by careful consideration of ch 5–6. Although the Messiah's self-giving death was itself once-for-all, yet in being united to Christ, one is joined to Him in that death but also bound to His own self-giving pattern by the Spirit.

This means practically living out of the Messiah's πίστις in something more than theory; it means finding power and pattern to "fulfill the law of the Messiah," as Paul will put it so potently in 6:2. Remember that in the context, Paul is not concerned merely with what constitutes the basis for forgiveness of sins; he is setting forth the way of the Messiah over against the way of Torah. Life in the flesh is now no longer to be governed by Torah; the new creation is to invade even life in the flesh, so that one is now governed by the acting and active love of the Messiah, which led Him to offer Himself in death.[18]

In all of this, Gal 2:20 should be compared to Phi 3:9–10, which shares a number of similar features. There too, Paul employs a subjective genitive to refer to "the faith of the Messiah" as the means through which "the righteousness from God" comes. Through the intimate knowledge of the Messiah which arises from that, Paul participates both in the Messiah's sufferings to the point of becoming like Jesus in His death. In both passages, connection to the Messiah reshapes the believer according to the Messiah's death—and in both passages, the Messiah's resurrection life is communicated to the believer. The *pistis* of the Messiah is not simply a past accomplishment embodied in the suffering of the cross. It certainly is that! But it is also *life;* and it is communicated to the believer by the Spirit through Jesus' own resurrection life. The righteous one will not only *die,* but also *live* by the *pistis* of the Messiah (cf Hab 2:4).

18 For further on this, see the Exposition below on 5:6.

2:21 *I do not invalidate the grace of God: for if righteousness [is] through Torah, indeed the Messiah died for nothing.*

If one does not *walk straightly along the path of the truth of the good news* (cf v 14), that is to ***invalidate the grace of God***. It is to set it aside, reject it, nullify it.

In speaking of *the grace of God* here, there is an implicit echo of the opening benediction, when Paul pronounced *grace and peace* upon the Galatians (1:3). Thus when the hearers of this letter (which would have been read aloud to the congregations) reach this point, there will be this connotation: do not nullify, spurn the grace which has been pronounced upon you. Righteousness—whether vindication or rectification—cannot come through Torah, which indeed was given by God, but belongs to the age of flesh rather than the glorious age of the Spirit. The Messiah's death has transcended Torah; it is His act of faithfulness through which righteousness has come.

Thus ***if righteousness is through Torah, indeed the Messiah died for nothing***. Note that this follows on from vv 19–20. The point is that righteousness in fact comes through the death of the Messiah, who loved His people and gave Himself for them. *God's* righteousness is embodied in that death; the *righteous response* He seeks is (as always) that of faith in Himself as the One who brings life in the face of death (implied in the upcoming mention of Abraham in 3:6ff, and explored further in Rom 4; here in Gal, God the Father is first of all identified by His action of raising Jesus from death, 1:1); and *righteous action* arises out of union with the Messiah: in being *crucified with the Messiah,* one is raised with Him through the Spirit and shares in His new creation life. (More on this at ch 5–6.)

This centrality of the cross explains why Paul immediately, in 3:1, breaks off from his response to Peter and refocuses the Galatians' attention on the fact that Jesus the Messiah was placarded before them as *crucified.*

GALATIANS 3:1–4:7

Proven to be Heirs

WITH 3:1–4:7, PAUL LAUNCHES INTO THE MEAT OF HIS ARGUMENT. Almost the entirety of this major section is devoted to demonstrating that the Galatians already are accepted by God as His full heirs, and that Torah can add nothing to the status they have already been granted in grace. Indeed, Paul points out the lengths God went to in order to liberate Jews themselves from Torah. The various further facets to Paul's argument range from what can be ascertained from the Galatians' own experience, to the structure of God's covenant with Abraham from the beginning, and on through the implications of union with the Messiah, in view of what His coming was designed to accomplish.

Appeal to a Good Beginning (3:1–5)

Chapter three may be read as an ABCABC pattern, with repeated "appeals" according to three major themes:

Appeal to the Spirit	*3:1–5*	>	*3:13–14*
Appeal to Abraham/promise	*3:6–9*	>	*3:15–18*
Appeal to Torah's limitations	*3:10–12*	>	*3:19–25*

These three threads are summarized and implications drawn, particularly in 3:26–29.

The opening subsection, 3:1–5, presses home the Galatians' folly in failing to consider that their own initial experience of the Spirit implies that they do not need Torah to complete them.

The verses have something of a Trinitarian structure. Paul says that the Galatians have entered into their inheritance through the *Son* (3:1), and that the firstfruits of this inheritance consists of enjoyment of the *Holy Spirit* (3:2–4). Back of that is *God the Father,* who provides the Spirit (3:5).

3:1 *O foolish Galatians, who has bewitched you, before whose eyes Jesus the Messiah was placarded crucified?*

The vocative ***foolish Galatians*** has misled some interpreters to suggest that this must imply the hearers are from north Galatia (ethnic Galatians), since people from southern Asia Minor would not have described themselves this way, and would likely have been offended by it. However, this overlooks, first, that there would be no other single unifying term to identify the people from the cities in view; and second, that Paul was never reticent about offending if it helped him carry his point. Surely the term *foolish* (ἀνόητοι) would have been far more offensive, in any case!

Paul asks, ***who has bewitched you?*** Bewitching was customarily thought to be caused by "the evil eye." Consequently, Paul may be engaged in a minor wordplay by pairing bewitching with ***before whose eyes***. What *they* had beheld should have had greater power over them than how someone else had beheld them.

An official, public royal notice has been provided, ***placarded*** before them. ***Jesus the Messiah*** the crucified One was placarded before the Galatians *via* the Word preached (see v 2, "message of faith"). The public proclamation, the legal notice of a new age has been posted in the preaching of Paul. Royal notice has been given regarding the reign of the crucified Messiah.

The reference to their *eyes* indicates that preaching paints Christ in His person and work, particularly with reference to His cross. (Compare 1 Cor 2:1–5.)[1]

"Placarded ***crucified***." Compare to 2:19: it is *via* the cross that *through Torah I died to Torah.*

The clause, ***that you should not obey the truth***, appears in the Byz/MT tradition. It is the royal proclamation of the Messiah's reign that is "the truth," and it is authoritative, calling forth obedience. (Note the resonance to *the truth of the good news* in 2:5, 14.) The good news of freedom is found in the Messiah's liberating kingship, and by heeding the

1 On Paul's usage of this word, cf Eph 3:3; Rom 15:4, where the meaning is "write beforehand" (unlikely here).

bewitchers, the Galatians were disobeying their liberating King.

This only I wish to learn from you: Did you receive the Spirit from works of Torah, or from the message of faith? 3:2

As Paul has taught them, now he says, ***this only I wish to learn from you.***

The apostle does not ask merely *did you receive the Spirit*, but rather, ***did you receive the Spirit from works of Torah?*** In other words, he acknowledges and indeed emphasizes their receipt of the Spirit; the question is how that reception came about.

The introduction of the Spirit here is to be unpacked further in the context of 3:14 (cf also 4:6–7). There is perhaps also an implicit contrast to the (in this instance, metaphorical?) unholy spirits which would have been involved in the "bewitching" of Paul's hearers (v 1).

The *received* theme is involved with the idea of inheritance which will be brought up presently (3:18, 29; 4:7; cf 3:14). The Galatians are already heirs who have begun receiving their inheritance. Elsewhere, Paul identifies the gift of the Spirit as the first installment or down payment upon the inheritance of believers, which seals or guarantees the ultimate provision of the inheritance in its entirety (Eph 1:13–14; cf 2 Cor 5:5).

The phrase ***the message of faith*** can legitimately be translated in a variety of ways, since both the key terms have multiple viable meanings. The first of these, ἀκοῆς, can be rendered either *hearing* or as *message* or *report*. The second, πίστεως (the genitive of pistis), could be accenting the act of believing; it could refer to "the faith" as the received body of Christian teaching (as in 1:23); or it could refer to *the faithfulness of Christ Himself.*[2]

Given the similar usage in Rom 10:16–17 and 1 Thess 2:13, ἀκοῆς

2 Surprisingly, Hays does not suggest this last option in his extended discussion in *Faith* 124–132, despite the fact that the work as a whole is a defense of the subjective genitive reading of *the faith of Christ*. Nonetheless, his discussion of the phrase is very helpful.

should likely be rendered *message,* as we have done here. Paul is interested, not merely in the human action of faith over against the human activity involved in carrying out the works of Torah; rather, he is defending the power of the preached gospel in bringing life.

What of Paul's use of πίστεως here? Does it refer to the subjective response ("believing"), as the "just as" in 3:6 might indicate? Or does it refer to the hearing of *the faith,* along the lines of how πίστις is employed later in the chapter? This is more difficult to choose from, given the strength of both senses in the close context; and perhaps the ambiguity on Paul's part is in fact intentional. In other words, perhaps he means both. The message which imparted the Spirit is the message of the Messiah's faithfulness; and that message is one which aims at and elicits faith.

I tend, however, to give slight primacy to the former point, given that in the immediately preceding verse, Paul has reminded the Galatians of how he has placarded Jesus the Messiah as the crucified one before their eyes. This is the "message of the Messiah's faithfulness," implicit in 2:20 ("I live by the faith of the Son of God, who loved me and gave Himself for me").

Regardless, the major point is clear enough: The reception of the Spirit, which they had indeed been granted, is the fruit of the proclamation of the Messiah's good news (cf v 1) received in faith, not the result of Torah observance.

We must stress that Paul's argument presupposes a sort of objective verifiability regarding the Galatians' participation in the Spirit. This involves, at the bare minimum, the working of various signs within their midst, as v 5 with its reference to "power-works" makes clear. Whatever we may say of Paul's interior life or that of the early Christians, the Spirit's activity was no mere secret assumption.

Whether or not we are "cessationist" in our view of certain gifts of the Spirit, we should all agree that everywhere the Scripture depicts the Spirit both as life-giving and powerful. The close association between the Spirit and the resurrection of Jesus provides eloquent testimony to both. Indeed, in Rom 8:2 He is described simply as "the Spirit of life" just shortly before being credited both with Jesus' resurrection as well as that promised to believers (Rom 8:11). Indeed, even now "the Spirit is life because of righteousness" (Rom 8:10), in the very face of our present mortality and weakness.

In view of this life-giving and powerful character of the Spirit, our lives should be lived with the expectancy of His work having a practical and powerful effect upon and through us.

Are you so foolish? Having begun in the Spirit, are you now being completed 3:3
in the flesh?

Are you so foolish is an echo of v 1; Paul first charged them with folly, and now indicates what form that folly took.

Paul speaks of them ***having begun in the Spirit***. In Greek, the form of the question is chiastic:

having begun
    in the Spirit
    now in the flesh
are you being completed?

On the concept of *beginning*, see esp 5:7: "You ran well; who impeded you, that you should not [continue to] follow the truth?" They began with a "sense of blessing" (4:15). As elsewhere in Paul's writings, he seems to have in mind the thought of the beginning and ending of a race (cf 1 Cor 9:24–27).

It is difficult to choose between rendering *in* and *by* (*in* the Spirit/flesh *vs by* the Spirit/flesh). While the modal reading (*by*) initially looks attractive on the basis of the second clause (being completed by the flesh), circumcision was "*in* your flesh" (Gen 17:13). Moreover, Paul tends to see "flesh" as a *realm*. Having entered the eschatological age in the Messiah, the Galatians have returned to the flesh-age in hopes of bringing their salvation to completion. Compare Heb 7:19: "The law made nothing perfect," i.e. *complete*.

In connection with beginning and continuing in/by the Spirit, see especially 5:16–25. The "good things" are fruit of the Spirit, performed when one "walks in/by the Spirit."

After the good beginning, Paul rhetorically asks, ***are you now being completed in the flesh?*** Given the contrast with *begun,* the frequent translation *perfected* is misleading, at least in modern usage. Such a reading tends to lead us into thinking the Galatians were adopting a form of perfectionism regarding which we have no actual evidence.

Generally, ἐπιτελέω focuses upon *completion, finishing,* and corresponds to *starting.* They *began in the Spirit;* consequently, Paul says in 5:7 that they had been *running well.* His question implies that if the proper *beginning* is *in the Spirit,* the proper way to *complete* the course is likewise in the Spirit rather than *in the flesh.*

The term also can be used in the sense of *completeness* in the sense of *wholeness* (probably, 2 Cor 7:1), and Paul may intend overtones of that here, as well. In that light, the question would be exposing the folly of their mistaken assumption that they could be *completed* "in their flesh" (cf Gen 17:13) by the *making incomplete* of their flesh (i.e. circumcision). "Are you now being completed in the flesh by being made incomplete in your flesh?"

On the broader level, the point of the chiasm is that, in line with 1:4, in the reign of the Messiah the Galatians have been delivered from "this present evil age," the realm of flesh (which is in turn the realm of foreskins and removed foreskins), and have been transferred into the beginning of their inheritance, the realm of the Spirit. Having had that good beginning, Paul questions why the Galatians would return to the very realm from which they had been delivered, in order to complete their journey.

Paul of course is not unique in making a contrast between (weak) flesh and (powerful) Spirit. These elements are prominent in Jesus' theme of birth in John 3; and back of that stands the OT with a number of passages contrasting the might of the Spirit over against the weakness of mere men of flesh. (See especially Isa 31:3; cf Gen 6:3.)

In this light, the promise of Joel 2:28 becomes almost ironic, as do the new covenant prophecies of Ezek 11:19; 36:26: God promises to pour out His mighty Spirit upon weak flesh. He gives infinitely more than we can hold.

Did you experience so much in vain?—if indeed yet [it was] in vain.... 3:4

Paul asks again, ***Did you experience so much in vain?*** The term I have translated *experience* here is frequently rendered *suffer. Experience,* however, was apparently the original meaning of the term, and is favoured here by the fact that the Galatians' experience of the Spirit is the concern in the immediate context.

Suffer too has some plausibility, given that in the more distant context, we learn that it was in order to avoid persecution that the "Judaizers" were attempting to get the Galatians circumcised (6:12). However, (1) that has more to do with potential suffering of others, not the Galatians themselves; and (2) the near context should likely be given greater weight, particularly since the Spirit theme is much more to the forefront in this letter. Thus I take the reference to be to the Galatians' experience of the Spirit and their new life in the Messiah.

Paul modifies the question with the half-hopeful, ***if indeed yet [it was] in vain***. He frequently expresses concern about receiving the grace of God in vain (cf e.g. 2 Cor 6:1 etc). Note also the issue in Heb 6:5, where there is a question whether the Hebrews have tasted of "the powers of the age to come" (i.e. the Spirit) for nought.

This sequence of thought thus indicates that certain approaches regarding "true conversion" are unhelpful in understanding Paul's thought here. His viewpoint is not that if they were "really converted," they would stick it out. Rather, he has been emphatic that they did indeed receive the Spirit and had experienced the Messiah. Again, as he says in 5:7, they "ran well." The danger is not in an insufficient past, but a misguided present which would make their past experience vain; a return to the flesh after having been ensconced in the Spirit.

He therefore who supplies the Spirit to you and works power-works among 3:5
you, [does He do so] from works of Torah, or from the message of faith?

He who supplies the Spirit is of course God the Father. The participle serves to characterize God as the Spirit-supplier. Compare to ὁ ἐνεργήσας in 2:8, where the Father is the one who equipped Paul and

Peter for apostolic service, but here it is ***to you***, a repeated affirmation of what the Galatians have already received.

Paul's contrast is between how God ***works*** (ἐνεργέω) ***power-works*** and his semi-technical phrase ***works*** (ἔργα) ***of Torah***. The law, Paul says elsewhere, was "weak through the flesh" (Rom 8:3). As in the Gospels, where Jesus clashes with the scribes and Pharisees in the context of Torah's Sabbath by doing things impossible for the law to accomplish, here too Paul stresses the way in which God's provision of the Spirit transcends Torah in its weakness.

The provision of the Spirit is *via* ***the message of faith***, again a probable reference to the message of the Messiah's faithfulness. See above on 3:2.

Appeal to Abraham's Promise (3:6–9)

The experience of the Spirit the Galatians have already enjoyed bears witness to their relationship to Abraham as covenant father. For they, like him, have been accepted by God by faith, and are thus participants in the ancient promise that the nations would be blessed in Abraham.

3:6 *Just as Abraham believed God, and it was accounted to him unto righteousness.*

Just as likely connects justification here with reception of the Spirit in v 5. The Spirit, as the earnest of the inheritance, was appealed to as evidence of God's acceptance elsewhere, e.g. Acts 10:44–47; 11:15–18; cf Acts 5:31–32. Note too that it is the Spirit who causes us to address God: *Abba, Father* (4:6). This again links the Spirit with justification, since it is by the Spirit we address the Father who has accepted us as His children.

The Galatians' experience to which Paul has just appealed (3:1–5) is not something novel; it conforms to the pattern God established with Abraham, by declaring him righteous prior to the advent of Torah. Thus Paul absolutizes not Torah, but the prior and underlying covenant with Abraham (cf 3:15–18).

It was accounted to him unto righteousness is a citation of Gen

15:6, but Paul deploys the patriarch's later name, *Abraham,* rather than *Abram.* This fits with the underlying notion of Abraham as the covenant father to whom one must be connected.

It should be underscored that while Gen 15:6 says that ***Abraham believed God***, at that point he was already a believer. The verse therefore should not be understood in some static sense ("At precisely one point, Abraham believed God and was justified") but as characteristic ("Abraham, as he typically did, received God's word with belief; God counted this to him as righteousness"). In correspondence with this, God continued to elaborate the promise by reminding Abraham that He was going to cause him to possess the land of Canaan (Gen 15:7).

This is significant, because Paul here is not denying that the Galatians initially believed and were justified. His concern rather is that now, having believed, they no longer are acting as sons of Abraham. They have assumed that there is another pathway to the possession of full salvation rather than the one upon which they had begun.

In the original Genesis context, the particular promise in view was that Yahweh would provide Abram with seed like the stars of heaven in number (Gen 15:5). This undergirds and informs Paul's discussion of *the seed of Abraham* in this chapter; while he makes that a singular *seed* in 3:16, by the end of the chapter, he opens it up to all those who have been baptized into the Messiah (3:26–29).

Thus the Galatians, now attempting to *finish in the flesh* (5:3), are not imitating father Abraham by their circumcision, after all. Further, their reception of the Spirit and experience of His powers (2, 5) are to be explained by the simple fact that God had indeed already justified (reckoned righteous) the Galatians by way of their faith. Thus this verse continues to appeal to their experience of the Spirit, while simultaneously shifting into the succeeding sections where Paul provides argument from Scripture (esp vv 6–14).

But the matter here is not simply imitation; as noted, the context is the promise of seed to Abraham. The experience and events of vv 1–5 are to be understood in fulfillment of the Abrahamic promises. (See below on vv 7–9.)

There is, however, even more beneath the surface. The passage Paul has quoted goes on to speak of the exodus from Egypt following a time of slavery and affliction (Gen 15:13–16). As will become increasingly clear as he proceeds through his argument, Paul has a new exodus in mind, one which liberates Israel from servitude to Torah.

3:7 *You know, then, that those from faith, these are the sons of Abraham.*

The familiar Pauline epistolary formula ***you know, then*** suggests the verb is indicative rather than imperative. Paul has provided ample proof (in v 6) for them to know what he says here: the characteristic faith of Abraham (peeked at through the quotation of Gen 15:6) is paradigmatic, so that we can speak of believers simply as ***those who are*** ἐκ πίστεως, ***from*** or by ***faith***. Compare to Gal 2:12, those from/of circumcision.

Paul's third person indicative poses a challenge to his hearers. *Those from/by faith*—are you Galatians indeed to be characterized in this way?

By employing the demonstrative pronoun, *these:* ***these are the sons of Abraham***, Paul places the emphasis upon those who believe, and in effect "exclusivizes" them. Since Abraham was thus characterized by faith-righteousness, the same character will belong to his sons (cf Jn 8:39). Implicitly, Paul is excommunicating those who are *of the works of Torah* (compare 4:30). Connection to Abraham is gained not by Torah but by faith.

But *whose faith?* The typical answer has been: *the believer*. While that is not wholly wrong, it overlooks the eschatological cast of the passage; as the next verse notes, the justification of the Gentiles was something not yet realized at the time. It was anticipated, *foreseen—it had to do with the future*. Moreover, what was in view was not the general fact that God accepts believing Gentiles (which was always true, as indicated by the stories of men such as Abimelech, Naaman, and Job).[3] Rather, Paul is concerned with a covenantal status connecting Gentiles to Abraham ("these are the *sons* of Abraham") in a way yet unforeseen at the time.

Abraham is thus not merely an exemplar: The one who would be

3 Gen 20; 2 Kgs 5; Job 1:1.

blessed must somehow be "in Abraham." He is not simply a *pattern* to these Gentiles; he is their *father.*

In view of all this, *faith* here is not simply borrowing Abraham's act of *believing* from the previous verse; it is referring to the substance of the promises made to Abraham. In particular (as seen from v 8), it is referring to promises that Gentiles would be incorporated into Abraham in the future. Throughout chapters 2–3, Paul identifies the faith through which this occurs: *the faith of the Son of God* (2:20), *the faith of Jesus the Messiah* which is now *given to those who believe* (3:22). The time of Torah was the time *before* [this] *faith came* (3:23), i.e. the time before *the Messiah came* (3:24); and in Him *faith has come* (3:25).

In short, it is through the *pistis* of the Messiah that sonship to Abraham arrives for Gentiles. The blessing promised to Abraham arrives in His faithful self-giving to death, and is appropriated in turn by faith.

> *Now the Scripture, foreseeing that God would justify the Gentiles from faith,* 3:8
> *announced the gospel beforehand to Abraham, "In you will all the Gentiles*
> *be blessed."*

Here Paul completes the shift from Abraham as exemplar to Abraham as recipient of the promise on behalf of those who were ultimately to be included "in him."

Scripture, as the living Word of the living God, is not meant to be interpreted atomistically, disconnectedly, as if addressed to the original situation and that situation only. Paul thus speaks of ***the Scripture, foreseeing***. The promise to Abraham was anticipatory, revealed with the eschatological event precisely in mind.

That which was foreseen through this living Word was ***that God would justify the Gentiles from faith***. In other words, that He would include Gentiles in His *from faith* activity in the Messiah.

The Scripture ***announced the gospel beforehand to Abraham***. The gospel is for Paul above all the spread of the good news to the Gentiles. Note the implication: it was the gospel, not Torah, which was "pre-announced" to Abraham. Paul wants to associate Abraham preeminently with the anticipation of new covenant blessings.

In you all the Gentiles shall be blessed. We're familiar with the translation *all the nations*, but so far as the Jewish understanding of the idiom, that is just the way of speaking of Gentiles. The underlying passages, in particular, would be Gen 12:3; 18:18; 22:18; cf 26:4; 28:14. Note the prominence of this promise: it was made no less than five times to the patriarchs alone.

Since Abraham was the recipient of the covenant (and its promises), the blessing must be *in him* in some way as a sort of federal head; presently we see that this headship is essentially passed on to the Messiah as his primary heir (3:16).

The work of justification God effected with Abraham (v 6) was a blessing which God was to extend to the nations in a fuller, eschatological sense. Apparently implicit in Paul's argument is the idea that Torah is what marks out Israel; a promise to justify the Gentiles assumes that this will not be through Torah. Submitting to Torah would make Israelites of foreigners, and thus the promise would not be fulfilled in the manner Abraham received it. Consequently, justification of the nations implies a bypassing of circumcision; and no circumcision likewise implies no Torah.

If this is so, it does raise the question of *why* God was so intent on including Gentiles in Abraham *as Gentiles*. Why would it not be appropriate for Gentiles to become Israelites *via* circumcision, even as the situation had been on a case by case basis for centuries?

For that matter, why did God introduce circumcision at all? Could not God have made it possible for a Gentile to become an Israelite (and thus become a participant in Abraham) apart from that?

Paul never explicitly answers these questions for us, and so far as I can tell, neither does the OT do so. On the other hand, Paul does deal with the other side of the equation: i.e. why it is so important that there be *one* people of God. To defend the necessity of that, Paul appeals to the *Shema* ("Hear O Israel, YHWH our God is *One*"). We see this most explicitly in Rom 3:29–30, where Paul proves that God is the God of both Jews and Gentiles by the fact that God is One. The *Shema* likewise underlies the discussion below, in 3:16ff (Paul references it directly in

3:20). We will explore that in its proper place.

This repeated appeal to the *Shema* shows that for Paul, the nature of God grounds the unity of Jew and Gentile in the Messiah. It is *because of who God is* that He aims to integrate Jew and Gentile together in one body.

This in turn suggests that the fundamental shape of things takes its point of departure, not from an arbitrary decision on God's part, but from the Trinity. Looked at in that way, we can suggest that both diversity and unity are important for God's purposes, and in His wisdom He desires that diversity to be reflected in a multiplicity of peoples within one fully unified body. Gentiles (again, meaning *the nations*) must remain Gentiles for that purpose to be maintained. Much more needs to be said, but I hope that can serve as a point of departure for further reflection.

As for the introduction of circumcision, it would take us far afield to explore its purpose in full, but in part it served to set Israel apart as a holy people. It clarified the distinction between them and the nations as they served as a priestly people for YHWH on behalf of the world.

Thus the removal of the distinction between hierarchical levels within Israel (descending authority for access to YHWH in the temple for the high priest, the regular priests, the Kohathites, the other Levites, and non-Levite Israelites) is of a piece with the full integration of Jew and Gentile in the Messiah. Israel no longer serves as a priestly nation on behalf of the nations; the Gentiles themselves are now inducted into the innermost presence of God, where previously only the high priest could enter. (See also below on 3:28.)

Stepping back and taking this verse as a whole, is Paul simply equating justification and the blessing given the nations? More likely, the blessing is grounded upon justification; the structure of the verse indicates that the promise that all the nations would be blessed in Abraham was due to Scripture foreseeing that God would justify the nations in Abraham. The blessing envisaged comes by way of God's prior acceptance (= justification); this understanding is confirmed by v 14, where the promise of the Spirit is (at least in part) epexegetical to the blessing of Abraham.

3:9 *So that those from faith are blessed with the faithful Abraham.*

The *in you* of the previous verse determines the ***so that*** here. It is not simply that others are blessed "like" Abraham had been blessed, or "in the same way." Rather, ***those from faith are blessed with*** (σὺν; cf Heb prefix *b*[e]) him. The promise is Abraham's promise, albeit eschatological, and it is by a covenantal relationship to Abraham that one enters into its enjoyment. The Gentiles are blessed *with* Abraham: *in, by means of*—by way of being in connection with him.

The proper translation of the adjective describing Abraham here is a good example of the difficulties attendant upon specifying narrowly what Paul has left ambiguous. Paul could be saying *believing Abraham* or *the believer Abraham,* or more generally ***faithful Abraham***. Or, he could be saying all of these. But either way, we are intended to connect the semantic association of *those from faith* (ἐκ πίστεως) in the early part of the verse with *the faithful Abraham* (τῷ πιστῷ Ἀβραάμ) in the latter.

In linking the argument of 3:1–5 with the Abrahamic content of 3:6–9, Paul stresses the normativity of the Abrahamic regime over against Torah. In terms of the OT revelation, the faith-message was most clearly manifest in him; the heart of the issue is clearest with Abraham.

It should not be thought that the justification available to Abraham was no longer accessible after the arrival of Torah. It certainly was—in Rom 4, Paul appeals to David as sharing Abrahamic justification. But part of what Paul is saying is that as Abraham was pre-Torah, so was the promise, and implicitly, then, Torah was not necessary to the fulfillment of the promise (i.e. it would not be Torah which would bring the blessing promised). Because Abraham's justification was prior to the law and promised something not promised by Torah, it is clear that Torah was in no sense instrumental to it.

Redemption from Torah (3:10–14)

This part of the argument is essentially an unpacking of 2:19 (*through Torah, I died to Torah*), as well as an exposition of how the Messiah has accomplished the blessing of the nations in Abraham, of which Paul has just spoken in 3:6–9.[4]

In essence, Paul is highlighting an impasse and depicting its resolution. Whereas God had promised a united family of Israelite and Gentile in Abraham, Torah with its fundamental separation of the two[5] posed an apparent obstacle to the fulfillment of that promise. This obstacle sealed Israel in by an oath, and thereby held those under Torah in a position that kept the promise in abeyance. Only the Messiah's oath-bearing death on Israel's behalf, taking the punishment of the disobedient son (His death "through Torah"), allows those under Torah to move into the era and administration of fulfillment, so that now Gentile and Jew can share in Abraham's inheritance together, participating in the new creation through the Holy Spirit.

> *For as many as are from works of Torah, are under curse: for it is written,* 3:10
> *"Cursed is everyone who does not remain in all the things written in the book of Torah, to do them."*

Paul speaks of ***as many as are from works of Torah***, which is frequently understood and even "translated"[6] as *as many as rely on works of Torah*. But this "from/by" is in contrastive parallel to "from/by faith" (vv 11, 12), and few would suggest that those verses mean, *rely on faith*. A more neutral reading (such as *those characterized by*) is preferable, especially in view of the usually overlooked fact that Paul clearly intends for v 13 to resolve the problem of v 10. If some curse that the self-righteous were under is the signal concern of v 10, then v 13 must be said to mean

4 Although 3:10–14 is itself an elaboration of a cryptic statement, it too is compact and will be further opened up later in the chapter and on into the one following. Modern interpreters bring various assumptions to the text, many of which are (so it seems to me) incorrect. Along with following the exposition below, the reader is strongly encouraged to read Appendix 1, "The Reverse of Ebal in Gal 3:10–14," in order to become fully engaged with the reading I have adopted, which will be fundamentally different from the most familiar interpretations.

5 Cf Eph 2:14, which speaks of Torah and its regulations as the dividing wall which intervened between Jews and Gentiles, prohibiting union and inhibiting peace.

6 I place "translated" in quotation marks, because such an eisegetical rendering scarcely deserves to be called a translation. At best, it is a highly tendentious—and wrong—paraphrase.

that the Messiah's death accomplishes redemption for the self-righteous. But it is clear that Paul intends something considerably more than that, and considerably *different,* as well.

Are under curse is usually taken as equivalent to "accursed." Thus, according to this reading, all who are of works of Torah are accursed. But this too is problematic, as we will see momentarily.

Paul's ***for it is written*** is a quotation of Deut 27:26: ***Cursed [is] everyone who does not remain in all the things which are written in the book of Torah, to do them.***

For years, the assumption has been that there is an unstated underlying premise: "And no one does do all the things written in the law"—thus implying the conclusion, "and therefore they are accursed." But this is problematic for several reasons.

1. In its original context, the passage Paul cites did not mean that failure to obey perfectly would summon down a curse. The text is drawn from the Gerizim/Ebal covenant renewal ceremony, and although deeds are certainly in view (see the curses against specific sins in vv 15–25), the point of the pronouncement surely is that those who fail to continue under Torah (i.e. maintain covenant) are accursed, not that those who fail in any respect are so cursed. Thus the issue is *apostasy from the Mosaic covenant.*
2. The OT explicitly records instances where people *did* fulfill the requirements of this verse. See esp 2 Chron 34:32: "the inhabitants of Jerusalem *did* according to the covenant of God"; cf the confession in v 21 of that chapter: "Great is the wrath of the Lord which has become inflamed among us, because our fathers did not obey the words of the Lord, to do according to all the things written in this book." Surely these two verses in conjunction imply that (in contrast to preceding generations) under Josiah, Jerusalem did indeed fulfill the requirements of Deut 27:26.
3. Luke 1:6 speaks similarly and even more explicitly regarding Zacharias and Elizabeth, whom it describes as ἄμεμπτοι

(*blameless*) in their walking in all (!) the commandments and righteous deeds required by the Lord (πορευόμενοι ἐν πάσαις ταῖς ἐντολαῖς καὶ δικαιώμασιν τοῦ κυρίου).

4 On the usual reading, the movement from v 13 to v 14 becomes obscure: the Messiah redeemed "us" from the curse of the law, *in order that* the blessing of Abraham might come to the Gentiles. It is not at all clear how the latter follows directly from the former, if the former is taken as "Christ has redeemed us from the curse of the law, which we universally have broken." (More on that later.)

5 In the closest parallel to 3:10, 13, Paul speaks in 4:4–5 of Jesus as being "born under Torah, in order to redeem those under Torah." Note that both passages have to do with association to the law, and redemption from it. This suggests that "those who are of the works of Torah" (3:10) is equivalent to "those under Torah" (4:5), which in fact at one time *included Jesus Himself.* But that means the *redemption* language is tied above all to release from slavery, in the form of a new exodus. And in that case, Torah has become a sort of stand-in for Pharaoh.

6 The usual reading overlooks the fact that, though his direct target is Gentiles, Paul himself is throughout Galatians presupposing that Christian Jews should *not* "remain in all the things which are written in the book of Torah"—he wants them to modify their practice wherever it is required for the sake of being one with believing Gentiles. But more to the point, it overlooks the fact that the goal of the covenant promise made to Abraham is that the *Gentiles* were to be blessed *in* him. Thus in context, Paul's concern is to get "Abraham" (his seed) out from under Torah so that *Gentiles qua Gentiles* (i.e. not Gentiles who became circumcised and therefore would not be, strictly speaking, *Gentiles* at all) could be *in* Abraham.

The resolution involves the removal of the unstated premise, and the refusal to over-read what Paul actually says. He does not say that all those under Torah are *accursed* (Gk. *epikataratos*), but that they are *under curse* (ὑπὸ κατάραν). Meaning: *bound by the curses pronounced on Ebal.* Those who are *accursed* (not just *under the threat* of being cursed) are those who *break* from Torah.[7] (Note the flexibility of the language; in Deut 11:29, for example, we're told that the curse is to be *placed upon* Mount Ebal, yet no one thinks that Mount Ebal was accursed.)

The point, therefore, is that those under Torah are "locked in" by an oath, creating a dilemma: the new covenant—which is supposed to include Gentiles in Abraham—has arrived, and yet Israel is bound to the old by an oath. This crisis will be heightened rhetorically in vv 11–12, before finding resolution in vv 13–14.

The accent on *all the things* written in Torah, highlighted in the LXX which Paul quotes, rather than the Hebrew, further underscores the dilemma. Loyalty to Torah involved comprehensive loyalty to its *details*—which would include the full spectrum of laws which would keep Israelites from maintaining full concourse with Gentiles, as well as continued observance of temple rituals such as animal offerings. In 5:3, Paul draws attention to the fact that circumcision would bind the Galatians to observance of *the whole Torah,* precisely to *all the things* implied here.

3:11 *Now that in/by Torah no one is justified before God is evident, since "The just one from faith shall live."*

Correctly understanding verse 11 requires reading it closely in connection with verse 12, because Paul is engaging in a rhetorical parallel.

With the statement, ***now that in Torah no one is justified before God is evident***, Paul makes an apparently audacious claim: Israel's justification before God is not in Torah at all. Torah makes promises of righteousness—but these promises are not "self-referential."

Since "The just one from faith shall live" is a citation of Hab 2:4. The backdrop there is an impending judgment upon Israel at the hands of a sinful nation. In the face of that conundrum, the righteous one must trust God, whose eschatological promise is that the knowledge of the glory of Yahweh will fill the earth as the waters cover the sea (Hab

7 See especially Joseph Braswell, "'The Blessing of Abraham' Versus 'The Curse of the Law.'" Cf Fee, *God's Empowering Presence,* 390–395, especially 391, footnote 86.

2:14).

The source of life lies outside of Torah, and always has. Certainly this is so with regard to the eschatological life which concerns both Habakkuk and Paul. It is the God who intervenes on the basis of His own promise who will cause the knowledge of His glory to flood the nations (Gentiles). And in that action, it is faith, *pistis,* rather than living in terms of Torah, which will be vindicated.

Hays *Faith* 132–141 has an intriguing discussion regarding whether Paul takes *the just one* messianically, an argument bolstered in 277–281, which is material new for the second edition. A key point is that *the righteous one* (ὁ δίκαιος) is widely used within the NT to refer to the Messiah (see e.g. Acts 3:14; 7:52; 22:14; 1 Pet 3:18; 1 Jn 2:1), as well as in extrabiblical literature of the period.

If a messianic reading of Hab 2:4 is Paul's intention here, it would make good sense within my overall reading of vv 11–12, which highlights the contrast between eschatological faith and the detailed requirements and *ethos* of Torah. In the Messiah Himself is righteousness disclosed and obtained, not *via* Torah.

With regard to this verse itself, arguably the point is very nearly moot, since in 2:20 Paul has said that he *lives* by the faith of the Son of God, i.e. the Messiah. Thus, even if ὁ δίκαιος here refers to the individual believer, ultimately the *pistis* which brings life is that of the Messiah.

But Torah is not from faith, but: "The one doing them shall live in them." 3:12

When Paul says that ***Torah is not from faith***, he surely is not claiming that the one living under the Mosaic covenant was not called to live by "faith," as defined by believing God's promises for forgiveness and so on. Nor yet is he conceiving some abstract construction called "law" that has at best a theoretical relationship to the actual total covenantal relationship which God established with His people.

Surely, Paul is using *faith* here in a more eschatological sense, as he increasingly does as he moves further into this chapter's argument. (Indeed, even the discussion of faith in connection with Abraham in 3:6–9, although looking back, should be taken as largely eschatological, since it has to do with an eschatological promise, a "pre-proclamation" of the new creation gospel.)

Torah, as Paul shortly will say quite frankly, was not the object of hope, and nor could it bring the object of hope. It was not eschatological nor even permanent; it rather was a temporary measure given to govern life under it.

This can be better understood when we carefully consider Paul's ensuing quotation of Leviticus 18:5, ***"The one doing them shall live in them."***

What is being asserted and denied here? To understand that, we must see the parallel structure of verses 11–12:

3:11	*the righteous one*	*from faith*	*shall live*	
3:12	*the doing one*	*these things*	*shall live*	*by/in them*

The primary contrast is not between *faith* and *doing* but between faith and *these things,* which is underscored by the repetition of the things of the law with the unmatched phrase from Lev 18, "by/in them." For Paul, the central concern in Lev 18:5 is not so much *doing* as *Torah and its details.*

Moreover, the notion of pitting *believing vs doing* is in fact wrong theologically as well, as demonstrated by Paul himself in this very letter, in 6:7–9, where he links reaping eternal *life* to *doing* good!

What then is the contrast? "The contrast is not between generalized 'doing" and generalized 'faith,' but between Torah's commandments and eschatological faith—in short, between Torah and the Messiah, between old covenant and new."[8] To put it another way, any movement into a fulfillment of the promises given Abraham cannot be accomplished simply by carrying on in obedience to the existing law; God brings His new covenant in, from outside, as a gift.

3:13 *Christ redeemed us from the curse of Torah, becoming a curse for us, because it is written, "Cursed [is] everyone who hangs upon a tree."*

8 *These Are Two Covenants,* 91–92.

Christ redeemed us from the curse of Torah. Who is *us?* Not all believers, but as also in 4:5, "we Jews," i.e. those who were "of the works of Torah" in v 10. The Messiah was born under Torah, not to remain under Torah, but to "redeem" (liberate) those who were under Torah (4:4–5) by dying under the curse pronounced against those who would depart from Torah.

Toward the end of the chapter, Paul explains further why such departure from Torah was necessary. It was a child custodian (*paidagogos*), a temporary caregiver given to manage Israel in her minority; and so long as Israel was under that caregiver, she could not inherit the promises.

The *curse of Torah* therefore is not God's general curse against sin. It is true that God does judge sin, and will bring an ultimate and final judgment to all, Gentiles included (cf Rom 2:6–11). But those not under Torah were never subject to the curse *of Torah;* and that is not Paul's concern here.

Here, Paul's concern is liberation from the curse-bearing oath mentioned in v 10. Because God's purpose for Abraham was a united family of Israelite and Gentile in him, Israel must be released from Torah, which kept Israelite and Gentile apart.

This liberation takes place by the Messiah ***becoming a curse for us.*** This phrase is apparently a Hebraism drawn from the ensuing quotation, and we probably should not try to make too much theological hay from the fact that Paul says "becoming a curse" rather than "becoming accursed." The underlying Hebrew can mean either (compare e.g. Num 5:27).

Paul now ties two Deuteronomic texts together: his use of 27:26 in the foregoing, and now a quotation of 21:23: ***Because it is written, "Cursed [is] everyone who hangs upon a tree."***

This verse is a reference to the penalty of an intransigent son, an impenitent rebel who refuses to hear the counsel of his parents (and back of them, the law). His parents describe him as someone who "is stubborn and rebellious; he will not obey our voice; he is a glutton, and a drunkard" (Deut 21:20). What is depicted is, in essence, a self-willed apostate.

It is no accident that one of the charges against Jesus was that He was *a glutton and a drunkard,* which is tied in Matt 11:19 to His friendship with publicans and "sinners," i.e. those who were considered by the most observant Jews to be covenant-breakers. Jesus' friendship with "sinners" was not merely seen as "keeping the wrong company"; it was taken to be part of a total program of undermining fealty to Torah.

The case of the rebellious son in Deut 21 perhaps sounds relatively specific, but in v 21, the principles become generalized. Such a one shall be stoned by the men of his city, so that evil is put away from Israel, and all Israel shall hear, and fear. It is then added in 21:22–23,

> If a man has committed a sin worthy of death, and he is put to death, and you hang him on a tree, his body shall not remain overnight on the tree, but you shall surely bury him in the same day, because he who is hanged [*upon a tree,* LXX] is a curse of God, so that you do not defile the land which Yahweh your God is giving you as an inheritance.

By appealing to this passage, Paul is acknowledging that Jesus died under a charge of apostasy from Torah (which of course is integral to the Sabbath conflicts), and in effect died the death of a rebellious son of Israel (cf again Gal 4:4–5). Certainly, Paul is not saying that Jesus was guilty of those charges (had he been guilty, His death would have been deserved and accomplished nothing), but the point is that He really did bear those charges, including the cursing identified with hanging upon a tree.

Those charges, again, *were charges of apostasy from Torah, and the Messiah bore them in order to liberate His people from Torah.*

The reversal of Ebal is hereby complete, and it is thoroughgoing. Upon the entrance into Canaan, where Israel would dwell separately from the nations, and when the Ebal and Gerizim ceremony is finally carried out, Joshua (LXX 'Ιησοῦς, *Jesus*) hung the king of Ai on a tree. At evening he commanded his body taken down, thrown outside the city gate, and covered with a great heap of stones (Josh 8:29; the

Ebal–Gerizim ceremony is recorded in 8:30–34).[9] Jesus the Messiah was also hung on a tree, his body taken down at evening, and buried in a stone tomb, and these parallels reinforce my advocacy of a connection between the Gerizim–Ebal ceremony and this passage.

If Paul intends these intertextual echoes, a biblical-theological reading suitable to the context is not difficult to develop. The first Jesus accomplishes the separation of Israel from the *goyim* by hanging the Gentile king upon a tree; the last Jesus accomplishes the integration of Israel with the *goyim* by Himself hanging upon the tree, raised from the stone tomb outside the city gate in order to fashion a new people and a new creation.

Is this exegetical play, or does it make sense of Paul's actual argument? Indeed it does. We need to be careful to remember to take the wide angle lens and ask what Paul is doing here. Why is Paul saying all of this, and why is he saying it *now?*

Remember that the overall issue at stake is that believing Gentiles were being persuaded to become circumcised and come under Torah. Paul has argued from their own experience that this was unnecessary and counterproductive, since they themselves had already received the eschatological Spirit apart from circumcision and Torah (3:1–5). In other words, they had received more than Torah could offer.

But then there is more. Abraham himself had received the promise that Gentiles *qua* Gentiles would be incorporated into himself and be thus blessed (3:6–9).

But 3:10–13 takes this yet a step further. It is not the case that believing Gentiles are in a different relationship to Abraham than are believing Israelites.

To the contrary, *Jesus released Jews such as Paul himself from Torah at the cost of His own blood, taking the curse of apostasy upon Himself, so that Jew and Gentile could move into the new creation upon equal footing.* Even though believing Jews (including Paul himself) generally observe the outward forms of Torah wherever they do not interfere with their new reality (e.g. full unity with Gentiles), in truth they are not under

9 On the significance of the Ebal–Gerizim ceremony for this text, see Appendix 1: "The Reverse of Ebal in Gal 3:10–14."

Torah, which does not find its source in eschatological faith.

While this reading is Israel-specific, that does not mean there is no analogy whatsoever between this liberation from Torah and a broader salvation for all believers. Paul himself provides that analogy in the parallel passage in 4:4–5. The Messiah was *born under Torah* so that He could die under Torah, bearing its curse against covenantal apostasy, and thus release Israel from it. But more generally, He also was *born of a woman,* in order to enter into the *kosmos,* so that He could be crucified to it and it to Him,[10] thus rescuing all those in Him out of "this present evil age" (1:4) and placing them into new creation.

Moreover, it should be observed that Paul is presupposing that the Messiah's death was one bearing representative judgment. Bearing the curse against apostasy may seem specific, but behind that it means that He bore the penalty for transgression against Torah. And while Gentiles themselves were never under Torah (see Rom 2:12), yet Torah itself was God's means of judging sin *via* His priestly nation (cf Paul's argument in Rom 5:12–21).

Thus, back of the very specific role Paul ascribes to the death of Jesus here is a much bigger assumed picture. The way Jesus released Israel from Torah is the same way He rescued both Gentile and Jew from divine wrath against sin.

3:14 *In order that unto the Gentiles the blessing of Abraham might come in*
the Messiah Jesus, in order that the promise of the Spirit we might receive
through the faith.

Here now is the point of the liberation just described. The result is at least twofold.

By liberating Israel from Torah, Jesus ensured ***that unto the Gentiles the blessing of Abraham might come in the Messiah Jesus***. That is, with the reconstitution of Israel outside of Torah, they can welcome Gentiles into the same Abrahamic body, just as had been promised to Abraham

10 Paul says this regarding himself in 6:14, but surely it is so because he is "crucified with the Messiah" (2:20) and has thus become a participant in His death to the *kosmos* and *vice versa*.

long before.

Second, the liberation of believing Israel from Torah is ***in order that we might receive the promise of the Spirit through the faith***.

Here Paul goes further than he did in vv 1–5. There, he said that the Galatian Gentiles were made participants in the Spirit by the message of faith, not through Torah. But now he implicitly says that, far from being an *advantage* in terms of the promise, Torah was keeping Israel from receiving it. It is due only to the Messiah's liberation from Torah that now "we" (believing Israelites) are enabled to receive the promised Spirit.

This then is further vindication of the position already enjoyed by the Galatians. Not only did they receive the Spirit apart from Torah; even Israelites themselves could not receive the Spirit without getting rescued from Torah!

Paul does not here explain why Israel could not receive the eschatological Spirit while under Torah. It may simply be that he has recognized that, according to Jer 31, the Spirit is a *new covenant gift*, and therefore one remaining under the old covenant could not receive it.

Arguably, Paul may also have connected Isa 32:15–16 (which connects *fruitfulness* to the eschatological outpouring of God's Spirit) to Yahweh's promises to make Abraham "exceedingly fruitful" (Gen 17:6).[11] The fruit of the Spirit and the fruitfulness of Abraham becoming father to the nations are thus intertwined.

It may likewise be that Paul ties the "all flesh" in the promise of the Spirit of Joel 2:28 to the Abrahamic promise that in him all the families of the earth would be blessed, and consequently interpreted "your sons and daughters" in the prophet as "sons of Abraham." In view of that, the Spirit would be promised specifically to a situation where Gentiles share in Abraham, i.e. outside of Torah's norms.

What is at any rate clear is that for Paul the lines are clearly drawn. It must be Torah or the Messiah, not "both/and."

To summarize, the release of Israel from Torah means that now

11 Cf Barclay 122 (note 46), who tries to make the connection *via* Gen 28:3–4, which, however, appears to distinguish between fruitfulness and the blessing of Abraham. In any case, the connection is weak, since a similar "fruitful" promise is given concerning Ishmael in Gen 17:20.

"Abraham" is clear of the law and Gentiles *as Gentiles* can be included "in him," in fulfillment of the promise Paul has mentioned in 3:8b, and correspondingly, this movement from "this present evil age" (1:4) to the new creation means that the eschatological Spirit is poured out upon God's people.

The Priority of Abraham's Promise (3:15–18)

The covenant with Abraham cannot be revoked or qualified by the law, which came later. Moreover, the Abrahamic covenant promised blessing for the nations in him; Paul insists that this includes them among Abraham's seed.

3:15 *Brothers, according to man I speak: Although merely a covenant of man, if it has been ratified, no one invalidates it or adds conditions.*

Note the tenderness that remains in Paul, calling them ***brothers***, despite the fire so typical of his address to the Galatians. His fury is the angst of love, not merely an angry rant.

Paul continues his argument in terms of the customs of mere men: ***according to man I speak***. He is arguing from the lesser to the greater (*a minori ad maius*), i.e. if the custom of men has solidity and significance, much more so with the ways of God.

The case regards what is ***merely a covenant of man***. Even with this, ***if it has been ratified, no one invalidates it or adds conditions***. That is, a ratified covenant cannot be rejected or altered. Whatever may be said of a promise *simpliciter*, full covenants are irrevocable, because they are oath-bound.

One might say that Paul has set a subtle trap. He is about to argue this point on behalf of the covenant with Abraham. But what is particularly ingenious is that Paul's argument in 3:10–13 has already presupposed the point being made here. In those preceding verses, the entire substructure of the argument assumes that Torah is a covenant and its force cannot simply be rejected or qualified by subsequent conditions. That is precisely why release required the Messiah's liberating death.

But now the trap is sprung, and Paul will take that same datum and point out that even prior to Torah, there was an existing covenantal arrangement. If Torah cannot simply be abandoned or modified, but requires redemption through the death of the Messiah, even less is it possible for Torah in its turn to qualify, still less invalidate, the earlier Abrahamic covenant.

> *Now to Abraham the promises were spoken, and to his seed. It does not say,* 3:16
> *"and to seeds," as upon many, but as upon one, "and to your seed," which is*
> *the Messiah.*

To whom were the promises spoken? ***To Abraham the promises were spoken, and to his seed.*** Recall that certain promises have already been mentioned in the context, *viz*, the blessing of the Gentiles in Abraham (vv 8–9). Thus there is an implicit affirmation here that the Gentiles would be blessed by Abraham only by a covenantal inclusion in him—i.e. by becoming part of his seed.

Paul's statement in v 16b, ***it does not say, "And to seeds," as upon many, but as upon one, "and to your seed,"*** has been analyzed virtually to death, and on one level is difficult to understand. Critical scholars have tended to imply that Paul is playing fast and loose with the text.

But at base, there is an important point to be made, which is that *seed* is a collective plural, rather than a distributive plural. And Paul wishes to make a point about the unifying factor in that collectivity. The promise is ***"and to your seed," which is the Messiah.***

Again, it rather sounds like Paul is saying that the original promise did not have in view Abraham's plural descendants, but rather referred to Jesus Christ individually—an interpretation that would be difficult to sustain from the immediate context of the Genesis promises.

However obvious it may appear that Paul is making such an ambitious assertion, that supposedly obvious take on things is surely incorrect. This is not simply because such a reading puts a bad light on Paul for handling the Genesis text irresponsibly, but even more so because Paul himself identifies all those who are in the Messiah to be the seed of Abraham later in this very chapter (v 29).

Consequently, whatever difficulties we may have in analyzing Paul's statement here,[12] fundamentally, he is stressing *the solidarity of the seed.* There are not multiple seeds, but *one;* a significant point, given his prior insistence that Gentiles will be blessed in Abraham. The eschatological anticipation is not that there will be multiple seeds for Abraham, whether the Gentiles be separate but equal, or separate but *in*equal. Rather, the promise is that there will be but one seed which unites Israelites and Gentiles. This solidarity is secured in the Messiah, who is both born of a woman and born under Torah (4:4), and ultimately becomes the primary and defining recipient of the promises. This is why Paul's argument on this score comes to culmination in v 28: "you are all *one,*" i.e. identified with the *one seed,* the Messiah.

3:17 *Now this I say: A covenant earlier ratified by God, the after-four-hundred-and-thirty-years-coming Torah does not revoke it, so as to nullify the promise.*

Paul now again takes up the ratified covenant theme of v 15: ***Now this I say: A covenant earlier ratified by God***, i.e. the covenant made with Abraham involving promises to him and to his seed.

Over against this Abrahamic covenant, due to what Paul has just argued in v 15, Torah's preeminence is undermined by the chronology: Paul defines the Mosaic law with a participial phrase, as ***the after-four-hundred-and-thirty-years-coming Torah.***

As a consequence of its very timing over against an existing covenant, Torah therefore ***does not revoke*** the former, which would serve ***to nullify the promise.***

God had established the promises to Abraham as a covenant to him and to his seed. Since a covenant cannot simply be repudiated or conditions added to it, even Torah cannot be considered a new wrinkle that simply updated the Abrahamic covenant 430 years later. It was something else; as Paul will say in v 19, it "came in alongside."

This builds from the preceding verse. If there is one "seed" which

12 For a detailed treatment of this verse, see my essay, "Abraham's One True Heir? Galatians 3:16 and 'Identity Interchange,'" Available online at: http://biblicalstudiescenter.org/interpretation/gal3_16.htm.

receives the promise, the inheritance cannot come through Torah, since Torah separates Israel from the *goyim*. If Torah is the permanent norm, the promise is nullified, not simply because illegal conditions were added, but because the very identity of the recipients to the promise was altered.

Paul's argument here, as elsewhere, serves in part to counter a common first-century Jewish notion that the messianic age would arrive in response to Israel's faithful keeping of Torah. To the contrary, such a condition would serve to add a codicil to the Abrahamic covenant, which is impossible.

Deuteronomy 34:4 may also be in the back of Paul's mind here. At the entrance to the land of Canaan, YHWH stops Moses short and says, "This is the land which I swore to Abraham, Isaac, and Jacob, saying, 'To your seed [LXX σπέρμα, *sperma*] I will give it.' I have caused you to see it with the eye, but you shall not pass over there." That entrance is left to Moses' heir, Joshua (Jesus). Moses cannot enter into the Abrahamic promise. The promise is reserved for Jesus, the true Heir.

There remains a significant difficulty in understanding Paul's argument, however. The crux of the matter in Galatia is circumcision, and circumcision was not introduced by Moses; it was given to Abraham and even identified as "the covenant you shall keep" (Gen 17:10).

While Paul's argument initially appears somewhat mystifying in light of the undisputed connection between Abraham and circumcision, these difficulties are not insuperable.

The key datum to remember is that for Paul the distinguishing feature of the Abrahamic covenant is not circumcision (which in fact he ties more closely to Torah) but promise, which is seen clearly in v 18 below. It may be that Paul distinguishes at some level between "the covenant that you shall keep" in Gen 17 and the covenantal promises which YHWH had already made Abraham many years before instituting circumcision. (It is important to note that in Rom 4:10, Paul finds a great deal of significance in the timing of Abraham's circumcision.) Seen in this light, this distinction could be a subset of his thought here that Torah cannot alter the Abrahamic covenant because it comes later. So too, circumcision cannot materially alter the initial promise arrangement God made with

Abraham, because it too comes later.

Furthermore, it is to be noted that at any rate, the removal of circumcision does not in any sense represent the addition of a condition or a codicil to the Abrahamic covenant, but the opposite. If I covenant to do something for you, and say you must do x, and then later say you don't need to do x, that is not the addition of anything at all.

Finally, for Paul's purposes here, the point is how the promises get fulfilled, which wasn't really the initial point of circumcision to begin with. (Nor was it really the initial point of Torah, either, but that was a live misunderstanding of his contemporaries in Judaism.) So while his Pharisaic contemporaries as a whole were saying that the Messiah would come in reponse to Israel's lawkeeping, and the "Judaizers" were saying that Gentiles could participate in covenant blessing only by transferring into Israel *via* circumcision, Paul is saying that to the contrary, the revelation of the Messiah is wholly the act of God's righteousness and covenant faithfulness, and that the blessing of the new covenant is a gift from outside. Moreover, because a key aspect of that blessing is that the Gentiles are to be blessed in Abraham, the answer cannot be circumcision, by the nature of the case. Why? Again, because circumcision makes a Gentile no longer a Gentile. The eschatological promise to Abraham has to ensure that Israel and the Gentiles become one in Abraham without the Gentiles ceasing to be Gentiles.

3:18 *For if the inheritance is from Torah, it is no longer from [the] promise: but God has given [the inheritance] to Abraham through promise.*

Paul throughout the letter has posited a contrast between Torah and the Messiah; here he likewise posits that same contrast between Torah and the Abrahamic promise: ***For if the inheritance is from Torah, it is no longer from [the] promise.***

As seen already above (see on v 17), God did not tie the provision of the inheritance to the keeping of Torah. Rather, God had given an unconditional promise. This does not mean that faithful living is unimportant to ultimate enjoyment of covenantal blessings; Paul goes on to say in ch 6 that what is reaped will be sown, and that doing good will issue in eternal life. But the inheritance itself comes to Israel, not because they have adequately kept the law, but because God Himself sends His Son "in the fullness of time" (4:4).

Again, Paul is apparently correcting mistaken first-century notions that God would bring in the age to come, marked by the arrival of the Messiah, in response to Israel keeping Torah faithfully. Such a manner of fulfillment, would, Paul suggests, entail God imposing new conditions on the Abrahamic covenant—which in turn would be illegitimate.

Paul's eschatological sense of the time is reflected in his countering clause, ***but God has given [the inheritance] to Abraham through promise***. It is not merely that the *promise* has been given to Abraham. Clearly the referent for what is given to Abraham here is κληρονομία, the inheritance. Moreover, Paul uses the perfect tense: this is something that has effectively been given. In the new creation gift in the Messiah, Abraham has now finally received what was promised him so many centuries earlier.

Age of the Custodian (3:19–25)

> *Why Torah, then? It was added for the sake of transgressions, until the time should arrive when the seed should come to whom [it] was promised, and it was ordained through angels by the instrumentality of a mediator.* 3:19

The foregoing argument, which sounds so negative toward Torah, particularly in comparison to the general viewpoint of Paul's fellow first-century Jews, spurs a very apt question: ***Why Torah, then?*** If God already had a covenantal arrangement with Abraham that could not be invalidated or modified, why was Torah introduced at all?

In answering this, Paul says ***it was added***—already a controversial way of putting it, since it was (and is) common to think of Torah as eternal, a transcription of God's character—***for the sake of transgressions***.

As so frequently occurs in Galatians, Paul has tossed out a phrase that could be taken in more than one way. One of the popular understandings of this phrase is that Torah was added *in order to restrain sin,* which is a sound enough thought, so far as it goes (cf 1 Tim 1:8ff).

Another interpretation (also a sound thought) is that through its sacrificial system, Torah provided a temporary mechanism for dealing with transgressions (likely part of the thought behind Heb 9:15 and elsewhere).

In this context, another somewhat startling reason is more likely: Torah was added for the sake (or at least, with the *effect*), not of restraining transgressions, but of defining and multiplying them. This would not be a unique statement for Paul; he says something very similar in Rom 5:20: "the law came in, in order to make the trespass increase." He likely has the same thought here, since he goes on in v 22 to speak of how Scripture has "imprisoned all things under Sin."

If this reading is correct, Paul's argument constitutes a double whammy against the view of Torah held by his contemporaries. Not only is Torah not eternal; neither is it a weapon against the evil impulse. Rather it is an agent that provokes Sin and keeps those under Torah imprisoned to it!

The non-eternality of Torah is further affirmed with the ensuing delimitation of its time: ***until the time should arrive when the seed should come to whom [it] was promised.*** Torah *entered* at a particular time, 430 years after Abraham, and was scheduled to be terminated at a particular time: the arrival of the promised one seed of Abraham. Whether we take this to refer to the Messiah individually as the head and representative of the reconstituted people of God, or as a collective noun to refer to all those whom He heads and represents, the point is that the arrival of the eschatological time was always intended to terminate the rule of Torah over the people of God.

Torah was not a mere work of men, nor an ultimate entity. It was ***ordained through angels.*** The mention of angels is perhaps an indication of its transcendence, but it is also a reminder of its limitations. While man's pre-eschatological condition is that he is "a little lower than the heavenly beings" (Ps 8:5), his purpose is dominion over *all* the works of God's creation (Ps 8:6).[13] Thus the connection between Torah and

13 On this view of man's calling as the canonical reading of Ps 8, see esp Heb 2:5–8. It is only Jesus, who has become firstfruits of the new creation, who has already now moved from being "for a little while" lower than the angels, with the goal of bringing

angels indicates that Torah's governance is a preliminary condition.

The ordination of Torah was ***by the instrumentality of a mediator*** or *intermediary,* i.e. Moses. This is in contrast to Abraham and his Seed, who were the recipients of direct promises. Paul is quietly implying the inferiority of Torah, along the lines of Jn 1:17.

Now he is not the mediator of [that] one, but God is one. 3:20

Paul continues regarding Moses, ***now he is not the mediator of [that] one***. Here again we have one of Paul's infamously cryptic statements. Like Wright,[14] my take assumes that Paul's unexplained "one" refers back to his usage of the term just a few verses earlier (3:16). With Wright, I take the initial article substantivally in the sense of "he," but even if instead we should take the article to be directly modifying μεσίτης (*mediator*), the implied statement should still be taken in similar fashion, i.e. *now the mediator is not [the mediator] of [that] one.*

Paul's claim is that while Moses was the intermediary through whose hand Torah came, he is not the intermediary through whom the seed of promise comes. Nor can he be; the Torah he mediates is a wall of division rather than a bridge of unity between the peoples of promise, between Israel and the Gentiles. Therefore, Moses (and by implication, the law) cannot be the instrument who brings to fruition the collective seed of promise (cf v 16).

The contrasting clause, ***but God is one***, reflects Paul's conviction that God's ultimate purposes reflect His own character. The unity of the people of God, Israelite and Gentile, is an implication of the *Shema:* "Yahweh our God, Yahweh is one" (Deut 6:4). Paul argues similarly in Rom 3:28–29: since God is one, He is God of both Jews and Gentiles. Who God is dictates the sort of gospel which Paul preaches.

Is Torah, then, against the promises of God? Impossible! For if Torah was 3:21
given as able to give life, truly righteousness would have resulted from Torah.

---

many sons to the same glory (Heb 2:9–10).

14 N. T. Wright, *The Climax of the Covenant,* 168–172; *Paul and the Faithfulness of God,* 387–389, 641–643.

Once again Paul's unrelenting chain of argument raises questions about the place and goodness of Torah: ***Is Torah, then, against the promises of God?*** And given what Paul has just said, we would almost think that the answer would be, "It certainly is!" After all, Paul *has* been setting Torah and promise in contrast to one another.

However, *contrast* is not the same thing as *opposition;* and the true answer is emphatic: ***Impossible!*** Since both the Abrahamic promise and Torah are God-given, they cannot have opposing purposes to one another, since, after all, God is one, as Paul has just reaffirmed.

The issue, therefore is not that the promise set out to accomplish one thing, and then that Torah was given to accomplish the same thing in a contradictory way: ***For if Torah was given as able to give life, truly righteousness would have resulted from Torah***. The life promised to Abraham was never assigned as a function of Torah; if it had been, eschatological righteousness would indeed have come that way, since God succeeds in His purposes.

But no, contrary to then-popular thought (which opined, "more Torah, more life"), the gift of life—and particularly, eschatological life—was *not* Torah's purpose, and certainly not its effect.

Rather, Jesus Himself is the way, the truth, and *the life* (Jn 14:6), and in Him is life (Jn 1:4). Unlike Torah, merely a word *imparted,* the Messiah the eternal Word is life itself. Thus Torah was *given* through Moses, but grace and truth *came* through Jesus the Messiah (Jn 1:17), even as faith (*pistis*) *came* in Him here (vv 23–24).

3:22 *But the Scripture has imprisoned all things under sin, so that the promise might be given from the faith of Jesus the Messiah to those who believe.*

Rather than providing eschatological life, through Torah ***the Scripture has imprisoned all things under Sin***. God delivered Israel from Egypt and gave Israel Torah, but the effect of Torah has not been further liberation but a confirmation in slavery. This was collectively manifested through various military defeats, and ultimately, exile, but those events were symptomatic of a broader issue. Torah was "weak through the flesh"; it did not deal with the fundamental fact that life under itself was still old creation life.

Here, as in esp Rom 5–6, Paul writes regarding sin in a fashion which is cosmic in scope. Sin is a power, a force of the old creation world.

But this imprisonment and slavery is not reflective of malevolence on God's part, nor of failure. The particular form of Torah's imprisonment leaves open the way for God to fulfill His promises in the way in which He has always intended, ***so that the promise might be given from the faith of Jesus the Messiah to those who believe.***

Here again we see the complementary "faith to faith" theme in play (cf Rom 1:17: the righteousness of God is revealed in the gospel *ek pisteos eis pistin,* from faith to faith). The promise which is first of all received by the Messiah as its true recipient, is communicated from His faithfulness to all those who believe, i.e. whose faith is in Him.[15]

Now before the faith came, we were confined under Torah, because we were 3:23
imprisoned until the revelation of the impending faith.

The eschatological character of *pistis* for Paul in this context is very clear in his phrase ***before the faith came****. Faith,* which is articular, is specific, and is something whose arrival corresponds with the advent of the Messiah. It seems most reasonable, therefore, that it principally refers back to the *faith[fulness] of Jesus the Messiah* in the preceding verse. Certainly, the posture of belief was the longstanding righteous posture of the saints throughout the successive ages, but what is new here is the Messiah Himself. Thus *faith* in this instance cannot refer generically to characteristic belief. It is the eschatological faithfulness of God revealed in the Messiah.

Thus, this *pistis* is so definitive that Paul can refer to it simply as "*the* faith." The *pistis* of Jesus is the supreme *pistis;* like the writer of Hebrews (see Heb 12:2), Paul sees Jesus as the embodiment, originator, and completer of *pistis.* The arrival of Jesus in history is at the same time the arrival of true, full, mature, and complete faith and faithfulness; it is the supreme manifestation of God's fidelity and of the representative Man's

15 For a summary defense of the "faith[fulness] of the Messiah" reading of *pistis Christou,* see the Excursus above, "The Faith of Jesus Christ," pp 89–98.

ready and willing response to God and His Word of promise.

Prior to that advent, Paul (speaking as a Jew) writes, ***we were confined under Torah, because we were imprisoned***. The imagery of imprisonment correlates to and magnifies the slavery theme that increasingly dominates the context as Paul proceeds. The confinement was implicit in 3:10–13, where Paul developed the movement from being bound to Torah under a curse-bearing oath until the granting of liberation through the Messiah vicariously bearing the curse against apostasy. Here, Paul moves from Torah assigning all under Sin (v 22), to Torah itself being the *locus* of confinement. Torah functioned not only as a third-party witness against Israel; it also functioned as the place or sphere where Israel was imprisoned.

The final phrase, ***until the revelation of the impending faith***, completes the neat chiasm:

Now before the faith came
under Torah we were confined
because we were imprisoned
until the revelation of the coming faith.

This again pairs well with Rom 1:17, where the disclosure of the gospel is a *revelation* of God's righteousness.[16] The faithfulness of the Messiah is the apocalyptic, eschatological embodiment of God's righteousness, and that in-history revelation brings confinement under Torah to an end (just as Paul has explained in 3:13).

3:24 *So that Torah became our custodian until the Messiah, that we might be justified from faith.*

16 To be sure, in Gal 3:23, *the revelation* is an aorist passive infinitive, ἀποκαλυφθῆναι; in Rom 1:17, the verb is a passive present, ἀποκαλύπτεται. The difference is due to the fact that in Romans, Paul is primarily speaking of the revelation of the Messiah in the preached gospel, whereas in Galatians, it is Christ's own now-accomplished ministerial activity, especially His self-giving death, that is principally in view. But in both, the concern is with the eschatological revelation of God in the Messiah.

The effect of all this is ***that Torah became our custodian until the Messiah.***

The term *custodian* is important. What Paul has in view is not "a *tutor* unto Christ." The *paidagogos* was not an educator, tutor or schoolmaster (as the KJV and NKJV would have it), and thus was not offering an education "to bring us to Christ" in the sense of *leading the way, introducing.*

The *paidagogos* was usually a household slave (!) who was entrusted with keeping custody of the child. Although it could be said that he "taught," it was more a matter of teaching manners than of what we would identify as "education." His main connection with school was that he accompanied his charge to the academy and back. He was a disciplinarian, an instiller of manners, and a protector. He was, in short, a *child custodian,* overseeing his charge until the child was of age.[17]

The stress, therefore, is on the *temporary* character of a child custodian as well as his role in *confinement* of the minor child. Implicit in the idea of a *custodian* is that he is keeping something or someone *in custody,* and that English connection conveniently illustrates the imprisoning character of Torah which Paul has already introduced (vv 22–23).

As with the literal role of the *paidagogos,* Torah's role therefore is a temporary measure, ***until the Messiah***, unto the era or time of the Messiah (*eis Christon*).

It should be noted that these observations undercut a traditional use of this verse, wherein pounding home "the law" is thought necessary in order to drive the sinner to Christ. On this take, the law is a tutor to give experiential instruction in guilt, which then forces the "student" to look to Christ for relief.

While there are certain elements in that notion which are not wholly incorrect (men do need to recognize their sin and their need for the Messiah), this usage is extremely far removed from what Paul is saying, and he *never* tries to get anyone under "the law." Gentiles never were under the law (cf Rom 2:12; 3:29), and unless they wanted to join Israel, they were never *supposed* to be, and Paul certainly never takes that route

17 For detailed discussion of the *paidagogos,* see especially Norman H. Young, "Paidagogos: The Social Setting of a Pauline Metaphor."

in the examples of his preaching in Acts. The so-called "pedagogical" role of Torah simply is not "pedagogical" in *our* modern (educational) sense of the term. The role is custodial, and Paul certainly does not want to bring anyone under the custodial power of Torah, even temporarily.

Paul's treatment of the limited place of Torah here again follows the pattern of 3:22 earlier. As there, through Torah Scripture imprisoned all under Sin, so that the promise might be given from the faith[fulness] of Jesus, so again here, Torah served as a child custodian temporarily, so ***that we might be justified from faith.***

In this text, justification comes in the Messiah as an eschatological event. Paul has in view more than individual forgiveness of sins, *simpliciter*. Yes, God has always made provisions for believers to be reconciled to Himself despite their sins. But in the prophets God promised a day when God would bring a new covenant and forgive the sins of Israel (Jer 31:34), and certainly those promises must have meant more than that individual salvation would suddenly become available—since it already *was* available, and always had been.

What is in view is manifold, and I can provide only initial thoughts here. The writer to the Hebrews gets at an aspect of it by noting that under Torah, there was still consciousness of sins, because sacrifices were repeated, and therefore the conscience of believers was not fully liberated (Heb 10:1–3). The sacrifices of Torah could not actually themselves take sins away (Heb 10:4). So the justification that awaits the Messiah's coming is one which vindicates His people in a way in which Torah never could.

Then too, whereas Israel's sins had caused her to run aground as a people, God promised a day when He would put away her sins, and what that would entail would be a corporate resurrection (see e.g. Ezek 37). That resurrection (which is vindication) finds its center in the Messiah, whom God raised on account of our justification (Rom 4:25).

In all of this is justification and vindication *from faith*. In this context, what is in view is not the posture of individual belief (which is indeed the proper and necessary response to God's saving act in Christ). Rather, Paul is referring to the God-revealing, lifegiving *pistis* of the Messiah, in whom God and His righteousness is perfectly revealed (cf Rom 3:22).

For this, Torah must be set aside as provisional and impermanent.[18]

But because the faith has come, we are no longer under a custodian. 3:25

Paul continues to work with the "sequentiality" of faith: ***because the faith has come***. Throughout vv 23–25, *the Messiah* and *faith* are essentially synonymous. The Messiah and faith come, arrive.

Due to this arrival, ***we are no longer under a custodian***. Paul will develop this thought further as he proceeds into making explicit the *Sonship* of the Messiah toward the end of this chapter and into the beginning of chapter four. But the groundwork for his logic has been ongoing for some time. Already in v 16, he has identified the Messiah as the seed, the recipient of the Abrahamic promise. In some ways, he is both the content and the heir of that promise, and therefore His arrival necessitates the deprecation of Torah's custody. But there is more: since this seed is the *mature Son* (4:4), He cannot remain subject to a *child custodian*. A man is not ruled by a *paidagogos*.

But then further, if the Messiah is the true seed who defines inheritance, that affects how others are to stand in relation to Torah, as well. Paul explains this in the following verse.

Sons in the Son (3:26–29)

For you are all sons of God through the faith, in the Messiah Jesus. 3:26

Paul now shows how so much of what he has been saying fits together: ***you are all sons of God***. Because the Messiah, the mature seed and mature Son, has now come, sonship for His people has also arrived.

The idea of sonship is paramount in the immediately preceding context. (See also the immediately following context in 4:1–7.) This is not simply about a new familial relationship. The point is that believers are not merely *children* of God (minors); they are mature sons who are qualified to inherit. Witherington 270 notes that this phrase in Jewish

18 For more on eschatological justification, see the Exposition on 2:16.

literature was predicated especially of eschatological Israel.

In Greek, *all* is the first word of the verse; there is emphasis here, relating to the issue of full Gentile equality in the inheritance. This equality is not limited to exceptional Gentiles; it is an unreserved affirmation of full sonship for all those in the Messiah.

With the phrase *for you,* Paul makes a shift in focus. After spending so much time with "we" (Israelites), Paul includes Gentiles in the discussion. This is about the matter of inheritance—believing Gentiles find sonship in the same way believing Jews do.

The remaining two phrases, ***through the faith, in the Messiah Jesus***, are often understood as "through *faith in* Christ Jesus." But believing in someone typically (although not universally) involves the preposition *eis;* here is *en.* Accordingly, the second prepositional phrase appears to be an instance of Paul's recurring *in Christ* (ἐν Χριστῷ) theme, not an object for "faith." Rather, *faith* in the context surely refers to the faithfulness of the Messiah.

It therefore seems likely that we have here two parallel prepositional phrases which mutually define one another:[19]

For you are all sons of God
through the faith,
in the Messiah Jesus

Sonship to God comes through the faithfulness of God displayed in the Messiah; the believer's sonship derives from the Messiah's own status. We have access to the Messiah's *pistis* by being in Him.

These parallel phrases largely point backward and forward at Paul's surrounding argument; *through the faith* essentially summarizes vv 23–25, while *in the Messiah Jesus* summarizes vv 27–28.

This verse clarifies how the Messiah's status affects the status of God's people. The Messiah is the seed of promise, the Man of *pistis;* therefore, through the faith that has arrived in Him, believers are participants in His inheritance. The Messiah is the Son; by being "in the Messiah Jesus,"

19 This has become the consensus grammatical analysis among modern commentators.

therefore, the believer is likewise a son.

For as many of you as into the Messiah were baptized, are clothed with the Messiah. 3:27

Reinforcing v 26, Paul says as many of you ***as were baptized into the Messiah, are clothed with the Messiah***. The believer is clothed with the mature Son in baptism, and therefore shares in His status.

Paul's argument is both personal and objective; he sees no tension between the two. He speaks, not of "those" (third party) who have been baptized, but of *you*. Meanwhile, the very action referenced is objective, which is underscored by the correlative pronoun *as many* (ὅσοι): "*as many* of you as were baptized." Far from being an empty symbol or illustration, therefore, baptism is both personal and objective, and provides the Galatians with demonstration of their true status. Paul's heavy emphasis on the Spirit elsewhere in the context, therefore, is not so that the Galatians' hope will become intangible and thus harder to grasp, but rather that they would see the contrast between old and new creation. Christian baptism is the definitive entry rite into the people of God and circumcision is unnecessary (and indeed, for Gentiles, counterproductive).

Paul's argument is not based on a notion of baptism as magical, but neither is it merely a reference to something else (e.g. "spiritual regeneration"), concerning which baptism is an empty symbol or illustration. Consider the example of a wedding ceremony, a ritual act which has performative force due to its integration within a larger cultural reality. The wedding ceremony effects a new relationship between a man and a woman without any hint of magical or occult activity, simply due to what such ceremonies mean in the cultures that practice them. So likewise, in Paul's view, the new creation represents a new cosmological culture, within which baptism is no mere human action, but an act of God whereby He transfers a person from the realm of flesh (or from the state of being in *Adam*, to borrow Paul's terminology in Rom 5 and 1 Cor 15) and places that person into the Messiah.

This ritual act is neither in competition with faith nor something that sits uneasily alongside faith. To the contrary, God's *pistis* (and of course the *pistis* of the Messiah) and that of the disciple meet in baptism. Baptism is not a rival "way to get saved," but the place where faith goes[20] at the point of transition from the old creation to the new. This is why Paul can expand upon v 26's comment about becoming sons of God *through the faith, in the Messiah Jesus,* by referring to baptism here. He is still talking about Jesus; it is *into the Messiah* [you] *were baptized.* Equally, he is still talking about faith. Baptism is the form taken by faith and repentance when one moves from darkness to light (cf Acts 2:38).[21]

In a certain sense, it sounds like Paul is saying that baptism amounts to "playing dressup"—being clothed with something (Someone!) we are not. Not so. Paul is speaking, not merely of an outward pretense, but a reconstitution of one's whole reality. What is accomplished in baptism is an identification with the Messiah, putting Him on to the degree that what is true of Him in His representative role is thus also true of the believer. The one baptized is inserted into Him and clothed with Him, and therefore the rights and inheritance of the Messiah become the rights and inheritance of the believer.

Paul's core principle here is one of unity and identity between Jesus and those belonging to Him. This relationship implies that *to require the new covenant believer to submit to Torah is tantamount to subjecting the crucified and resurrected Messiah Himself to Torah.*[22] Those in the Messiah share His status and identity; subjugation to Torah, therefore, implies the superiority of Torah to the Messiah. Since this cannot be, union with Christ necessarily means a status outside of the governance

---

20 Luther liked to call the sacraments "trysting places" (spots where lovers meet), which is helpful in some respects, but the notion of God or Jesus and the believer as lovers is an unfortunate one. The marital relationship depicted in Scripture is not between the Messiah and the individual believer, but between the Messiah and the Church, corporately. Failure to appreciate this point adequately has frequently led to widespread damage to both corporate worship and individual Christian experience.

21 For further exegetical and biblical-theological reflection on the non-magical but effectual character of baptism, see the work of Peter Leithart, particularly *The Baptized Body.*

22 Paul of course believes that the Messiah was "born under Torah" (4:4)—but precisely in order to bring liberation from its hegemony (4:5) through His death (cf 3:13), not to become permanently subjected to it.

of the Mosaic law.

There is neither Jew nor Greek, neither slave nor free, there is not male and 3:28
female: for you are all one [man] in the Messiah Jesus.

There is a sense in which Paul's argument is "egalitarian," but not in the way this verse is frequently now put in service to agendas such as women's ordination to authoritative teaching positions, for example. It must be remembered that in the context, Paul is not simply obliterating all natural and social distinctions, period. If natural distinctions were invalid, then the removal of roles for male and female would make homosexuality a matter of indifference at worst, and a great sign of progress at best. But in fact, Paul vehemently opposes homosexuality elsewhere, e.g. Rom 1:26–27; 1 Cor 6:9.

The three pairings of the verse are apparently all direct counterpoints to corresponding phrases of the Jewish benediction, where the free Jewish male thanks God he is not a Gentile, not a slave, and not a woman—each of whom had either less rights or less responsibilities in terms of Torah. Thus, along with placing all believers on equal footing as full heirs to the Abrahamic promises, Paul here is once again providing a counter-narrative to the predominant view of Torah among his Jewish contemporaries.

In the Messiah, there is ***neither Jew nor Greek***. The Jew has no advantage over the Greek regarding inheritance rights. For both, inheritance comes *via* the Messiah (v 26), and connection to the Messiah is union to (in some sense) the point of identity, and there can be no gradations here—the Messiah is the Messiah. Thus circumcision offers nothing; baptism has done all.

In the Messiah, there is ***neither slave nor free***. Inferior or fewer rights or responsibilities for slaves regarding Torah no longer come into play in the new covenant inheritance, since the inheritance comes outside of Torah (3:15–18). Although Paul is not revolutionary, elsewhere he treats masters and slaves as equal brothers in the Messiah (see esp Phlm 16; note also that in Eph 6:9, Paul says that there is no partiality with God between slaves and masters).

In the Messiah, there is ***not male and female***. Note the altered form here (καὶ rather than οὐδὲ), as over against the other contrasts—this seems to be an allusion to Gen 1:27, an indication that in the Messiah the new creation in some way supersedes the first creation. The trick is: How so? Paul certainly believes in marriage (e.g. 1 Cor 7) and there is a great deal of continuity between his explicit teaching regarding male-female roles and that of the OT. Paul doesn't obliterate roles; cf 1 Tim 2; Eph 5. In fact, given the basis Paul provides in v 27, flattening roles would implicitly entail destroying parental governance of the home, which is obviously far from his mind (cf Eph 6:1–4).

In view of the phrase's background in Gen 1–2, it seems to me that Paul is suggesting there is a sense of completeness for both male and female apart from one another (or, more precisely, apart from *marriage*) that wasn't possible under the OT. There are more possibilities for fullness as a single person, because one is joined to the Messiah.

And yet this is not an individualistic turn, since being joined to the Messiah entails being joined to all who have put on the Messiah—"you are all one man in the Messiah Jesus." The sufficiency leads, not to isolation, but to deeper community.

But the key point in Paul's argument regards *inheritance*. Whereas Israelites and Gentiles were previously not equal heirs in covenantal status, that is no longer the case; and the same can be said regarding men and women. In baptism, both men and women have been clothed with the Messiah and are identified with His status of sonship.

Under Torah, there was a hierarchical chain of access to the presence of God, with the high priests at the top, then the priests and Kohathites (all male), and then the common people. Further, under Torah, aside from childbirth, women were unclean on a monthly basis and automatically disqualified from access to the tabernacle or temple.

Now, however, there is full and equal access to the presence of God in His Son. The arguments Paul makes elsewhere against authoritative teaching positions for women (e.g. 1 Tim 2:11ff) are not based upon any notion that women are inferior, inequal, or have less access to God or the promises of God.[23]

Ironically, the contemporary stress upon women's ordination assumes a sort of clericalism. For as all recognize, not *all* in fact are qualified for church office, whether by reason of youth, spiritual immaturity etc. In the meantime, the equality Paul envisions is a head-for-head, all-encompassing unity. Thus if church office is the goal of egalitarianism, either all in the Messiah's household, children included, must qualify for it (an impossibility), or egalitarianism is not as egalitarian as it looks.

The basis of the new position of equality for all of God's people is this: ***for you are all one in the Messiah Jesus***. The term *one* once again harkens back to v 16 as well as v 20. In being baptized into the Messiah, all have been clothed with the one seed of promise, have all been identified with Him. Each of His people—Jew, Gentile, slave, free, man, woman—and yes, young and old, brilliant and self-aware or severely handicapped—all are equal participants in His heritage.

Even as Paul has written above in v 27 that all those baptized into the Messiah have put Him on, he has written elsewhere that the bread of the Lord's table and the body of the Messiah are coextensive (1 Cor 10:17). Those clothed with the Messiah are all full participants in His life—not individually or atomistically, but *together*. This is a key datum in the matter of communing baptized children.[24] The issue is whether the new covenant allows for a hierarchy of access to the heart of worship, where God gives Himself to His people. Closing the communion table off from the children of the worshiping assembly implies that they are not in fact the children of God—that they are outside the body of the Messiah.

This principle of equality and unity extends also to the treatment of visitors belonging to churches of other denominations. Many ecclesiastical traditions bar such visitors from celebration of the sacrament. (There are a spectrum of practices, from the complete insularity of "closed" communion, to the slighly more inclusive "close" communion,

23 For expansion on the matter of leadership roles in connection with this passage, see *Sermons on Galatians*, 168–173.

24 On this subject, see my book, *Feed My Lambs*.

which reserves table participation for those holding to the same or similar confessions.) As with the matter of barring the congregation's children from the *Lord's* table—and we must emphasize that the table is *His* rather than our own—this represents a serious failure to appreciate the unity of Jesus Christ and His body. The Messiah's work has effected a new unity among the people of God, and such follies of denominationalism arise out of the divisions engendered by the old creation.

It would be fruitful to consider the relationship between this verse in context and Eph 4:13, where Paul writes of the *unity* of the *faith* and of the knowledge of the Son of God. That verse raises a further future ongoing and even eschatological dimension to the matter at hand. Whereas here in Galatians, Paul is addressing the present status of believers as those made one in the mature Son, in Ephesians, he is addressing the ongoing practical growth into the fruit of that status, which ultimately results in the manifestation of the Church as *the complete* or *mature man* (ἄνδρα τέλειον)—confirming the notion that the masculine "one" here is implicitly "the one Man, the Messiah."

Of further pertinence in this comparison is the question of whether both *the faith* and *the knowledge* in Eph 4:13 modify *of the Son of God*, which seems likely. In that case, we have an analogous construction to Gal 2:20, where Paul says that he lives *by the faith(fulness) of the Son of God*. The indwelling of the Messiah "in your hearts" through (His?) *pistis* (Eph 3:17) bears fruit in the mature expression of being one in the one fully mature and complete Man.

3:29 *Now if you are the Messiah's, indeed you are the seed of Abraham, and heirs according to [the] promise.*

Arguing from their established status, Paul continues with the first-class conditional clause, ***Now if you are the Messiah's***. The first-class form does not call their status into question, but builds on it; one could translate: *since you are the Messiah's*.

The Galatians are *the Messiah's* or *of the Messiah,* as determined by being clothed with Him in baptism (v 27).

Given this connection to the Messiah, who is the one Seed of Abrahamic promise (v 16), then, ***indeed you are the seed of Abraham.*** The identity of the seed is located in the Messiah, and so are you.

Remember again that Paul is primarily writing to Gentiles. He is therefore affirming the fulfillment of what God had promised to Abraham. Those who are "of the faith," *of the Messiah,* are now blessed *with* and *in* Abraham. Apart from either circumcision or Israelite extraction, these Gentiles have become the fruit of the promise which was pre-preached to Abraham (cf 3:8): "*In you* shall all the Gentiles be blessed." And thus, Abraham has now received the children promised to him (cf 3:8).

This new relationship to Abraham and the seed of promise likewise implies that they are ***heirs according to the promise.*** As the Messiah is recipient of the fully realized promises given Abraham, those who belong to Him are, with Him, full partakers—whether Jew or Gentile.

As heirs according to the promise, everything that Paul has said in vv 15–18 therefore comes into play. There is full partnership in the Messiah and in Abraham—and indeed, there is a whole new creation (2 Cor 5:17).

From Slavery to Public Heirs (4:1–7)

Paul now continues along the same vein in which he has been speaking, but backs up a bit in order to get a sort of a running start to address the Galatians' current situation.

The passage describes the transition from childhood and slavery to adoptive sonship, by means of the sending of the Son and Spirit by God the Father. This transition has clear eschatological overtones, as seen in the themes of τὰ στοιχεῖα τοῦ κόσμου (*the elements of the world*), fullness of time, and so on. The Son accomplishes the transition; the Spirit effects it and is Himself the first installment of the inheritance.

Lightfoot observes the chiasm of 4–5:

A. God sent Son

B. Born under law

B-. Redeeming those under law

A-. We receive adoption as sons.

4:1 *Now, I say, as long as the heir is a child, he differs nothing from a slave, [though] being master of all.*

Reverting to the time prior to the Messiah's coming, Paul writes, ***Now, I say, as long as the heir is a child***. Paul does implicitly acknowledge that prior to the Messiah, there was a difference between Israelites and Gentiles. The former were indeed heirs, but they were children. Israel under Torah had not yet reached its inheritance.

Under these circumstances for the heir, ***he differs nothing from a slave***. Now, of course, Paul does not mean this exhaustively, as if a free child had no more privileges than a slave. The context primarily has to do with the matter of inheritance as well as certain aspects of the household *ethos*. The child is so slave-like that he is kept in custody by a slave, after all.

The *heir* and *slave* themes reappear in 4:30: "Cast out the *slave* woman and her son, for the son of the slave woman shall not *inherit* with the son of the free woman." (But contrast to Jacob's sons by Bilhah and Zilpah.)

The child is in this position, ***though being master of all***. It is interesting to note that the Greek term for *master* is κύριος (*lord*); in the context, Paul is developing a symbiotic relationship between the Messiah and His people. As in Psalm 8, God has placed all things under the feet of mankind (i.e. His people). Here, however, while the heir is in fact a lord, so long as he is a child, he cannot enter into the exercise of his mastery.

4:2 *But is under guardians and managers until the set time of the father.*

The lord of all ***is under guardians and managers*** during his childhood. The former term is clearly a reference to the παιδαγωγός discussed explicitly in 3:24–25. The preposition *under* further relates this statement to 3:22–23, where Israel is said to have been imprisoned, both under Sin (22) and under Torah (23). This again emphasizes the heir's temporarily subservient role.

In comparison to the *paidagogos,* Witherington says the term *manager* refers to a more important household manager, usually a close family friend (albeit still a slave).

This subservience has a terminal point, ***until the set time of the father***. No wealthy father would have placed his child under the direction of a slave and just leave him there. The child's subservience was due to the fact that he was not yet ready to enter upon and enjoy his rightful role; and likewise, Paul is saying that the hegemony of the old creation generally, and Torah specifically, was part of God's design—but not intended to be permanent.

> *Thus also we, when we were children, we had been enslaved under the* 4:3
> *elements of the world.*

Paul now explicitly moves from the analogy to his actual point of reference: ***Thus also we, when we were children***, i.e. experiencing the status outlined in 3:23ff.

At that time, Paul says, ***we were enslaved***, like the heir who differs nothing from a slave in v 1, subject to his social inferiors.

Here Paul says that this slavery was ***under the elements of the world***. There have been many pages written regarding the intended meaning of *elements* (Gr *stoicheia*). Witherington, for example, makes a plausible case for *elemental teachings,* while others go farther afield with the thought of "elemental *spirits*."

While Witherington's view is plausible, it seems to me that it takes the *paidagogos* theme too far into the educational realm, and overlooks the letter's programmatic theme of new creation. In that light, a simple metaphorical use of the conventional classical elements (earth, air, fire and water) makes best sense.[25] Jews, like pagan Gentiles, shared a common κόσμος made of certain constitutive elements; Paul is affirming a new creation (cf 6:15). In comparison to the mature (and thus liberating)

---

25 Although she herself takes the present phrase in the sense of *elementary principles,* Linda Belleville "Under Law" 64 acknowledges, "Predominant usage in the religious literature of the NT period is to the physical concept of τὰ στοιχεῖα as the constituent elements of the world, generally specified as fire, air, earth and water."

new world which was to emerge, the old *kosmos* was one of childhood and relative slavery.

But what exactly *are* these constitutive elements of the *kosmos*? It is surely clear in this context that at least one of them is Torah itself; after all, Paul has been giving an extended discussion of Torah's custodial, imprisoning role (see especially 3:22–23). But back of that, and more generally, the primary constitutive element of the old *kosmos* is *flesh*, and for this reason, Paul can tie Israel's experience under Torah together with the Gentiles' experience serving idols (vv 8–9). The point of that analogy is not that Torah is evil, along with the rest of the old creation (a thought Paul vehemently denies, implicitly in 3:21 and most explicitly in Rom 7:12). Rather, the point is that Torah belongs to the first creation, because although coming from God who is powerful Spirit, it is a covenant made with mere flesh, old creation human beings, men of the *kosmos*, and its characteristics reflect that situation. (See below on vv 8–10.) Torah is what it is because it is a first creation administration for a fleshly era.

4:4 *But when the fullness of time came, God sent forth His Son, born from a woman, born under Torah.*

In the case of an heir, presumably the *terminus* for his time under a *paidagogos* would have been at a certain age or perhaps demonstration of maturity (cf v 2). But so far as salvation history goes, ***when the fullness of time came, God sent forth His Son***, i.e. He brought maturity into the *kosmos* from the outside, sending His own eternal Son.

This Son enters fully into the experience of the *kosmos*—He is ***born from a woman;*** and fully into the experience of Israel—He is ***born under Torah.***

By being born from a woman, the Son is fully man, fully a part of the *kosmos*—a matter to which Paul will turn explicitly in a moment.

The phrase also echoes the original promise of Gen 3:15: "I will put enmity between you and the *woman*, and between your seed and her seed; he shall bruise your head, and you shall bruise his heel." (This of course connects to the promised seed of 3:16 here.)

By being *born under Torah,* the Son became heir to the common (enslaved) condition of Israel. It must therefore be underscored once again that the Messiah Himself was *of Torah* in the terms of 3:10, and thus subject to its curse. So far as the closer context goes, the mature Son entered into the experience of immature Israel, the people enslaved to Torah, subject to the custodian.

This insight provides an important window into the conflicts of the Gospels. Jesus is born under Torah, but He lives in its context as the mature Son whose actions transcend it and expose its limitations, and repeatedly He is accused of lawbreaking.

In order that He might redeem those under Torah, in order that we might 4:5
receive the adoption.

The entrance of the Son as one born from a woman and under Torah was ***in order that He might redeem those under Torah.*** The redemption language goes back to 3:13, and reinforces again the point of that passage. The Messiah was born under Torah, so that He could liberate (i.e. from it) those who were under it.

This redemption opens up a new possibility: ***that we might receive the adoption.*** Paul, in a twist, says that "we" Jews—the heirs!—had to receive adoption! Their mature sonship is not something automatic, but a gift of God's grace in the sending and delivering up of His beloved Son.

Even if υἱοθεσία should be translated along the lines of *public designation as sons,* rather than *adoption,*[26] the statement here is indeed surprising. For after all, one expects that a child will grow up and inherit almost automatically. We should remember, however, that Paul has laid groundwork for all of this in 3:16. The eschatological Abrahamic promise was to the seed "as of one," which Israel under Torah could not be. It is only in the Messiah that the promise can come to fruition, and that

26 The classicist Matthew Colvin suggests that υἱοθεσία does not mean here what we do with *adoption* terminology. In Paul's usage, he argues, it "really means the acknowledgment of a son, the entry of the child into the public eye as the heir of his Father." See the article, "Eschatology and the Fatherhood of God," online at http://colvinism.wordpress.com/2013/05/03/eschatology-and-the-fatherhood-of-god/

Israel can become what she was called to be as the seed of promise. And here, there is *one* seed, Israelite and Gentile.

4:6 *Now because you are sons, God sent forth the Spirit of His Son into our hearts, crying out, "Abba, Father."*

This now opens up the logic of Paul's shift from first person plural to second person address in v 6:[27] ***Now because you are sons***. In the very act of redemption that provided adoption to believing Israel, God in His Son likewise provided equal adoption to Gentiles. Just as liberation for Israel from Torah is made possible because the Son is *born under Torah,* so too liberation for Gentiles from the bondage of the first *kosmos* is made possible because the Son is *born from a woman,* has entered into the constitution of the old creation.

The matter of Jews and Gentiles continues to be one of mutuality. Because *you* are sons, ***God sent forth the Spirit of His Son into our hearts***. Just as in 3:13–14, where the redemption of Jews from Torah brings them the Spirit and blessing to the Gentiles, so again here, the redemption of Jews from Torah brings them the Spirit and sonship to Gentiles. The sonship of Gentiles and the gift of the Spirit are parallel benefits of the new creation, aspects of the eschatological promise provided Abraham.

The relationship between these blessings is not merely incidental; the sending of the Spirit to Israel is confirmation that God has adopted Gentiles. See especially Joel 2:28–29:

> And it shall come to pass afterward that I will *pour out My Spirit on all flesh;* your sons and your daughters shall prophesy, your old men shall dream dreams, and your young men shall see visions. Even on the male and female *servants* in those days I will pour out My Spirit.

---

27 As hinted by the mild movement of the conjunction δέ (*now*).

The prophecy in Joel includes at least three elements present in Gal 3–4: (1) the outpouring of the Spirit; (2) the inclusion of Gentiles (all flesh); (3) the breaking of the inheritance barrier between slave and free.

The Spirit is spoken of specifically as *the Spirit of His Son*. Why this phrase? Witherington 290: "focus is on the fact that the Holy Spirit is the one who forms Christ in the believer, conforming the believer to the image of the Son" (cf Rom 8:9).

Through the Spirit's work, those receiving him are ***crying out, "Abba, Father."*** The adoption is not merely some formal legal relationship, but a warm familial bond. (The endearing term is not, however, a childish "Daddy"; the context has to do with mature heirs entering their inheritance—even if their maturity is not in fact their own, but granted as the Messiah's gift.) Having the Spirit of the Son prompts us to pray as the Son did (Witherington 291). See Mk 14:36: this is how Christ prays. (Cf above on 3:27–28: believers are the one Man, the Messiah.) Witherington notes, "What greater proof could there be that [these Gentiles] already had, through the Spirit, all the benefits of an intimate and loving relationship with God they ever could need or ask for without having to submit to the Mosaic law?"

So that no longer are you a slave, but a son; but if a son, also an heir through 4:7
God.

In v 7, Paul again shifts from Israel to Gentiles: ***So that no longer are you a slave but a son***. The fact that Jews now participate in the Spirit has as its necessary implication that so do Gentiles, as the sending of the eschatological Spirit involves "all flesh" (see quote above from Joel 2), and the seed into which both have been incorporated is *one;* the gifts of the one are the gifts of the other. By inclusion into the Messiah, believing Gentiles are not foster children, but full sons.

And this means, ***but if a son, also an heir through God***. Sonship entails becoming Abraham's heirs, together the seed of promise.

This all has happened to those who really were *slaves*. While Israel in her immaturity "differed nothing from a slave," Paul says that the Galatians really were slaves. He individualizes in this case; *you* is singular.

What has come about is personal as well as corporate reality. And that reality is that those who were slaves are now made full sons and heirs, full participants in Abraham and all the promises belonging to him.

Unstated: all without circumcision, all apart from Torah. Indeed, all because God has sent His Son to liberate those who were under Torah, just as (more generally) He sent His Son to be born from a woman under the elements of the world in order to liberate those born from women to enter into new creation.

This change of status is ***through God*** (Byz *heir of God through the Messiah*). Just as the first creation was created by God, although marred by men, the emergence of the new creation likewise is His handiwork, and entrance into its inheritance is His gift.

The Conflict for the Covenant

THE MAJOR SUBSECTION WHICH FOLLOWS THE HEART of Paul's narrative is largely devoted to exploring the conflict that has arisen within the community in Galatia, and what should be done about it. This is a "conflict for the covenant" because, as Paul explains, it is those who live by the *pistis* of the Messiah (cf 2:20) and thus live by faith in Him, rather than those who cling to circumcision and Torah, who are heirs of the Abrahamic covenant.

The false teachers have pushed the Galatians off course and alienated them from the apostle and his message. The proper response to this conflict is to expel the teachers and return to the Messiah and the pathway upon which the Galatians had begun in the Spirit.

Return to Slavery (4:8–12)

But then indeed, not knowing God, you were enslaved to those which by 4:8
nature are not gods.

As he had done earlier in connection with Israel, Paul momentarily backtracks with the previous status and experience of the Gentiles: ***then indeed***, they were ***not knowing God***. In an absolute sense, this of course was not universally true of all Gentiles; there were scattered God-fearers among the nations at various points (and perhaps continuously) throughout ancient history. But by and large, the Gentiles did not know the one true God.

In this condition, ***you were enslaved***. Paul here picks up the slavery language which he has used mostly in connection with Torah to this point, but of course it is far from his thought to imply that Israel under Torah was enslaved while others were free. Far from it, Torah was a kind governor compared to the things that ruled over Gentiles. Nonetheless, for Paul, the old creation as a whole is an era of relative slavery.

In this case, the slavery is more fundamental and serious than being subject to a child custodian; it refers to enslavement ***to those which by nature are not gods***. These Gentiles were enslaved, *via* false worship, to demons—and indeed, to Caesar.

4:9 *But now, knowing God, or rather, having been known by God, how do you return again upon the weak and poor elements to which again you wish to be enslaved?*

Note the τότε ... νῦν leading v 8 and v 9, respectively. *Then* you didn't know God, but ***now*** you are indeed ***knowing God***—or rather, are those who have ***been known by God***. This of course is not a reference merely to divine awareness, but is an example of the biblical *knowledge* terminology being employed for God having love toward someone. In this case, as sons and heirs.

Paul uses this remarkable blessing of rescue and reconciliation as the basis for his plea: ***how do you return again upon the weak and poor elements?***

Given that Paul uses the language of *return* here, we may almost expect that these Gentiles are going back to their previous idols; but of course, the context of the letter is Jewish circumcision, and the ensuing charge in the next verse has to do with keeping the calendrical observances of Torah. If, however, they had never been under Torah, how can they be said to be *returning?*

Paul's point is that while their previous experience of the old creation was indeed different, what they are now doing is making a return to the old creation, becoming entangled with it.

With the simple term *elements,* Paul refers to v 3's full phrase *the elements of the world* (τὰ στοιχεῖα τοῦ κόσμου). This is a Pauline theme elsewhere, as well. In Col 2:20, the apostle says that believers died with the Messiah to *the elements of the world;* therefore (again in reference to matters of Torah) why are they submitting to regulations as if they were still alive in the *kosmos?* He considers Torah and its regulations to be constitutive elements of the old world, the old creation; and the new creation is not composed of these elements. As noted above (see on v 3), these elements included Torah, but back of that, *flesh* and all things belonging to the old *kosmos*.

Paul characterizes these elements as *weak and poor,* which stands in contrast to the age of the Spirit; throughout the Scriptures, God's Spirit is mighty and is contrasted to *flesh*—the weakness and mortality of men and things (see e.g. Isa 31:3; cf Gen 6:3; Mt 26:41 etc).[1] Indeed, this is one of the startling juxtapositions of the Joel prophecy referenced above: God pours out His Spirit on all *flesh,* His power upon men in weakness (Joel 2:28).

Consequently, a return from the new creation to the old is a departure from the age and realm of authority and power to an age and realm of weakness and poverty.

Paul speaks of these elements and questions why, through them, ***again you wish to be enslaved.*** While previously they had been enslaved to idols, Paul does not see a turning to Torah as a comparatively minor matter. Whereas God had once governed Israel through Torah, He now does so through His Son, and Torah is no longer blessing. The negative things concerning Torah remain, but none of the good things, and for Gentile believers to seek Torah represents a pursuit of slavery in a world from which they had been rescued.

You are observing days, and months and seasons and years. 4:10

While the movement to circumcision is apparently still a work in process, in the meantime, ***You are observing days***, i.e. they have already begun to keep the Jewish Sabbath. And not only the weekly Sabbath, but the wider Jewish calendar: ***months and seasons and years.*** The items of observation here are all clearly delineated in Torah: Sabbaths (days), new moons (months), festivals (seasons), Jubilee (years). Paul uses a slightly more explicit but less complete list in Col 2:16, which refers to

1 *Flesh* is of course a dominant theme in Galatians and elsewhere in Paul, and in part is singularly apt terminology because of its connection to the institution of circumcision (Gen 17:11, 13–14, 23–25). One wonders if the vulnerability of men's reproductive organs are part of the array of connotations at play.

festival, new moon, and Sabbaths, as well as matters of food and drink.

Witherington 298 notes that this is analogous to the calendar of the imperial cult, which was loaded with various observations, but of course the other various idolatries also had their own markings of time. What all this implies is that in effect, the Galatians have traded in one old world calendar for another.

It should be understood that observance of the Sabbath was the single most defining practice of Judaism. Unlike circumcision, it applied to both men and women; and it was public and observable. To observe Sabbath told the world that one was Torah-observant.

4:11 *I am afraid of you, lest somehow I have laboured among you in vain.*

Paul watches this turning to sabbatical observance with trepidation: ***I am afraid of you***. As a mother watching her daughter giving her heart to an unsuitable suitor, it is with dread that Paul considers where his disciples have drifted.

His concern is that ***somehow I have laboured among you in vain***. Such a return to the elements of the world—even if to Torah rather than to paganism—would mean nullification of Paul's work. The effort he had expended was not in order to make Jewish proselytes (albeit ostensibly Messiah-believing ones), but to win them squarely for the service and grace of the crucified and risen Lord. The Messiah whom Paul had preached was the liberator from *this present evil age* (1:4), and the embrace of Torah implied abandonment of His eschatological realm in favour of the *kosmos* they had left behind.

4:12 *Become as I am—for I also became as you—brothers, I beg you—you have not harmed me at all.*

In response to the direction they have turned, Paul urges the Galatians, ***Become as I am***. This is not a generic reference to his holiness of life, but rather an indication of his liberation from Torah, which is confirmed by his next statement: ***for I also became as you***. While he once had been fiercely Torah-observant to the degree which would shame them, he counted that dung (cf Phi 3:8) in view of the Messiah's riches. If he, then, who had surpassed his contemporaries in zealous Torah observance, had moved *outside* Torah, surely they should not move *inside* it. As Witherington says, he calls upon them to "become as I am"—not "as I was," as he had described in ch 1.

In addressing them so, he writes, ***brothers, I beg you***. Once again, he appeals to familial tenderness, while at the same time vindicating their established status apart from Torah: they are already *brothers,* fellow sons of Abraham and sons of God. It is therefore fitting that he should *beg* them, implore them not to make the huge mistake which they are making.

The final clause of v 12, ***you have not harmed me at all***, is rather obscure. It may look forward to vv 13ff and refer to their prior good relationship to Paul. But the reference to not wronging/harming him seems a bit abrupt and understated in that context.

Alternatively, perhaps it is linked to the earlier part of v 12. If there is a conceptual connection to the second clause, the implication would be that Paul became like them (i.e. Torah-free), and despite the pressures of their own situation, he has remained so, unharmed by the call of deceit. Against this reading is the aorist (suggesting a single past event), and the fact that another clause intervenes (*brothers, I beg you*).

A Harmful Courtship (4:13–20)

Now you know that because of weakness of the flesh I proclaimed the gospel 4:13
to you at the first.

Paul now backtracks again, but not as far as previously, reminding the Galatians of their initial enthusiasm in response to his ministry. In mentioning the ***weakness of the flesh***, Paul could be referring to an unspecified physical infirmity that forced his original itinerary to get sidetracked, leading him on a different course that took him through South Galatia. Against this, however, is the fact that there is no hint of a change of course in Acts 13.

Rather, Paul is probably referring to when he was struck blind on the road to Damascus, and in the process implying that his healing at the hands of Ananias was only partial (on the likelihood of eyesight being at issue, see v 15). It was due to Jesus exposing his weakness and indeed, bringing him to further weakness, that Paul was brought to his knees and reoriented to a different life and different call.

It was therefore precisely because of that weakening of the flesh at the hands of the Messiah Himself that Paul became an apostle and consequently, ***I proclaimed the gospel to you at the first.***

Thus there is an almost ironic assertion here: life in the old creation is lived in "the weakness of the flesh," but it was precisely due to a weakness of the flesh imposed upon him by the Messiah Himself that Paul came into the new creation and was commissioned to preach. The antidote to the weakness of the flesh is not the provision of superpowers for the flesh, but the strength of the Messiah being made complete in weakness (cf 2 Cor 12:9).

4:14 *And your/my trial in my flesh you did not despise nor disdain/loathe, but as an angel of God you received me—as the Messiah, Jesus [Himself].*

Paul now notes that this weakness which was either ***your trial in my flesh*** or ***my trial in my flesh*** (Byz), ***you did not despise nor loathe.*** If the former, the point is that while his suffering would have been a trial for them, given contemporary associations between followers and leaders, they embraced that trial. If the latter, the reading is more straightforward: they did not despise him on account of the trial which he endured.

In the ancient world, the authority of orators was almost universally considered dependent upon the impressiveness of their personal presence. Paul elsewhere says he does not have that (cf 1 Cor), although in that context, he is speaking primarily of the fineness of his speech, whereas here the focus is on his physical infirmity.

Despite Paul's distance from the rhetorical ideal, he was received, not merely as a philosopher or great speaker, ***but as an angel of God you received me—[indeed] as the Messiah, Jesus.***

The reference to *an angel* echoes Paul's earlier warning that they should not receive any different gospel, even if proclaimed by an angel.

He himself had received a reception not inferior to that of an angel; indeed, they had received him *as the Messiah Jesus* Himself. In truth, that was fitting; in Mt 10:40, Jesus said, "Whoever receives you receives me, and whoever receives me receives Him who sent me."

Therefore, where is your blessing? For I bear witness to you that if possible, 4:15
you would have gouged your eyes out and given [them] to me.

In view of their prior joyful reception of him, Paul asks now, ***Therefore, where is your blessing?***

Paul has his day in court now: ***For I bear witness to you***. They may have forgotten the powerful effect of his preaching upon them, but he has not; and he is ready to make that impact part of his case.

They embraced Paul fully as God's messenger; ***if possible, you would have gouged your eyes out and given [them] to me***.

Apparently, although God restored Paul's sight when Ananias laid hands on him, recurring and visible problems remained with Paul's eyes. Nonetheless, the Galatians' response to Paul was so positive that they would have provided him with their own, had that been possible. They were thus willing to be disgraced to share in Paul's disgrace. (Cf Nahash's intention to bring disgrace on Jabesh-gilead by gouging out their right eyes, 1 Sam 11:2.)

Therefore, have I become your enemy, by telling truth to you? 4:16

In contrast to the Galatians' previous devotion, Paul asks, ***have I become your enemy?*** Whereas they had looked at him as one whom they would have sacrificed their eyes and dignity on his behalf, apparently now they are offended by him.

This change in stance has transpired ***by telling truth to you***. If a wise man is rebuked, he will love the one who speaks the truth to him (Prov 9:8), but the Galatians are foolish rather than wise (3:1).

One of Paul's chief concerns in the letter is *walking in line with the truth of the gospel* (cf 2:14; 5:7). As he continues to provide counsel consistent with that, in the face of those who would deviate from this path, he challenges the Galatians to return to their original blessing (v 15).

4:17 *They are zealously courting you in a manner not good, but they wish to exclude you, so that you may zealously court them.*

Paul's metaphor shifts more directly to one of courtship as he takes on the role of pleading mother (v 19): ***They are zealously courting you in a manner not good.*** In contrast to his sacrificial motherly love, the teachers in Galatia are ill-intentioned suitors, zealously eager and persistent in their quest to deflower their prey. The mention of zealotry is an echo of Paul's own former life, when he was surpassing his fellow Jews in zeal for Torah and Judaism generally (1:14). He associates that zeal with his attempt to destroy the Church of God (1:13), and recognizes that the effect of the circumcision party's teaching in Galatia would be the same.

The teachers ***wish to exclude you***, shut you out. This has numerous possible overtones, including exclusion of the Galatians from Paul's influence, as well as exclusion from the people of God until such time as they are circumcised. But Paul's position is the reverse: they wish to exclude you from the true people of God precisely *by* having you circumcised.

Shutting the Galatians off from Paul's care is ***so that you may zealously court them.*** Just as an ill-intentioned young man may try to weaken a daughter's trust in her parents' protection and counsel, so that she will fall for him and do as he wishes, the false teachers likewise wish to isolate the Galatians from Paul. This isolation will leave the Galatians vulnerable to the teachers and their destructive hopes.

Paul in turn of course is implicitly engaging in an attempted exclusion of his own; by exposing the teachers' hopes using this harshly negative metaphor, he is attempting to wrest the Galatians away from the false teachers. Toward the end of the chapter, he will call for expulsion of such people (v 30).

4:18 *But it is good to be zealously courted in good always, and not only in my presence with you.*

While Paul often associates zeal with devotion to Torah, including in the near context, that is not exclusively the case. Actually, ***it is good to be zealously courted in good always.*** When the Messiah overtook him on the Damascus road, Paul didn't get the zeal smacked out of him. But the direction and character of his zeal fundamentally changed.

Paul has exercised that zeal in Galatia, and the Galatians were courted and won precisely by that zeal for good. But that past is insufficient; he wants them consistently won over by that sort of zeal, ***and not only in my presence with you.*** Be trustworthy when mother is away.

My children, whom again I am birthing with travail, until the Messiah may 4:19
be formed in you.

With the motherhood theme now to the fore, Paul addresses them, not as *brothers,* as previously, but even more tenderly, ***My children.*** They are his beloved offspring, whom he has birthed.

For as it turns out, the ill-intentioned suitors in Galatia are not simply threatening the Galatians' virginity; the effect of their teaching has reversed the birthing process, so that now ***again I am birthing with travail*** (see also on v 24). *Whom,* referring to the Galatians, is the direct object of the verb; not simply Paul's suffering as such, but the act of childbearing itself is in view. Through this letter of emergency and desperation (and no doubt his prayers), Paul seeks to rebirth his children. This is indeed *Paul's travail.*

Paul depicts himself as a mother in pain, and certainly the folly of the Galatians has brought him sorrow (cf Prov 10:1: A wise son gladdens his father, while a foolish son brings his mother sorrow). Here, however, the pain is birthing pain, the result of his own labours. He is attempting to push the Galatians back into the open world of the new creation; the false teachers are attempting to push them back into the old *kosmos.*

Paul's activity, this renewed process of birthing travail, is ongoing ***until the Messiah may be formed in you.*** For Paul the "in the Messiah" (*in Christ*) relationship is *perichoretic,* a matter of mutual indwelling between the Messiah and His people (cf Jn 17:20–23). In baptism, believers have been clothed with the Messiah and are thus in Him (3:27); and likewise, the Messiah is formed in them: He is in them, and they bear His shape, His form (cf Rev 12: the Man-Child is born from the woman, i.e. the people of God).

In 2:20, Paul contrasts being shaped by Torah with his new condition: *now I live no longer, but the Messiah lives in me.* The Galatians have become Torah-formed to the point where it is the law rather than the Messiah which is recognizable in them.[2]

4:20 *But I wish to be present with you now, and alter my voice, because I am uncertain concerning you.*

Although it is good for them to be zealously courted for good even in his absence (v 18), ***I wish to be present with you now***, just a mother does not want to deal with her daughter's danger from a distance. If only I could be present, Paul says, perhaps I could ***alter my voice***, speak to you in a different tone.

As it is, ***I am uncertain concerning you***. Paul is in perplexity, and is imploring them: give me assurances of your zeal for good and your repudiation of the agitators, so that I can speak to you with certainty and not with complaint and rebuke.

Children of Promise (4:21–5:1)

Paul is now ready to double down on his long chain of argument in chapter 3 and the early part of chapter 4. As he has shown, the Mosaic covenant is not merely an adumbration that permanently "sticks" to God's one covenant (3:15); it was an administration for Israel in the time between Moses and the advent of the mature Seed. Since it was for the immature and not for the fullness of time, it participates in the slavery of the child-era and cannot remain in the promise-era, the era of the Spirit. Now, Paul will make it plain: those who embrace Torah are *sarx* and must be cast out. By no means are the Messiah's heirs to return to the bondage from which they have been delivered.

Since Torah is the *paidagogos* (a slave), and those in the Messiah are

2 For more on this verse, see also the comments below on v 27.

in the mature Son, and therefore inheriting heirs, then anyone submitting to the *paidagogos* must be a slave, for it is only when the genuine heir is a minor that he differs nothing from a slave.

Tell me, the ones wishing to be under Torah: do you not hear Torah? 4:21

Paul addresses his hearers as ***the ones wishing to be under Torah.*** Whether the false teachers were encouraging them to keep Torah fully (which is in fact open to question; see on 5:3), that is in fact what circumcision entailed and what Sabbath observance implied. Certainly, even if the Galatians thought that they could obey Torah in a limited way, what they were prepared to embrace would have been in response to Torah, a commitment to it.

Given, then, that ostensible commitment to Torah, Paul asks, ***do you not hear Torah?*** The apostle is offering a play on words. As elsewhere (e.g. Rom 3:19, 31), he glides between two distinct uses of *nomos:* law as *covenant* (Torah, the Mosaic administration), and law as OT *Scripture*. In this case, those desiring to be subject to the Torah covenant need to consider the significance of the *Genesis narrative* of Abraham, Sarah, Hagar, Isaac, and Ishmael (vv 22–23). Torah provides a lesson that they must heed; and in the context of Paul's argument, the ironic lesson is that the Galatians must repudiate Torah and expel those who are sold to its service.[3]

Paul's "polemic against Torah" is not a swerving from the authority of Scripture. Rather, it is all about reading Scripture through the lens of Jesus the Messiah (and *vice versa*). Torah as covenant is relativized, not at all because Scripture is relativized, but because the consummate "grace and truth" have come in the Messiah (Jn 1:17).

For it is written, Abraham had two sons, one from the slave woman, and 4:22
one from the free woman.

Although Abraham had later sons (Gen 25:1–2), for Paul's present

3 "If the Galatians listen to what the Law actually says, they will hear it speaking the words 'Throw out the slave woman and her child'" (Hays, *Galatians*, 300).

purposes, ***Abraham had two sons.***

The elder of these sons, Ishmael, was ***from the slave woman.*** It should be noted that the slave woman became Abraham's concubine, not because of Abraham's dissatisfaction with Sarah, but because Sarah herself did not see how to procure the promise due to her barrenness. This cannot be pressed too far—it was God Himself who gave the law; it was not Israel's brainchild. Nonetheless it remains true that just as God's promise to Sarah preceded and transcended the relationship between Abraham and Hagar, so too God's promise to Abraham preceded and transcended the Mosaic covenant (cf 3:17). That it was given by God demonstrates that it was indeed good; but that it followed in time demonstrated that it was temporary (3:15–19).

Abraham's younger son, Isaac, was ***one from the free woman.***

It may be that Paul's use of *one* for each of the sons intends to allude back to his use of the term in the previous chapter (3:16, 20, 28). If so, the placement of two "ones" side by side indicates that something has to give; one *one* must go (cf v 30).

4:23 *But the one indeed from the slave woman was born according to [the] flesh,*
but the one from the free woman, [was born] through [the] promise.

The juxtaposition of the two sons gives Paul opportunity to return to his flesh–Spirit contrast. ***The one indeed from the slave woman was born according to [the] flesh.*** Note well that Paul's point is not that Ishmael was born as the result of a sexual union (that was true of Isaac, as well), and this made him *fleshly.*

The center of the matter here has to do, first, with the slavery–freedom contrast which Paul has been developing since at least 3:22; and second, with the fact that it is by God's Spirit that life is brought to those free heirs (even when such looks impossible). Even if the one in slavery receives various blessings, those do not give equal status to the one whose life is merely *flesh.*[4]

4 On the importance, however, of not over-reading Paul, as if he were saying that Ishmael was an unsaved unbeliever, see Jordan, "Ishmael." Note particularly the "Immanuel statement" (*God with us*) of Gen 21:20, "*God was with* the lad." Paul's

Meanwhile, the *flesh* terminology (*sarx*), as throughout, has connotations of the flesh of the foreskin and therefore a "direct" allusion to circumcision.

Paul says of Isaac, ***the one from the free woman [was born] through [the] promise.***

We should recall that various promises were attached to Ishmael too (Gen 17:20). But the matter before us has to do with *whose birth* was effected *via* the promise. That was true only of Isaac, not Ishmael (or for that matter, the later sons of Abraham through Keturah).

The birth of Isaac, which was intended to carry forward the seed, required pneumatic intervention, birth by the power of the Spirit, effected within Sarah's lifeless womb. That pointed forward to the eschatological birth of the heirs to the new creation.

The Spirit is the giver of eschatological life. Torah does not bring the Spirit; it works death, and correspondingly, wrath, rather than life (cf Rom 4:15). The most Torah can do is perpetuate life under the old *kosmos*. This is no longer good enough.

These observations undercut the anti-paedobaptist argument that this verse implies that the children of believers are merely "children of the flesh" and not heirs. That has nothing to do with Paul's argument, and violates the actual narrative thread of Genesis. (Jacob carried forward the line of the promised seed in the next generation, and all twelve of his sons did so in the one following; many of these births had no "miraculous" elements.) The matter at issue here is that the heirs are those who belong to the Messiah, rather than to the old creation. This passage does not pretend to answer whether the offspring of believers belong to the Messiah or to the old creation; that is a question that must be answered from elsewhere.

> *Which things are an allegory: for these are two covenants, one from Mount Sinai which bears children into slavery, which is Hagar.* 4:24

---

concern here is not one of election *vs* reprobation, but of the salvation-historical and eschatological significance of Isaac over against Ishmael, just as is his discussion of the Abrahamic promises over against the Torah covenant concern the same matters.

Paul says that the facets of the Genesis narrative ***are an allegory***. He uses this term in a sense similar to *typology*. Typological interpretation recognizes patterns within the reality of the texts, and invariably perceives those patterns in later contexts of fulfillment. Because God controls both history and the authoritative literature describing His works, in an early event, He establishes a stamp or die which sets a pattern or matrix for later events.

So it is that Paul sees the history of Hagar and Ishmael, on one side, and Sarah and Isaac, on the other. The event establishes a typology; and therein ***these are two covenants.***[5]

Paul's language is important. He does not say (as some insist he means), "one covenant looked at in two different ways," but *two different covenantal administrations*—as he has already delineated at some length in chapter 3.[6] One of these covenants was designed to come into its own as a matter of full inheritance; the other was designed as a form of governance for minors. They are different entities, not merely different views of the same thing.

The two covenants Paul sees in the story are not his own fabrication. Leithart ("Mother Paul" 213) notes that there are indeed two covenants in the Genesis narrative; Ishmael and Hagar received promises alongside of, and differentiated from, those given to Isaac (see Gen 16:10–12; 17:20; cf 21:18).

Paul does not dwell here on those original covenants in the Genesis context; his concern is typological, how the bifurcation plays out presently, in terms of his Messiah-centered eschatology.

One of these covenants is the one from ***Mount Sinai which bears children into slavery, which is Hagar***.

---

5 On this theme in Paul, see especially my work devoted to Paul and the law, *These Are Two Covenants*.

6 Note that there is a difference between the two covenants here and those in 2 Corinthians 3—the latter deals with the Mosaic law and the *new* covenant, whereas Paul here is dealing with a contrast between the Mosaic law and the covenant with Abraham. That Abrahamic covenant is of course bound up with the new covenant and forms its "matrix"; the new covenant is its fulfillment in a somewhat different sense than the new covenant is a fulfillment of Torah (which is also true in certain respects, e.g. Matt 5:17; cf Rom 10:4).

Torah of course was delivered from *Sinai*. As a slave itself, Torah/ Mount Sinai bears children into slavery, which is why Paul again travails in birth for the Galatians (v 19): by coming under Torah's influence, they have been reborn, as it were, into slavery.

Paul's description of Torah corresponds to ***Hagar***. Witherington 324 notes that for Philo, Hagar symbolizes elementary learning or education, and compares that to Paul's use of *stoicheia* in the preceding. But Paul is not really working in terms of lower and higher education; his point regarding the *paidagogos* is not focused upon the sort of learning communicated, but by the *ethos* of slavery and temporality implied in life under a child custodian.

In this case, the connection between Hagar and Torah is at least fourfold, having to do with status (which is to the fore), experience, geography, and chronology.

The first point, centering upon the *status of slavery*, is clear enough: Hagar was a household slave, and Paul has already identified Torah as a *paidagogos*, a slave devoted to managing children.

Second, with regard to *experience*, it is often overlooked that like Moses at Sinai (Ex 33:18–23), *Hagar saw God* (Gen 16:13), although doubtless with less attending glory.[7] The connection between Hagar and Sinai/Torah is not simply one of denigration for either; rather it is an explication of the salvation-historical significance of the Abrahamic promise and the eschatologically-weighted route it takes in history *versus* the temporary role of Torah and the old creation as a whole.

Third, the *geographical* connection is clear enough. Hagar fled to Shur—just north of Sinai—when Sarah mistreated her (Gen 16:7); and took Ishmael to the wilderness of Paran—next to Sinai—after the permanent expulsion (Gen 21:21). Moreover, she was originally from Egypt, on the far side of Sinai. Outside of Abraham's household, therefore, Hagar's life circled around Sinai. Thus it is not surprising that Paul connects her to Sinai in the next verse.

---

7 I owe this insight to Jordan, "Ishmael," Pt 2. Moses of course saw "the back" of YHWH, while Hagar saw the *Angel of YHWH,* which we learn, not only from her response in Gen 16:13 but also from elsewhere, was an angelic manifestation of God Himself.

Hagar's Egyptian nativity may also be part of the slavery/redemption theme: just as God liberated Israel from slavery in Egypt, now He has liberated true Israel from slavery to Torah. In other words, the Messiah has provided a new exodus from Egypt, and Hagar's Egyptian ancestry fits Sinai/Torah neatly into that narrative.

Fourth, there is the matter of *chronology*. Leithart ("Mother Paul" 214) points out how the Abraham narrative concerning Hagar and Sarah "previews Israel's history." Once that is granted, the sequence connecting Hagar to Torah becomes significant:[8]

> Abram is married to the free wife first; Hagar the slave woman has the first, fleshly seed; then Yahweh fulfills his initial promise to Abraham and Sarah. Because Hagar comes in as the "second" bride, she is linked with the law, the Sinai covenant that came after the promise. She is fertile before the promise bears fruit, just as Israel after the flesh grew before the arrival of the Israel of the Spirit.

How can it be said that Hagar *bore children into slavery?* Although there is no hint in Genesis that Hagar's son Ishmael was granted second-class (slave) status in Abraham's household, yet it is clear that God was not satisfied with him *as the heir* to the promises He had made to Abraham, or as the seed through whom the covenant would be established (see especially Gen 17:18–21).[9] This thus ties directly into Paul's argument; inheritance does not come through Torah, but through the truly free Son. In Isaac Abraham's "seed" would be called (Gen 21:12; cf Rom 9:7; Heb 11:18). But if that is so, Isaac is connected to the true Seed for whom the promise was made (3:16), and inheritance comes only through Him as the free and proper Heir.

---

8 And of course, we know from 3:15–18 that sequence is highly important to Paul's argument (cf also Rom 4:10).

9 The exclusion of the son of a slave wife from inheritance (at least when there were children from a free wife) was apparently common practice in Abraham's time. Cf the *Lipit-Ishtar Code,* line 25.

Paul therefore is not merely engaging in what *we* would call "allegory"; he is tying the Genesis narrative quite intelligibly to his own connection of Abraham and the Messiah (cf 3:6–9, 16). Isaac is the chosen seed through whom the Abrahamic covenant is established, the son of freedom (both God's freedom and Sarah's), whereas Ishmael (blessed as he may be in other respects) is the one left outside the great eschatological inheritance, the son of slavery—heir to the old creation alone, and not the new.

Now this Hagar is mount Sinai in Arabia: now it corresponds to the present 4:25
Jerusalem, for it is enslaved with her children.

Paul again asserts ***this Hagar is Mount Sinai in Arabia***, a point already made in the preceding verse, in reference to Torah (see comments there).

In the typology, Hagar now ***corresponds to the present Jerusalem***. Here the logic is not geographical, but inevitable. Since the present Jerusalem is under Torah, and Torah is a slave who governs children as slaves, the correspondence is straightforward enough. Jerusalem, despite being populated by God's people Israel, is present Jerusalem, i.e. the Jerusalem which belongs to *this present evil age* (1:4).

Just as Ishmael was in some sense not freeborn, since his mother was a slave, Paul says that the present Jerusalem ***is enslaved with her children***. She is not simply enslaved to the Roman empire, although in terms of the Deuteronomic curses, that is also an *apropos* observation. More crucially and fundamentally, she is enslaved to the old *kosmos*, the first creation. As Paul has explained in 3:19ff, Torah was a *paidagogos*, and those under it, even if legitimate children, differed nothing from slaves (4:1). Because the present Jerusalem remains under Torah, she is not free, and her children are not free.

But the above-Jerusalem is free, which is our mother [Byz: which is the 4:26
mother of all of us].

In contrast to the present Jerusalem, however, ***the above-Jerusalem***

is free. The terms *present* (or *now,* νῦν) and *above* are of course not exact as opposites, because the once-future Jerusalem has become present, but she is "above," transcending the old *kosmos*. Paul frequently uses the *above* concept to refer to life in the Messiah, whether present or future; cf Phi 3:14 (*upward* call); Col 3:1–2 (seek the things *above,* think on things *above,* where the Messiah is). Since the ascension of Jesus, the locus of "Jerusalem" has shifted; the "present Jerusalem" is the old creation Jerusalem; the resurrected Jerusalem is wherever the Messiah is present.

This *above-Jerusalem,* rather than the *present Jerusalem* locked under Torah, ***is our mother***. Paul has been depicting himself as mother in the preceding section. This has not been arbitrary. He sees himself as a sort of proxy for the free Jerusalem; he has been identifying himself with the presence of the Messiah and the *above-Jerusalem*. Paul's ministry engenders freedom (cf 2 Cor 3:8, 17), because the free Jerusalem bears free children, while similarly the Judaizers' efforts engender slavery, because the present Torah-bound Jerusalem bears enslaved children.

4:27 *For it is written, "Rejoice, barren woman who does not bear; break forth and shout, one who does not suffer birth-pains, because more are the children of the wilderness than of the one having a husband."*

Paul does recognize that in some respects, there is something of an unexpected character to this turn of events, and so turns to a quotation of Isa 54:1. This is a text about Jerusalem, linked to Abraham and Sarah by the context of Isa 51:2 (Witherington 335). In Isaiah's context, "your Maker is your husband" (Isa 54:5).

Although Paul's usage in connection with the Abraham narrative seems a bit of an ironic inversion in the context—after all, Sarah the free woman was the one with a husband, and Hagar was the one sent into the wilderness—his instincts are more sure than it appears at first glance. For the first matter in Isaiah is the ***barren woman who does not bear***, and it was Sarah who was barren. And her laughter perhaps fits with the commendation to ***break forth and shout***.

In the present case, Leithart ("Mother Paul" 218) points out that the

Spirit's work in Galatia is manifest in the fact that he himself is their "mother" (v 19), meaning their birth is even more a work of the Spirit than that of Isaac (Sarah, after all, was at least a woman). "If his ministry gives birth to children of God, they must be children belonging in the column with Sarah, freedom, the Spirit, and promise."

The more difficult section of the quotation is the final two clauses, ***because more are the children of the wilderness than of the one having a husband***. For who repeatedly kept ending up in the wilderness, if not Hagar? And Sarah was the one who had a husband. However, it should be remembered that Sarah in a sense gave up her husband to Hagar in order to bear through her.[10]

At any rate, the overall point is made. Fruitfulness does not always come from where it is expected, as repeatedly God vindicates the barren and rejected. This is what He has done with the gospel of His Son, bringing outsiders into His new creation, while most of Israel remains under Torah's bondage.

Now, you [Byz we], brothers, corresponding to Isaac, are the children of 4:28
promise.

Paul continues his treatment of the Genesis narrative by referring to ***you*** (or perhaps, ***we***, in which case, he refers not now to *we Jews*, but to *we believers together*) as those who are ***corresponding to Isaac*** in the typology which he has been exploring. Isaac was the child of promise—i.e. the designated heir of God's promise to Abraham. These Gentiles are not merely *analogies* to Isaac, but represent in person the *fulfillment* of the prophecies given Abraham, as well as the antitypes to the types in play over the course of Abraham's life. The promise has always been pointed in their direction.[11]

In this typology, the Galatians ***are the children of promise***. Paul has

10 Witherington 336 makes sense of the passage thus: Paul is the barren woman; Paul as the "desert" woman who spent time in Arabia, has more numerous children than those wedded to "the present Jerusalem."

11 Hays 305: "They are the heirs for whom the promise was destined from the first (cf. 3:8)."

already asserted this in other words in 3:29 by identifying them as *the seed of Abraham,* but his intention here is to relate this datum to the Genesis narrative of Abraham, Hagar, Ishmael, Sarah and Isaac, from which he is about to make a point (vv 29–31).

4:29 *But just as then the one born according to [the] flesh persecuted the one [born] according to [the] Spirit, so also now.*

Some things never change. In a world where Jews and Gentiles persecuted one another, much more those born of the *kosmos* persecute those born of *pneuma*. ***Just as then the one born according to [the] flesh persecuted the one [born] according to the Spirit*** apparently refers to Gen 21:9. The original text provides little detail, but the laughter of Ishmael, perhaps in mockery of Isaac, led to the ultimate expulsion of Hagar and her son. *Isaac* means laughter, and whatever the nature of Ishmael's action, the latter's laughter somehow seems to encroach upon Isaac's prerogatives. As Leithart ("Mother Paul" 214) puts it, by "Isaacing," Ishmael was "claiming to be the true heir."

And ***so also now;*** those with full inheritance as the seed of promise are being pressured and persecuted by those making the claim to be the true heirs, but who in fact are not.

Again, the contrast is not, as often supposed, between those who are born into a covenant family ("flesh") and those who undergo a conversion experience ("Spirit"). Both Isaac and Ishmael were *born* in the same way in that sense. Moreover, the Judaizers' argument was not that one must be "born a Jew"—arguably, it is possible that they themselves were not (cf on 6:13a), and they obviously were not requiring that impossibility from Galatian Gentiles.

Nonetheless, Ishmael was born *via* a "fleshy stratagem" (Hays 301), an attempt to "force" the arrival of the divine promise. Isaac, on the other hand, was "resurrection"—the gift of life in the face of death (Sarah's barrenness).

4:30 *But what does the Scripture say? "Cast out the slave woman and her son, for the son of the slave woman shall not inherit with the son of the free woman."*

Paul has finally arrived at the hortatory point of his journey into the history and typology of this particular Genesis narrative. Alluding back to his question of v 21, *do you not hear Torah,* Paul asks, ***But what does the Scripture say?***

And what "Scripture" says, it turns out, is what Sarah says. While readers sometimes see Sarah's words as bitter, in fact Yahweh affirms her request (see Gen 21:12). Whatever her own motivation, what she requests is God's own purpose. And thus the weight of Scripture rests upon her words, lightly paraphrased by Paul: ***Cast out the slave woman and her son, for the son of the slave woman shall not inherit with the son of the free woman.***

Thus, on the authority of Scripture, Paul is calling for the expulsion of the false teachers from the new covenant communities, his Galatian churches. The *cast out* language has some relationship to 1:4, where the term *deliver* sometimes has the meaning of *cast out.* The alternatives are deliverance from the present evil age, or casting out of the sphere of covenant blessing (in the terminology of the near context, life in the community of the *above-Jerusalem*). On expulsion/church discipline, see also 5:9–10.

The separation of the sons of the slave and free demonstrates that a new time has arrived. Whereas previously the minor heir did not differ from a slave (v 1), now the time for inheritance has come, and those who remain defined by slavery (as marked out here by Torah) must be cast off.

Therefore, brothers, you are not children of the slave woman, but of the free 4:31
woman.

Paul sums up this section of the argument, ***Therefore, brothers***, i.e. for the reasons we have explored, ***you are not children of the slave woman***. Your identity is not with Torah, the present Jerusalem, or the old *kosmos*. You are the children ***of the free woman;*** you belong to the free city, the above-Jerusalem, and the new creation. Indeed, you are *my* children, says Paul (cf v 19); and I am one who has personally been liberated from Torah.

5:1 *For the freedom, the Messiah has freed you: stand firm therefore and do not again be subject to the yoke of slavery.*

Since they are children of the free woman (4:31), the calling of the Galatians therefore is defined by the liberation which the Messiah has won: ***For the freedom, the Messiah has freed you***. There is an emphasis on *you*. Yes, you Galatians have been freed in the liberation of the Messiah in order to live in the freedom of the new creation, not to move from one bondage—that of idols—to another—that of Torah (cf 4:8–10).

With such freedom at the center of their calling and identity, Paul calls them to ***stand firm therefore***. Stand firm in the new creation; be vigilant with regard to the gift and standing you have been granted through the Messiah's liberating action, ***and do not again be subject to the yoke of slavery***.

Paul's phrase *the yoke of slavery* is almost certainly a subversion of the familiar Jewish reference to *the yoke of Torah* (cf Acts 15:10). While he himself will presently call his liberated brothers to a new form of service, for Paul Torah is an inappropriate yoke, a weight of bondage, rather than a calling to be borne by free men.

Sundry commentators also point out that the *yoke* terminology is used in the LXX to refer to the oppression of Israel under e.g. the Seleucids (1 Macc 13:41; 8:18). Just as Greeks oppressed Israel, now Judaizers are seeking to oppress Greeks and other Gentiles.

The emphasis on freedom in this verse has led some to posit some sort of faith without rules or structure. That, however, is foreign to Paul, as will be seen shortly. Paul's freedom is not autonomy, but rather liberation to new life. Namely, the new life of 2:20: I no longer live *my* life, flesh-life, but the Messiah lives in me. In Pauline theology, the Messiah died and lives in service to His body. Therefore, I am free "for life in community, a freedom for mutual service in love" (Hays 310).

Interestingly, Paul moves in chapter 5 from v 1's *stand* to the metaphors both of *running* (v 7) and *walking* (v 16)—perhaps an echo of Ps 1:1. If so, delighting in the Torah of YHWH still means meditating upon the Scripture (see 4:21 above), but now delighting in "the law of the Messiah" (cf 6:2) rather than undertaking the yoke of Moses.

The Cost of Circumcision (5:2–6)

Look! I Paul say to you that if you become circumcised, the Messiah will 5:2
benefit you nothing.

Most commentators take the rather emphatic, ***Look! I Paul*** to be an appeal to apostolic authority. But Bruce 229 says:

> ... he does not expressly invoke his apostolic authority in giving them the serious warning which immediately follows. 'This is Paul speaking to you'—Paul whom you know, Paul your friend and father in Christ, not 'the brothers who are with me' (1:2) but I, Paul, myself. Others had apparently undertaken to say what Paul believed or practiced in the matter of circumcision (cf. v 11); here is Paul's own account.

The conditional ***if you become circumcised*** (subjunctive) indicates that although there was already widespread Sabbath observance (see above on 4:10), circumcision was widely still a matter under contemplation. This is not surprising, given the painfulness of the procedure for grown men. It was the final and decisive step in converting to Judaism.[12]

At any rate, if you follow through with that, Paul says, ***the Messiah will benefit you nothing***. This is the conclusion implied throughout Galatians; e.g. *I do not nullify the grace of God; if righteousness comes by Torah, the Messiah died in vain* (2:21). Cf 4:11: *I fear lest I have laboured over you in vain.*

Unlike with physical health, where some may think it prudent to "hedge your bets," following the doctor's orders while also eating organic foods and imbibing herbal supplements, for example, there is no hedging one's bets with the Messiah. To lean elsewhere is to lean away from Him and His new creation.

12 Thus Paul here is not addressing the widespread modern practice of circumcising infant males for the sake of health or hygiene, which must be evaluated on its own merits (or lack thereof).

5:3 *Now I bear witness again to every man becoming circumcised, that he is under obligation to do the entire law.*

Paul invokes legal language, ***Now I bear witness again***. As one who has been under Torah and knows it well, Paul provides testimony to the significance of the direction in which the Galatians are going.

Paul's testimony is addressing ***every man becoming circumcised***. The passive participle is present tense, which indicates that most of his hearers had not yet taken the step. The sense is therefore probably along the lines of: *to every man contemplating becoming circumcised,* or *to every man who is committed to becoming circumcised.*

If such a man follows through with his intention, ***he is under obligation to do the entire law***. That is, if one enters the law, one is obligated to all of its requirements.

This is often taken to be principally a threat of condemnation: since no man can keep all the law's requirements, one will therefore be condemned. That however is not what Paul says, and elsewhere Paul refers to the viability of blamelessness before the law.

His point is rather different: Torah cannot be entered into and observed piecemeal; if the Messiah really is not sufficient, one must take on the whole Torah (contrary to what the Judaizers themselves apparently practiced; cf 6:13).

The stress on this implication of circumcision may be because Paul wishes to accent things such as guilt and trespass offerings and the like, in order to highlight even more that Torah now, at this eschatological time, offers something not merely ancillary to the Messiah, but in competition to what He has accomplished. (Hence the lead-in to v 4.) After the Messiah has come, sacrifices for atonement constitute a repudiation of the value of His death. To turn from the Messiah in order to pursue Torah is a turn from the place of true sacrifice to one where there is no more sacrifice for sins remaining (Heb 10:26).

At any rate, in context, Paul's point is that they cannot accept *partial* bondage to Torah; they will be in wholesale servitude if they become circumcised (cf Bruce 231).

Bruce 229–230 and others suggest that the Judaizers were insisting on circumcision primarily for their own benefit; they themselves would then not be "fraternizing with the uncircumcised" and thus guard themselves against persecution. This view fits with 6:12–13, although it should be noted that more was in view than circumcision narrowly considered, since by and large the Galatians were already observing the levitical calendar (4:10).

You are severed from the Messiah, whoever is justified in Torah; you have 5:4
fallen away from the grace.

The seriousness of circumcision is not simply a binding commitment to keep the entirety of Torah (v 3); even more significantly, it means ***You are severed from the Messiah***. The terminology puts forth the inverse situation of that envisioned in Rom 7:2, 6, where the term κατηργέω (*katargeo—severed, released*) is used to express how a married woman is *released* from the law of her husband if he dies (Rom 7:2) and likewise "we" are released from Torah, having died to it (7:6). We learn here that the converse is also true: just as union with the Messiah is death to and liberation from Torah, so too union with Torah is "liberation" from the Messiah. Gal 3 is about how the Messiah enables Israel to "apostatize" from Torah by taking the penalty of apostasy upon Himself in the curse-death of the cross; now Paul says that embracing Torah means apostasy from "the grace."

The term *severed* has the idea of being *cut off,* and thus a play on words with circumcision is likely ("you're cutting off a piece of skin, but really you yourselves are being cut off—from the Messiah Himself").

The idea here is reminiscent of John 15, where Jesus warns that whoever does not "remain in Him" will be cast away as a branch (Jn 15:6). The Galatians are departing from the Messiah rather than remaining in Him.

Calvin reminds us that this was not the intention of the Galatians; they were "Christian" in their outlook: "They were not so grossly mistaken that they believed that they were justified by the observance of the law alone; but they wanted to mix the Messiah with the law. Otherwise Paul would have been threatening them without effect" (95).

Wright (*Justification* 138) aptly notes the ecclesiological aspects of this: "This is the Messiah's family. And if you separate yourself from this family, you separate yourself from the Messiah." This of course is why Paul could say in 2:11 that Peter's action in Antioch was one of self-condemnation: he was severing himself from the justified people of God.

Paul addresses this warning to ***whoever is justified in Torah***. This for Paul is not a separate intention from the intention to get circumcised, and thus it is a mistake to read in notions of merit here. The point is that circumcision is an attempt to be *vindicated* as a member of the people of God, the people with whom God is in a right covenantal relationship.

Most commentators take the present verb to have a conative sense: "you *seek* to be justified by Torah," and that seems to be a sound instinct. Paul was not suggesting that one really *could* be justified in Torah, at least not beyond being vindicated in the minds of certain wrongheaded people.

Paul follows up the initial clause with the parallel ***you have fallen away from the grace***. Although Greek articular forms need not be translated with an explicit *the,* the article here does indicate a *particular* grace. It is not generic "grace" that one falls away from, but the specific embodied grace of God in the Messiah (see esp 2:20). It is the grace of the Messiah in which God has called them in 1:6.

It is important not to obliterate Paul's point. One does not fall from a mountain without being on the mountain; and so neither does one fall away from grace without being a participant in grace. One was not severed from the law without first having been subject to the law; and similarly, one cannot be severed from the Messiah without first having been united to Him. The people Paul has in view were those who *began in the Spirit* (3:3) and, as Paul will say shortly, were for a time *running well* (v 7). What the Galatians needed to hear was not a message about "really, truly" being converted, but a warning against departure from the Messiah.[13]

---

13 One of the problems with common approaches is that they are too static and impersonal. Paul does not frame things in terms of "losing one's salvation," but of departure from the Messiah.

For in the Spirit, from faith, we anticipate the hope of righteousness. 5:5

In 3:2, Paul has affirmed that God's open reception of the Galatians, sealed with the gift of the Spirit, occurred through the message of *faith,* and in 3:3, that they *began in the Spirit.* So now, consistently with that he insists that the follow-through must likewise be ***in the Spirit*** and ***from faith.***[14]

The Spirit is the down payment and seal of the gift of new creation, and therefore the ongoing life of the new creation must be carried out within His operative sphere and by His power. It is by the down-payment-Spirit that we await the fullness of our inheritance.

Once again the sense of *faith* is ambiguous, which is perhaps intentional. Both the πίστις that has come in the Messiah, and correspondingly *believing* upon Him, living faith-fully, shape our eschatological anticipation.

Paul says that in and through the Spirit and out of life-shaping faith, ***we anticipate the hope of righteousness.*** The sense of anticipation is that of *awaiting expectantly;* one looks forward in the strength and context of the Spirit and faith.

The genitival phrase, *the hope of righteousness,* raises the question: Is this *the hope-that-is-righteousness,* or *the thing hoped-for which righteousness awaits*? In other words, are we awaiting (a) righteousness, or are we in righteousness awaiting some other unstated object of hope?

We should not have an aversion to the former, which is probably a more natural reading than the latter. Certainly, Paul has a view that righteousness is now present, but there is also a future aspect, e.g. Rom 2:13; 5:9–10 etc. Also on future judgment, see e.g. 2 Cor 5:10; Mt 25 etc. Recall that righteousness is not only a present gift of God but also something that remains for Him yet to accomplish: He will bring forth a new

14 Alternatively, given the phraseology of 3:2, it is possible that *from faith* should be taken with reference to *the Spirit,* i.e. we anticipate the hope of righteousness in the Spirit, whom we have received from and in connection with faith. But since Paul immediately continues on to speak of a faith presently working through love (v 6), it seems more likely that the phrase *from faith* here is coordinate and parallel to the phrase *in the Spirit,* rather than modifying it.

heaven and earth in which righteousness dwells (2 Pet 3:13 etc).[15]

In contrast to the falling away he has just mentioned in v 4, Paul presses home the need for a persevering anticipation of the object of eschatological hope,[16] a perseverance that leans upon the Spirit and lives in Him. Just as they *began* in the Spirit, the Galatians must *continue* in the Spirit, persevering in the same course that started them off aright. The Spirit who is the initial gift of the new creation is the means and context within which one arrives at the full consummation of the new creation.

It should be underscored that on this view, perseverance is no less gift than is original faith. The Spirit was given as gift (3:2), and so too here perseverance in the Spirit must be received and patiently embraced as gift. For Paul, the possibility of apostasy in no way diminishes the fact that salvation from start to finish is pure gift, pure grace.

The pairing of *faith* and *hope* here is supplemented by the addition of *love* in the following verse. On faith, hope and love as a triad, see not only 1 Cor 13:13 but especially 1 Thess 1:3: "We give thanks to God always for all of you, constantly mentioning you in our prayers, remembering before our God and Father your *work of faith and labour of love and steadfastness of hope* in our Lord Jesus, the Messiah." Dunn also notes the triad in Rom 5:1–5 (although other characteristics are also present there: endurance, character).

5:6 *For in the Messiah, Jesus, neither circumcision is effectual for anything, nor uncircumcision, but faith working through love.*

As is thematic in his writings, Paul is speaking of what is true ***in the Messiah, Jesus*** (ἐν Χριστῷ). One begins (3:3) and continues with perseverance (v 5) in the Spirit, but the truth is that all this reality is *in the Messiah, Jesus*. He Himself is the *coming faith* of ch 3, and the One who

15 Similarly Bruce 231–232: "The law holds out no such sure hope as this. The 'hope of righteousness' is the hope of a favourable verdict in the last judgment (Rom. 2:5–16).... Their hope is not vague or uncertain; it is fostered and kept alive by the indwelling Spirit of God."

16 Citing Rom 8:19, 23, 25; 1 Cor 1:7; Phil 3:20, Garlington 222 notes that the term I have rendered *anticipate* is always used in Paul with an eschatological sense.

loved me and gave Himself up for me (2:20). And just as that *pistis* (*faith*) and love defined the Messiah in His self-giving, so that same form of faith and love avails for those who are in Him.

In Him, ***neither circumcision is effectual for anything, nor uncircumcision.*** The term I have rendered *effectual* (ἰσχύω) has the idea of *strength.* Paul is denying strength to the *flesh*—a thought which is scarcely new with him. The point of his overarching anti-circumcision, anti-Torah polemic is not a privileging of uncircumcision over circumcision, but the setting aside of the power of *sarx* altogether.

What avails rather than circumcision or uncircumcision is ***faith working through love.*** Paul frequently juxtaposes circumcision to new and, as it were, opposing realities. In 6:15, the contrast is to *a new creation;* in 1 Cor 7:19, it is the keeping of God's commandments, although the latter is not in a justification context.

Working is a present middle participle (ἐνεργουμένη). It is a faith which avails; and the sort of faith which avails is one which works through love. See again 1 Thess 1:3, where the Thessalonians are commended for their "labour [work] of love."

Paul's *in Christ* language is so customary that it becomes easy to overlook the fact that *faith working through love* is first of all a reference to the Messiah Himself. In 2:20b, Paul has written, *what life I now live in the flesh, I live in faith—the faith of the Son of God Himself, who loved me and gave Himself for me.*

Paul still must live in the weak *flesh,* but the life he lives there is still in the *pistis* (πίστις—*faith, faithfulness*) of the Son of God Himself. That *faith* of the Son *worked* through *love* to the point of self-giving in death, and it is this faith which is effectual, which is powerful over against the weakness of the flesh.

We should not, however, reduce Paul's point here merely to a piece of "representative theology," i.e. Christ's faith worked through love on our behalf, and therefore we need not concern ourselves with faith working through love in *us, today.*

Rather, when Paul speaks of life *in Christ,* the past accomplishments of the Messiah form a matrix, a pattern through which His life shapes the present life of the believer, the *life I now live in the flesh.* It is this present life that is now lived *in the faith of the Son of God Himself.*

Moreover, what is in view is more than the pattern of the Messiah's past work. The vital *in Christ* relationship communicates the powerful *pistis* of the *risen* Son to me, and it is that *pistis* which is effectual and powerful in the new creation inaugurated in the Messiah.

Among Protestants, there has frequently been a tendency to disassociate *faith working through love* from justification, which sounds rather like "works salvation."

The disassociation, however, is not exegetically tenable. Circumcision in this context is the action of those seeking to be justified in Torah (vv 2–4), and Paul's contrast here in v 6 is inextricably bound up with the matter of justification.

Furthermore, the immediate point is the manner in which one pursues *the hope of righteousness* (v 5), i.e. the eschatological goal of final vindication in God's judgment. And that *righteousness* in turn must be seen against the backdrop of 2:21 and 3:21, where Paul deploys the same term to refer to what is denied to Torah's power and purpose.

We must therefore follow Paul's argument, and not blink. What is effectual toward the end of final justification is that in the Spirit, we anticipate our hope—our goal of God's final verdict of *righteous*—through our connection to the vital *pistis*, the "faithful faith" of the Messiah, which works through love, even as it did in His self-giving on the cross. Just as God highly exalted the Messiah by vindicating Him in resurrection in view of His self-offering in death (Phi 2:8–9), He will vindicate those *in Christ* in view of the Messiah's own *pistis* establishing the same pattern within their lives. This occurs, once again, because the believer lives by the *pistis* of the Messiah (2:20) by the agency of the Holy Spirit, who re-creates Christ's character in the believer (see below on the fruit of the Spirit).

Paul's treatment of apostasy (vv 2–4), as well as his exposition of the vital relationship necessary between the Messiah and the believer (vv 5–6), is essentially a practical application of Christ's own words in John 15. Jesus said that those who *remained*[17] in Him would draw on His own

17 Here again we bear the misfortune of a tradition arising out of what has become a misleading translation in English, whereby the English word *abide* has been used in

life and bear much fruit (Jn 15:4–5), and correspondingly warned that those who did not *remain* in Him would be thrown away, wither, and ultimately be burned (Jn 15:6). Living in love and living in *the Messiah's* love are mutual (Jn 15:9–10). In short, live continually in the Messiah's life, and you will bear much fruit through love.

The reference to *love* is not an aside; it is the characteristic that largely shapes the discussion of the fruit of the Spirit shortly to follow (5:22–23), a discussion prepared for also by the call to serve one another in love as the proper exercise of gospel liberty (5:13). As is probably also implicit in 1 Cor 13:13, love is "the greatest of these" in that it is the mature and complete expression of faith, just as the Messiah's self-giving love on the cross was the great manifestation of God's πίστις in Him. Cf also 1 Tim 1:5: "The aim of our charge is love that issues from a pure heart and a good conscience and a sincere faith."

Impeded Runners (5:7–12)

Paul attributes the Galatians' severance from the Messiah and fall from grace (5:4) to the interference of "troublers" who have cut in and redirected the Galatians from following the truth of the Messiah. Even if the Galatians are ultimately recalled to the course, these troublers will suffer punishment; indeed, Paul expresses his wish that they would suffer such a punishment both in body and in relation to the covenant community even now, because they nullify the cross of the Messiah.

You were running well—who impeded you, to not follow the truth? 5:7

Paul's primary metaphor in ch 3–4 is *familial,* but early on, in referring to the Galatians *beginning in the Spirit,* the ambiguity in the phrase could lead in two directions: a theme of *maturity,* or a journeying or racing metaphor. Having dealt at length with the former, Paul now turns to the latter: ***You were running well.*** Paul frequently uses running/traveling motifs. Here the accent is on a race, as in 1 Cor 9:24ff; elsewhere the focus is more on walking a path *led* by the Spirit (see v 16's

an almost technical and pietistic sense. The Greek term *meno* (μένω), however, simply means *remain, stay* or *live,* and corresponds closely to how Paul uses *live* in 2:20.

walk in the Spirit; cf Rom 8:14).

Paul uses an imperfect tense (Ετρέχετε, *were running*), indicating that at least for some time, his hearers had been running the race in the proper way.

As with 3:3, Paul does not resort to explaining their apostasy as due to something defective or insincere in their initial response and walk, which was to be credited to the Holy Spirit Himself. The Spirit is both the power and gift of the new creation, as well as the pacesetter who leads the way and marks out the path to be run. The Galatians had received Him, and for some time followed the path upon which He led them.

Running well is the expectation of those who begin in the Spirit, but the Spirit's work also involves training for the course. In 1 Cor 9:24–27, Paul argues that one must discipline himself in order to obtain the imperishable prize. He says that he does not run aimlessly nor box by beating the air; rather he disciplines his body, so that he does not become "disqualified" after preaching to others. That is followed up in 1 Cor 10:1ff by recounting the story of Israel's apostasy in the wilderness. Taking Galatians together with that passage, we can see that *running well* does not simply mean avoiding egregious sins such as idolatry etc, but also cultivating our lives in such a way that we do not allow others to cut in and redirect our faith away from the Messiah.

Given the good beginning, Paul asks rhetorically, ***Who impeded you?*** *Who* is an indefinite singular—as in 5:10, Paul narrows from a generic group compelling circumcision to one individual. This could perhaps be the leader among the teachers who had come among them, or possibly even Peter, whose inadvertent example had apparently carried such weight in pushing them in the direction of circumcision and Torah.

Whoever it is has *impeded* or *hindered* the Galatians. Given the race theme, the idea seems to be of one cutting in and directing the runner off course.

The result of being thrown off course is that now they do ***not follow the truth***. The race's pacesetter and course-marker, the Spirit, is the Advocate who has come in the Messiah's place (Jn 16:7), and of course

Jesus Himself is *the* Truth (Jn 14:6). The Spirit is thus the "Spirit of truth," and His role is to *guide* the Messiah's disciples—His *followers*—into all truth by declaring the Messiah to them (Jn 16:13). By turning aside to Torah, the Galatians have left off following the Spirit's guidance and gone onto a different path (cf Acts 5:36–37, where people *followed* false messiahs).

This persuasion is not from the one calling you. 5:8

There are two possible ways to read v 8, given the relationship of the noun here, ***This persuasion***, to the term I have rendered *follow* in v 7:[18]

1. Perhaps in an ironic contrast, Paul contrasts this new "following" to the proper one. It is deceit, rather than the true following ordained by ***the one calling you***. The gist is thus: *This current persuasion you have adopted is not from the God who calls you.*
   On this reading, the verse is on one level an implicit encouragement; a reminder that God is *still* calling them (present participle).
2. *This persuasion* in fact refers to the following of the truth in v 7, and the point is that the one who calls you into circumcision is offering something very different from the persuasion of the truth. Thus the gist would be: *This persuasion of the truth is not what you are receiving from the one who is now calling you into something else.* On this second reading, the *one calling* is the same as the one troubling in v 10. Just as Paul contrasts Torah and the Messiah as mutually exclusive covenants, Paul is implicitly contrasting the God who has called the Galatians (1:6, 15; 5:13) to the "troubler" who is now "calling" them. There is thus false calling and false justification.

18 *Persuasion* (πεισμονή) here is the noun corresponding to the passive infinitive in 5:7, from the verb πείθω. The passive form can mean *obey* or *be a follower;* given the dominant running metaphor of the context, I opted to focus on the latter shade of meaning in v 7.

5:9 *A little leaven leavens the whole lump.*

Perhaps in recognition that the Galatians' departure from the Messiah is not in fact a self-conscious repudiation of Jesus as Messiah, Paul refers to ***A little leaven***. But the effect of a *little leaven* is not itself "little"; the nature of leaven is such that a even a small amount ***leavens the whole lump***.

The choice of leaven imagery here is *apropos*. Throughout Galatians, Paul has been contrasting the old *kosmos* to the new creation. In biblical usage, the primary characteristic of leaven is that it carries forward from an old batch of dough.[19]

Thus, mixing Paul's metaphors, the message of the false teachers in effect imports the old *kosmos* into the new creation community in Galatia, with the effect that the whole lump of dough is therefore now characterized by the old world they had left behind, rather than by the new creation in the Messiah.

The referent of the *leaven* itself could be either the false teachers, or their teaching. Either way, the body is spoiled with the effects of the leaven; the pure loaf of the Messiah has been corrupted into the sourdough of the old *kosmos*.

On the leaven metaphor in Paul, see especially 1 Cor 5:6–8. As there, part of the point is that the celebration of the Messiah's Passover necessitates the purging of the leaven from the house. In 1 Cor 5, it was the sexually immoral man who needed to be excommunicated; here, Paul has already implicitly called for the expulsion of the false teachers and their ultimate spiritual progeny as children of the slave woman (4:30).

5:10 *I am persuaded concerning you in the Lord, that you will not be otherwise minded; but the one troubling you will bear the judgment, whoever he may be.*

---

19 It is important to note that *leaven* in Scripture does not refer to *yeast,* but to the process of making sourdough bread, whereby a lump of dough from an earlier batch was retained to use in a new batch of bread. The warning is thus against an attempt to mix the old creation into the new.

Picking up again on the terminology he has used in the previous two verses, Paul writes, ***I am persuaded concerning you in the Lord.*** In the face of apparent evidence to the contrary, he expresses faith. Such expressions are not infrequent in Paul, e.g. Phi 1:6 (He who began a good work in them will complete it).

His persuasion is ***that you will not be otherwise minded***, which could refer to the general following of the truth laid before them, or more narrowly in the context, the necessity of expelling the false teachers along with repudiating their message—that is, of purging the house of leaven, as he has just implicitly called for in v 9.

Either way, ***the one troubling you will bear the judgment, whoever he may be.*** Cf Ezek 33:1–9. Paul is acting as the blameless watchman, sounding the warning, but the teachers will bear their judgment—indeed, even if the Galatians should come to correct their course.

The form is different, but *whoever he may be* bears some conceptual similarities to 2:6 (*whatever once they were, it makes no difference to me*). If Paul does have Peter in mind, this resonance is understandable. While it may seem difficult to conceive of Paul speaking in this way regarding Peter, it must be remembered that at the time of this letter, there has been no known change of course on Peter's part; and in 2:11, Paul has explicitly said that Peter was judicially *condemned* in connection with his actions in Antioch. Paul does not vacillate; he has made clear that *whoever* proclaims another gospel, whether it be an angel from heaven or even Paul himself, let him be anathema (1:8–9). Paul did not hold himself sacrosanct in this regard, and certainly neither did he hold Peter so, whom he had rebuked so strongly.

Peter did of course *bear his judgment* by repenting and speaking strongly, at the ensuing Jerusalem council in Acts 15, on behalf of Paul's Torah-free gospel for Gentiles.

As we have noted, however, it may be that Paul has in mind an unidentified leader of the teachers who is, or has been, actually present in Galatia.

Now I, brothers, if I still preach circumcision, why am I yet persecuted? then 5:11
the scandal of the cross has been nullified.

Alluding to his past zeal for Torah, which led to his persecution of the Messiah's Church, Paul writes, ***Now I, brothers, if I still preach circumcision.*** When he was advocating circumcision, he was the persecutor. If he still advocates circumcision, ***why am I yet persecuted?*** As Paul notes in 6:12, the teachers want the Galatians circumcised, not simply out of devotion to Torah, out of true integrity, but to avoid persecution themselves. If Paul dealt with Gentiles the way they do, he would not arouse such bitter Jewish opposition—opposition which his Galatian churches know all too well, as it has been in militant display before their own eyes (e.g. Acts 13:50; 14:5, 19).

If Paul, however, had retained his previous advocacy of circumcision, ***then the scandal of the cross has been nullified.*** How so? As Paul has just explained (v 3), circumcision obligates one to the entire Torah; that being the case, the cross of the Messiah can no longer be understood as definitive. For then one is back to Torah for atonement etc.

If Paul were saying that Jesus is the Messiah, but simultaneously had been calling upon Gentiles to become circumcised and follow Torah, scarcely any of his fellow Jews would likely have been offended. But Paul's message instead stands against their entire *kosmos;* it is that Jesus put to death the old world on the cross, and there is now no Jew nor Greek, circumcision nor uncircumcision (3:28). And this is indeed a *skandalon*—a stone of stumbling, as Paul puts it in Rom 9:32–33.

The implicit message here is that the false teachers have in effect abandoned the cross. A descandalized cross is no cross at all.

This is no insignificant point; as Paul says in 1 Cor 2:2, his determination was to "know nothing among you except Jesus the Messiah and Him crucified." It is only here that faith rests, "not in the wisdom of men but in the power of God" (1 Cor 2:5).

5:12 *Would that those disturbing you would also castrate themselves!*

Paul exclaims, ***Would that those disturbing you!*** The verse opens with an interjection that implies a wish that is not realistic.

The wish, essentially, is that the teachers would re-circumcise themselves, and slip in the process, that they ***would also castrate themselves.***

Just as their work has had the effect of cutting off the Galatians from the Messiah (v 4), Paul wishes the teachers too would experience a cutting-off.

There is likely also an allusion to 4:27, where Paul quotes the prophecy of the fruitfulness for the barren woman in the context of his own labours in childbirth (4:19). He does not want the teachers' corresponding efforts at childbearing to be fruitful. May they be eunuchs forevermore.

The Conflict for the Cosmos

IN THE PRECEDING, PAUL HAS GIVEN EXTENSIVE ATTENTION to the conflict with the false teachers. In this subsection, he does not quite change the subject, but he does broaden the discussion somewhat. The opponent now is the flesh, rather than the teachers; and the scope is more cosmological. That is, Paul's concern now is not so much the Abrahamic covenant (at least not directly), but the new creation and its antithesis to the old *kosmos*.[1]

Free to Love (5:13–15)

> *For you were called on the basis of freedom, brothers: only not the [sort of] freedom [serving] as an occasion for the flesh, but through the love serve one another.* 5:13

Paul now turns to build upon his statement of v 6, that what is effectual in the Messiah is neither circumcision nor uncircumcision, but faith working through love. He reminds the Galatians, ***For you were called on the basis of freedom, brothers***.

Rather than freedom being defined as a sort of autonomous anarchy, this love is depicted as the true shape of freedom—a liberty to serve others *via* the freedom to live responsibly in the Spirit.

The *called* language itself implies the above: to be called is to be destined for a particular role. Calling of necessity cannot be to some sort of absolutized "freedom," since a calling provides a direction, a destiny—indeed, a *responsibility*.

Paul (as is common) has already identified the Galatians as *called* in

1 These are not of course wholly different things, but they do nonetheless represent noticeable differences of emphasis.

1:6: "I marvel that you are turning away so soon from Him who *called you* in the grace of the Messiah...." In 1:15, Paul also mentions that God has called him by His grace. Thus calling is to God the Father; liberty is life with God through the Messiah. It is in the grace of the gospel that God provides freedom from the old *kosmos* and the life of true heirs. (Cf 1:4: rescued from *this present evil age.*)

The Galatians' calling is upon the basis of freedom—the freedom of the Son, the mature heir who is not under the governors of the *kosmos,* but is the fully-developed Man of the new creation.

Since they have been called, therefore, the freedom upon whose basis their call was given is ***not the sort of freedom serving as an occasion for the flesh.*** Given that the whole point of the liberation is removal from *this present evil age* (1:4), i.e. the realm that serves as the arena for *the flesh,* it should be obvious that the freedom in view cannot allow for marching orders dictated by the flesh. The term ἀφορμὴν, which I have rendered *occasion,* originally referred to military marching orders, although by the Koine period, it had become generalized, and can mean something like *pretext.* The contextual metaphor of travel here, however, lends itself to the original meaning; in view is what provides direction to the life of the freed man. Throughout, Paul has been saying the genuine provider of such direction is the Spirit, who marks out the course by means of the truth of the gospel.

"Liberty" *as an occasion for the flesh* is not in fact freedom, but slavery to *sarx* every bit as much as servitude to Torah was, if not more so. For at least Torah pointed forward to, sought fulfillment in, something greater: love (see next verse). Meanwhile the one who practices sin is its servant (see esp Jn 8:34 and Rom 6 etc). One of necessity is a "slave"—whether one of death or of life:

> Do you not know that if you present yourselves to anyone as obedient slaves, you are slaves of the one whom you obey, either of sin, which leads to death, or of obedience, which leads to righteousness.... now that you have been set free from sin and have become slaves of God, the fruit you get leads to sanctification and its end,

> eternal life. For the wages of sin is death, but the free gift of God is eternal life in the Messiah Jesus our Lord. (Rom 6:16, 22–23)

And in Galatians, Paul himself says he is a *doulos* of the Messiah (1:10), as Bruce 240–241 points out. Being a *doulos* of the Messiah leads to being *douloi* toward one another, since He is the Head and those baptized into Him have put Him on (3:27). If I am a servant of Christ, and you "are" Christ, I am your servant.

The apparent paradox of being freed (and emphatically given a call to be steadfast in that freedom; cf 5:1) in order to become a servant must be faced—and embraced. In view is not an incomprehensible, incoherent sort of double-talk that makes *freedom* just another word for *slavery*. Rather, what is in view is a fundamental implication of the doctrine of creation, an implication which stands squarely against the notion that human reality is a mere construct that we may shape as we see fit. One cannot genuinely be a "self-made man"; one can only embrace creation and its Creator, or slavery and destruction. As created beings, who and what we are have a decisive "givenness," and human freedom is only possible within a willing stance of faith within that context. It has been well said that just as a fish is not liberated by removing it from the water that constitutes its native habitat, neither is a man or a woman liberated by any attempt to transcend the constraints imposed by the Creator and Redeemer. It is the fish out of water that needs liberation; and it is humanity outside the Messiah that is in bondage, because it is only in Him that full humanity is found. Mankind was created to bear God's image, and the Son is the express image of God, the full revelation of the Godhead (cf Heb 1:3). Consequently, service to the Messiah is the only kind of freedom that matters.

This is essentially the theme the apostle expounds upon in Rom 1:18–32, where he describes deviance such as homosexuality and idolatry, not as freedom or creative autonomy, but as the outcome of exchanging of God-revealed and God-given glory for a futile lie. The suppression of the truth about God is the pathway to the loss of truth regarding ourselves, as well.

Thus it is that, rather than serving as an occasion for the flesh, freedom in the Messiah offers an imperative: ***through the love serve one another***. I have retained the somewhat awkward *the* to highlight the specificity of the Greek article. The love in view is not wispy sentiment or some generic form of affection. It is the love with which the Messiah gave Himself for us (2:20); it is through this very love that true service to one another occurs.

5:14 *For the whole law is fulfilled in one word—in this: Love your neighbour as yourself.*

Despite what Paul's argument rather sounds like, his viewpoint is not simply that the gospel is a nullification of Torah; rather, the gospel brings "fulfillment" (*filling up, completion*) to that which was lacking. In line with that, therefore, he writes, ***For the whole law is fulfilled in one word***.

The reference to *the whole law* (ὁ γὰρ πᾶς νόμος) contrasts and compares to v 3, where the one circumcised becomes indebted to keep *the entire law* (ὅλον τὸν νόμον); i.e. the full range of Torah's prescriptions. In place of that formal keeping of Torah, Paul argues for Torah's *fulfillment*, a filling-up of its fundamental intention and scope, always lacking under the old creation.

Paul is adamant about *not* keeping *the entire law* in v 3 (or even circumcision); here he does not contradict that. He does not even urge fulfillment of the law *directly*, as a command; rather, he says that fulfillment occurs ***in one word—in this: Love your neighbour as yourself***. The imperative is not therefore the fulfillment of Torah; the imperative is *love*, and the fulfillment of Torah happens by implication. As Witherington 381 adds, this fulfillment (as in Matthew) is eschatological: because the Messiah has acted decisively in fulfilling the law and the prophets (Mt 5:17), now our love through Him becomes an eschatological action.[2]

The specific *one word* in view is Lev 19:18 (cf Lev 19:34, which extends love of neighbour to sojourners). In the original context of Lev

2 On the eschatological fulfillment of Torah, see also Rom 8:4.

19:18, the application lists providing for the poor *via* the law of reaping (Lev 19:9–10); not stealing, dealing falsely or lying to one another (19:11); not swearing falsely by YHWH (19:12); not oppressing or robbing a neighbour, including withholding or delaying wages (19:13); not mistreating the disabled (19:14); judging righteously in court (19:15); avoiding slander and standing up "against the life of your neighbour" (19:16); not hating one's brother in the heart but reasoning frankly with him (19:17), and not taking vengeance or bearing a grudge (19:18).

Paul (following Jesus, Mk 12:28–31) sums up the ethical requirements of Torah the same way in Rom 13:8–10. Love does no harm to a neighbour; therefore it is the fulfilling of Torah.

Here again we draw attention to 2:20. Paul has more in mind than a recitation of Leviticus 19. The thoroughgoing love of the Messiah in His self-giving death is now the truest and fullest touchstone and pattern for love. By following in His pathway, His followers will *fulfill Torah*—not merely *obey Torah,* but fill it up, bring its best intentions to eschatological maturity.

Now if you bite and prey upon one another, beware lest you are consumed by 5:15
one another.

While the fulfillment of Torah is an implication of functioning, Christocentric love, it does not follow that love itself is merely an implication or something automatic. It is the calling of *pistis* (*faith, faithfulness*) in its outworking (cf v 6). Love is commanded; and the refusal to love is warned against severely, as indicated by Paul's caution, ***if you bite and prey upon one another***.

As Witherington 384 observes, the progression here is bestial. Whereas the new creation has inaugurated the era of the *Son of Man,* the life that is not driven by faith working through love ends with men behaving as *beasts* (cf Garlington 240, who notes not only the use of comparison to beasts in Greek diatribe literature, but also the beasts of e.g. Dan 7). And if one commences that progression of biting and preying upon one another, ***beware lest you are consumed by one another***, i.e. destroyed.

The upshot is that "unbridled freedom" (actually, slavery to the flesh) does not result in true liberty but in destruction. Animals are not more free than men, simply because they have no responsibilities. Rather, it is men created in the image of God who have the freedom of genuinely responsible agents. As those of the new creation, we serve the strength of responsible liberty rather than the weakness of *sarx*.

The Battle Between Spirit and Flesh (5:16–18)

Gordon Fee (*God's Empowering Presence* 429) aptly summarizes this passage this way:

> At issue ... is not some internal tension in the present life of the individual believer, but the sufficiency of the Spirit for life without Torah—a sufficiency that enables them to live so as not to revert to their *former* life as pagans (= life in the flesh, as vv. 19–21 make clear).

This mini-section prepares the way for what follows, which identifies the works of the flesh which must be resisted, as well as the actions that the Spirit empowers.

5:16 *Now I say, walk in the Spirit, and you will not carry to completion the longing of the flesh.*

Continuing with his journeying theme but moving away from the running motif, Paul writes, ***Now I say, walk in the Spirit***. The notion of behaviour in life as "walking" is familiar to the Old Testament, at least as early as Enoch ("Enoch walked with God," Gen 5:22, 24), Noah (Gen 6:9), and Abraham ("walk before Me and be blameless," Gen 17:1). Moreover, the Christian faith is simply described as *the Way* (ὁδός, *road, way*) frequently in Acts (e.g. Acts 9:2; 19:9, 23; 22:4; 24:14, 22).

The way that the Spirit marks out is the course or pathway of truth—the pathway from which the teachers have drawn the Galatians aside into a detour. Interestingly, *Torah* itself comes from a word group that can mean *guide*. Witherington 393 cites Ex 16:4; Lev 18:4; Jer 44:23; Ezek

5:6–7, and suggests that here is an implicit contrast between walking according to the statutes of the law, and walking by the Spirit. The realm of the Spirit and the realm of Torah offer modes of life that are alternatives, rather than complementary.

At least equally clear is the contrast to the behaviour mentioned in Psalm 1:1: "Blessed is the man who *walks not in the counsel of the wicked,* nor stands in the way of sinners, nor sits in the seat of scoffers"; the new covenant parallel to delighting in the law of Yahweh and meditating on His law day and night would thus be *walking in* (or *by*) *the Spirit.*

All of this is in context of Ps 1:6: "for YHWH knows *the way* of the righteous, but *the way* of the wicked will perish." I.e. where one "walks" is his "way," just as the course which he runs (see Gal 5:7; cf 1 Cor 9:24ff) is likewise his "way." As implied in the ensuing passage here in Galatians (5:21; 6:7–8), Psalm 1:5 says that the wicked will not stand in the judgment, nor sinners in the congregation of the righteous.

On *walking,* Fee 430 says:

> As usual with such imperatives, it comes in the present (iterative) tense and refers to "the long obedience in the same direction." Paul is not talking about what one does from time to time, but about a way of life in general. Thus, we might correctly translate, "go on walking in the Spirit."

As usual, it is difficult to choose between translating the dative as *by* (*walk* by *the Spirit*) or as *in* (*walk* in *the Spirit*). Given the analogy to Paul's *in Christ* language, as well as the implicit analogy to Torah, I take the primary sense of the dative to be locative (*in*), but once again it is probably not really a matter of one or the other. Since the Spirit is the powerful personal presence of God, even the locative would also spill over into an instrumental sense. It is by walking *within* the sphere of the Spirit that one is *empowered* to walk; there is a sort of reciprocal relationship between *in* and *by* (similar comments could be made in connection with v 5).

The sphere of the Spirit is the new creation, that path upon which the Galatians had been set when they first heard the proclamation of the Messiah crucified (cf 3:1ff). This sets up the ensuing discussion of "the fruit of the Spirit" (5:22–23). In terms of the preceding context, it is by walking in the Spirit that one fulfills the love command just given (v 14).

How does one so walk in the Spirit? Again, Fee 433 observes well:

> Life in the Spirit is not passive submission to the Spirit to do a supernatural work in one's life; rather, it requires conscious effort, so that the indwelling Spirit may accomplish his ends in one's life.... it means to rise up and follow the Spirit by walking in obedience to the Spirit's desire.

The Christian life in part consists of being "normed" to the new desires. As we are shaped by the Spirit-breathed Word and walk according to it, we learn in practice the shape of life in the Spirit.

When you thus *walk in the Spirit,* Paul says, ***you will not carry to completion the longing of the flesh***. The word I have rendered *carry to completion* is the subjunctive aorist version of *teleo* (τελέσητε), which is sometimes rendered *fulfill* but is not the same term generally used for eschatological fulfillment (that is accomplished by πληρόω, as in v 14 here). Nonetheless, both terms are primarily concerned with something coming to maturity or completion in some way, and in Scripture, lust bears fruit in mature sin. Cf especially Jam 1:15: when lust conceives, it begets sin, and fully grown sin brings forth death.

Walking in the Spirit "cuts short" this "natural" progression. Note also the context of destruction in v 15: If one does not walk in the Spirit, there is biting, devouring, and the prospect of being consumed and destroyed. Once again, the Spirit's work is to break this chain, to overcome the power of *sarx* to work death.

The term *longing* here is singular and relates to the plural *longings* (*lusts*)[3] which are about to be enumerated in vv 19–21. The singular likely

3 The term I have translated *longing* (ἐπιθυμία) is frequently rendered *lust,* but that seemed unsuitable here, since in the following verse the term is used to refer both to the activity of the flesh and of the Spirit. Therefore, a more neutral rendering such as

refers to the fundamental impulse of the flesh, from which the various sinful desires spring (Fee 432 uses the language of "the basic *perspective* of life in the flesh").

The one who walks in the Spirit doubtless wrestles with that impulse, but because he does walk in the Spirit, he *will not* (the construction is emphatic) carry out that impulse to its natural end. (A colloquial way of putting this is that through the Spirit, the longing of the flesh gets "nipped in the bud.")

This "shutting down" of the progression of the flesh's longings by the one walking in the Spirit stands in contrast to those under Torah (cf v 18), because Torah in fact has no value in opposition to the satisfaction of the flesh (Col 2:23).

The parallel and contrast to 3:3 ("having begun in the *Spirit,* are you now made *complete* in the *flesh?*") should not be missed. The earlier passage refers to the beginning of a *walk,* and in both verses there is an idea of *completion* (ἐπιτελέω in 3:3; τελέω here). In 3:3 of course, it is the *Galatians'* completion that is in view; here it is the works of the flesh, but this only further serves up the contrast. One cannot be made complete in life and godliness in the flesh, because the completion of the flesh is death and destruction.

As elsewhere, the backdrop for *flesh* is not only circumcision (see Gen 17; circumcision is "in your flesh" and of course has to do with the cutting of the flesh of the foreskin), but also Torah's rules of uncleanness (see esp Lev 12–15). In the flesh is defilement and death.

Flesh (*contra* some translations) does not mean "sinful nature." Fee 430–431 is on the right track to some degree in identifying it with "one's life before and outside of Christ"; however, it must be remembered that Paul says both that the believer is *not* "in the flesh" (Rom 8:9–10) and that he *is* (e.g. Gal 2:20), obviously in different senses. As we learn in 2 Cor 4, the inner man is renewed day by day and redeemed; the outer man is perishing. Moreover, in Rom 8 Paul says we *await* the redemption of the body.

The flesh in this sense (i.e. of the outer man of 2 Cor 4) is the mortal

desire or *longing* is appropriate. It is the character and object of ἐπιθυμία which makes it sinful.

and corrupted outer man. This does not mean that "the lusts of the flesh" are simply physical desires (e.g. sexual lust, gluttony etc), which we know from experience is false (we are tempted to pride, anger etc, as is also recounted in the list of the flesh's lusts here in vv 19–21); rather, the outer man is our fallen constitution exposed to the outside fallen world of Flesh, which includes temptation to all sorts of sins of body and spirit.

5:17 *For the flesh longs against the Spirit, but the Spirit against the flesh, for these oppose one another, so that not the things you might wish these things you might do.*

Paul has implied an antithesis between flesh and Spirit in the previous verse, and now he identifies this as an outright battle: ***For the flesh longs against the Spirit, but the Spirit against the flesh, for these oppose one another.***

This verse elaborates on and grounds v 16, as indicated by the *For*. Thus it does not blunt the force of the "will not" of v 16, but shows its basis (cf Fee 434). As Fee correctly stresses, the verse has nothing to do with the godly desires of the believer being thwarted by the flesh.

The flesh longs against the Spirit; its desires are in collision with and in antithesis to the Spirit. The flesh is tied to the old creation, and the Spirit is the master and firstfruits of the new; thus the two represent "kingdoms in conflict" or more precisely, creations in conflict.

Correspondingly, *the Spirit [longs] against the flesh.* The action attributed to the flesh in the first clause is attributed in the other direction to the Spirit. What I have translated *longs* is widely translated *lusts.* Some commentators stumble over bringing "lusts" into the second part of the parallel, but the term means *desire* and can have positive connotations. The point is that just as the desires of the flesh, its fundamental impulses, are at odds with the Spirit, and are indeed at war with Him, so the converse is also true. The Spirit's desires are in opposition to the flesh.

As a result of this antithesis, what would be carried out is not. The war between flesh and Spirit is ***so that not the things you might wish, these things you might do.***

Dunn 299–300 notes that the believer is both the recipient of the Spirit and "in the flesh" insofar as he/she lives in the present body. Therefore, both the desires of the flesh and of the Spirit are "us"; consequently, we have desires that are thwarted, no matter if we are walking in the Spirit or caving in to the flesh.

Fee however takes the verse to be exclusively on the other side: since the Spirit and flesh are in opposition, and he has urged walking in the Spirit, the (fleshly) desires one may have will not be carried out (e.g. eating and devouring one another, as in 5:15). I think this means, implicitly, that Fee's point is that if one were to follow the flesh, its desires would be such. Given the pair of subjunctive verbs, this verse itself does not address the question of whether the believer walking in the Spirit actually desires such things, only that the Spirit wages war against things that we *may* wish, i.e. if we are walking by the flesh. But that surely does not mean that even faithfully walking believers are not subject to temptations to sin.

In any case, contrary to common opinion, the point is not that the Spirit is powerless to act against the desires of the flesh (or *vice versa*)—that would be a direct contradiction of the previous verse (walk in the Spirit, and you *will not* fulfill the desires of the flesh), and would also imply that the mighty Spirit is in fact weaker than the weak flesh. Besides, as Fee 435 points out, the text says "may not," not "*cannot*." As Porter 56–57 explains, the subjunctive refers to "a projected realm," and does not indicate either affirmation or disavowal of the reality of what is in view.

Consequently, Paul is not suggesting that the Spirit-flesh conflict paralyzes the believer and makes good (or thoroughly bad) conduct impossible. Rather, the one led by the Spirit is compelled by His longings and impulses, and thus does not do the fleshly things he otherwise may desire to do; conversely, the one living according to the flesh is driven by its longings and cannot carry out the Spirit's will. Thus, neither here nor elsewhere[4] does Paul give countenance to those who are slaves to their sins. Such acquiescence is wrongly thought "pastoral"; it is in fact

4 On the often misused Rom 7:15 and context, see my *Two Covenants,* 41–47.

a denial of the biblical view of liberation from Sin's dominion through Jesus the Messiah and His life-giving Spirit (cf Rom 6:15–23). Being enslaved to Sin is not "the normal Christian life"; it is the way that leads to death (Rom 6:16; cf Rom 6:23).

None of this is to ascribe any sort of triumphalistic perfectionism to Paul. Far from it; for Paul the life led by the Spirit is both gift and difficult challenge. Being led by the Spirit entails sacrificing desires that are fleshly. In statements such as these, Paul is putting his own angle on Jesus' teaching: he who loves his life will lose it, and he who lays down his life will find it. Even as believers, we must "put to death the deeds of the body" (Rom 8:13), and Paul speaks of how he disciplines himself, so that he may remain approved of God (1 Cor 9:27). Paul does not confuse *battle against* Sin with *slavery to* Sin.

There is a surface contradiction in Paul that is important to deal with at this point. In Rom 8:8–9, he says that those in the flesh cannot please God, and that believers are *not* "in the flesh." Elsewhere, however, he repeatedly affirms that they *are* in the flesh (2 Cor 4:11; 10:3; Gal 2:20). This difficulty is resolved by recognizing that in Rom 8, Paul is speaking of the *domain* of flesh (as parallel to Sin etc), whereas in the other passages he is referring simply to the flesh as the mortal body ("death-body") within which each of us dwells. Paul's doctrine is that the believer has been transferred from the realm/kingdom of flesh and Sin into that of the Messiah and the Spirit ... but at the same time, the believer continues to live in the "mortal body of flesh"—a bodily existence conditioned by the old creation and suffering from its corruption. One's inner man has been redeemed, but according to Rom 8:23, the "redemption of the body" still awaits.

5:18 *Now if you are led by the Spirit, you are not under Torah.*

Now (δὲ) functions here to introduce a sort of concluding thought to the more general section as Paul prepares to move to a more specific discussion of the works of the flesh and the fruit of the Spirit.

If you are led by the Spirit closely echoes *walk in the Spirit* (v 16), although here the sense is a bit more clearly instrumental. Throughout the letter, the Spirit is the one who marks out the pathway for the believer (cf 3:3); and it is in Him and by Him that one anticipates the eschatological hope of righteousness (v 5).

Just as Yahweh led Israel into the wilderness, where He (ironically?) gave them Torah, so the Spirit led Jesus into the wilderness (Lk 4:1), and even now leads those who are *in the Messiah* through the trials of a road race. The Spirit leads the believer in the way and truth of the Messiah (cf again Jn 16:13–15).

While the Spirit led Israel to Sinai, now if you are subject to His leading, ***you are not under Torah.*** Torah was weak through the flesh (Rom 8:3), and since the Spirit and flesh are at war (v 17), Torah could not be the Spirit's long-term solution. Cf Rom 6:14—to be led by the Spirit means one is living in the Messiah and is not therefore subject to Torah's hegemony.

Although Paul does contrast "Spirit" and "letter" in 2 Cor 3, the primary point here is not about being led by an inward compulsion or feeling as opposed to something written. As Paul Himself writes in 2 Tim 3:16, Scripture is "God-breathed"—probably itself a reference to the Spirit, as the regular words for *wind, breath,* and *Spirit* are interchangeable in both Greek and Hebrew, and there are analogical concepts, as well (see e.g. the ambiguity of Ezek 37, where the "Son of Man" is told to prophesy to the breath/Spirit to come into the reconstituted bodies, in the context of the promise of the Spirit in Ezek 36:26–27).

The Spirit's work entails the invisible, but almost always uses means, and in particular the Word which He Himself inspired (cf 2 Pet 1:21: "men spoke from God as they were carried along by the Holy Spirit"). The Spirit–Torah contrast is less a contrast between inward motivation and outward letter than a contrast between new covenant gift and old covenant administration (Torah as covenant).[5]

The Galatians' temptation toward circumcision was being motivated at least in part by fear of persecution (v 11; 6:12). In this light, the echo of the Messiah's leading by the Spirit is important to note. When Jesus was baptized, the Spirit led Him into the wilderness to do battle

5 Note again Paul's appeal to the Genesis narrative as normative in the *nomos vs nomos* contrast of 4:21.

with Satan, and ultimately led Him to the cross. To be *in the Messiah* by virtue of baptism is to find solidarity with Him in His submission to the Spirit's leading, a leading whose pathway is defined by the cross.

The Works of the Flesh (5:19–21)

The section delineating some of *the works of the flesh* is not verbally chiastic, but it does appear that the heart of Paul's present concerns are in the center of his list. Garlington 252 suggests that the first and last sections are lists of things "that would have been deplored by everyone"; the central section enumerates the particular sins which most likely would have been manifesting themselves in Galatia, particularly in connection to the dissension and division arising from the "Judaizers." This is highlighted by the fact that many of the words in the central section would not have been common in conventional vice catalogues, although they do appear elsewhere in Paul— which is not surprising, given how frequent is his theme of the integrity and solidarity of the body of the Messiah.

With that idea of *koinonia* in the background, the comments of Witherington 397 are helpful: "the first and last ones listed have to do with sins associated with the sort of κοινωνία that went on in pagan temples... while those in the middle refer to sins that went on within the very fellowship of the community of faith."

That the central section is in fact the key one here[6] is further reinforced by the character of the *fruit of the Spirit* list which immediately follows.

Various modern scholars have charged Paul with inconsistency, since despite repudiating Torah, in passages such as this he prohibits various practices forbidden in the law. "He says this because he is Jewish," they say dismissively, as if the apostles' ethical values do not cohere with his overall theology. But this exhibits a fundamental failure to understand Paul. The freedom from Torah which he preaches refers to the

---

6 By *key*, I am not intending to imply that the sins enumerated in the middle are more significant or worse than the other sins listed. I am simply drawing attention to the fact that so far as matters in Galatia were concerned, the center of the list is the focus.

law's role of covenantal oversight; for him, the Hebrew Scriptures are indeed authoritative *Scripture*, and although he is adamantly opposed to Gentiles becoming subject to circumcision, the Jewish calendar, and so on, throughout his writings he demonstrates a thoroughgoing commitment to retain the Scriptures, albeit reinterpreting them in the light of the Messiah's advent.[7]

The fact that Paul overtly ties such prohibited actions to *the flesh* shows that his ethic is in fact self-conscious and fully integrated with his theological understanding.

> *Now the works of the flesh are evident, whatever is fornication, uncleanness, sensuality...* 5:19

Providing a rather startling implicit parallel to *the works of Torah* (cf 2:16; 3:2, 5, 10), Paul begins to enumerate a partial list of ***the works of the flesh***. The parallel is surely not incidental. Once again, the law is not a real antidote against the flesh because they belong to the same realm, the old creation.

In writing that *the works of the flesh* ***are evident***, Paul is not likely implying that the flesh's activities are obvious for everyone to see. For him, sins of the heart are very much the works of the flesh, and although one's heart bears fruit, that is not always *evident*.

The point rather would seem to be that at least for the one who is normed by the leading of the Spirit, it is generally not difficult to discern what sorts of deeds are in fact *works of the flesh*.

Paul commences the list with three or four sins related to sexuality: ***adultery*** [Byz only], ***fornication, uncleanness, sensuality***.

Adultery (μοιχεία) is included in the MT tradition, but not included in BNT. The term refers specifically to adultery, i.e. violation of the marriage covenant. E.g. the woman caught in adultery in Jn 8:3; vice lists of Matt 15:19 and Mk 7:22. The verbal form is a bit more frequent than the noun in the NT.

Fornication (πορνεία) has become quaint and very nearly archaic

7 On these two meanings of Torah, see above on 4:21. For further on how law functions in Paul, cf also below on the *law of Christ* in 6:2.

in modern usage. It frequently refers in Scripture (1) to sexual relationships that are prohibited by more than marital situation; and (2) to consorting with prostitutes/harlots (1 Cor 6:13, 18), and from there, to more general forms of sexual immorality.

Examples of the first instance could be e.g. a blood relationship such as siblings or between son and stepmother. In the case of 1 Cor 5:1, Paul uses πορνεία to refer to a sexual relationship with a man's father's wife.

With regard to the second instance, 1Cor 7:2 says that each man ought to have his own wife "on account of fornication." There is also probably a more general sense of "sexual immorality" in 1 Thess 4:3, where Paul in context is arguing for "sanctification," "that each of you know how to control his own body in holiness and honour, not in the passion of lust like the Gentiles who do not know God."

The Greco-Roman world had a quite widespread laxity toward sexuality, although it was not identical in form to modern sexual liberation. Single females other than prostitutes were better protected, while on the other hand being a passive partner in homosexual acts was considered degrading and unmanly. Moreover, in contrast to the modern West, prostitution was socially acceptable, particularly the almost ubiquitous cult prostitution.

That cultural milieu serves in part as a reminder that the Pauline vice lists are not simply mirror images of what was predominant in the notions of good behaviour which prevailed in the culture of the time, although in some respects his lists bear resemblance to the virtue lists of philosophers of the same time period. Even with regard to the latter, however, Paul is distinctive in some of the activities which he identifies either as vices or as virtues. (Humility and meekness, for example, were disdained by the philosophers.)

Such Pauline lists, therefore, should not be read as conditioned upon what was popular in the culture, nor by what was considered virtuous by other contemporary ethical thinkers. An implication of that is that Paul's warnings against sexual license are not time-bound prejudices which he would jettison were he alive today. His vision of both vice and virtue arises out of biblical understanding through the lens of the controlling narrative of the Messiah and the Spirit.

In view of this, the relative indifference to premarital sexual activity which pervades much of the modern Western Church is not a sign of deeper understanding of grace, but rather of declension from Paul's vision. Allowing the flourishing of fornication, along with the other sins mentioned in such lists, without due correction in firm meekness (cf 6:1), amounts to a countenancing within the Church of things on account of which those doing them do not inherit the kingdom of God (v 21b). When the works of the flesh are uncorrected within the Church, the Church thereby becomes every bit as characterized by *this present evil age* (1:4), the realm of *flesh,* as was the agenda of the false teachers in Galatia.

Uncleanness or *impurity* (ἀκαθαρσία) elsewhere in the NT does not always carry an apparent sexual sense.[8] Nonetheless, the connection of illicit sexuality to impurity is predominant. By way of illustrative example:

- Rom 1:24—God gave men up in the lusts of their hearts to the *impurity* of dishonouring their bodies among themselves;
- Rom 6:19—the Romans once gave their members as slaves to *impurity* and lawlessness;
- 2 Cor 12:21—Paul fears that when he comes he will find those who have not repented of "impurity," πορνεία and ἀσελγείᾳ (sensuality);
- Eph 4:19—the Gentiles have given themselves up to sensuality and greedily practice every kind of *impurity;*
- Eph 5:3—along with *porneia* and covetousness, *impurity* is not to be named among the saints;
- Col 3:5—put to death your members, the things upon the earth: *porneia, impurity,* passions, evil desires;
- 1 Thess 4:7—in the context of 1 Thess 4:3 (mentioned above), Paul summarizes the call against *porneia* by saying, "God has not called us for *impurity,* but in holiness."

8 E.g. Mt 23:27 where the Pharisees are "whitewashed tombs," beautiful outwardly but inside full of dead men's bones and "all uncleanness"; 1 Thess 2:3: "our appeal does not spring from error or *impurity* or any attempt to deceive."

While the thrust of Paul's vice list is surely the center section, by no means is the inclusion of terms such as *uncleanness* a haphazard or superfluous one. Not only does it generalize what the preceding term, *fornication,* may have made too specific to cover all intended sexual immorality. More particularly, one should note the connection to *uncleanness* under the Levitical law (Lev 12–15). That by itself ties neatly to Paul's *flesh* theme, but it also reflects the consequences of practicing wickedness. While ritual impurity of that sort barred one from the ritual presence of Yahweh in the tabernacle or temple, Paul will presently say in v 21 that those who practice "such things" as he lists here will not inherit the kingdom of God.

This fact further illustrates how Paul sees the relationship between Torah and what he elsewhere calls *the new covenant.* While the new covenant *is,* ultimately, the Abrahamic covenant, with its promises realized, the new covenant also fulfills Torah (cf v 14), albeit in a rather different way. The relationship is not one of promise and realization, but of shadow and immaturity over against substance and maturity (on the maturity theme, see above on 3:22–4:7; on the shadow and substance theme, cf Col 2:17).

Consequently, the passing of the Levitical norms regarding uncleanness does not dispense with the matter of liturgical and spiritual access to the presence of God altogether. Rather, the Levitical norms have been fulfilled, and in the process transformed, reinterpreted and clarified in the light of the advent of the Messiah and the gift of the Spirit. In reading his letters, we thus discover that the forms of uncleanness depicted in Lev 12–15 are not operative for Paul, but he still has his own Messiah-normed *uncleanness* classification which bars one from the Lord's table and the Lord's kingdom. This is why (for example) he calls for the excommunication of the adulterer in 1 Cor 5:1–8.

The next term in Paul's first subset in his vice list is *sensuality* (ἀσέλγεια), which apparently refers to sexual immorality in more extreme forms.[9] It is sometimes translated as *debauchery* or similar terminology which stresses a sense of excess. It is found elsewhere in the

9 Witherington 398 terms it as "extreme and public debauchery of a kind that would be shocking even to a pagan."

NT in Mk 7:22; Rom 13:13; 2 Cor 12:21; Eph 4:19; 1 Pet 4:3; 2 Pet 2:2, 7, 18; Jude 4.

Idolatry, sorcery, hostilities, strifes, zealotry, wraths, rivalries, divisions, factions... 5:20

The next two terms, ***idolatry, sorcery***, continue with the more general vices of the wider world. Both fall generally under the category of wrongdoing condemned by the first commandment of the Decalogue. As with eight of the other nine of those commandments, Paul has no more tolerance for the sins prohibited than does Torah.

Idolatry (εἰδωλολατρία) is found elsewhere in the NT at 1 Cor 10:14; Col 3:5; 1 Pet 4:3. It refers primarily to the worship of false gods, which unlike Yahweh, were generally represented by carved or graven images. Paul has already drawn attention to the fact that in their previous lives, the Galatians worshiped things which by nature really were not gods, i.e. they were idols (4:8).

The offense of idolatry under the new covenant is only further heightened, because God has been more openly and profoundly revealed in the Person of His Son, who is the true, ultimate, and express image of God (cf Heb 1:3).

In the NT, the present term for *sorcery* (φαρμακεία) is used only here and Rev 18:23 (speaking of "Babylon" the harlot, "all nations were deceived by your sorcery"). Related terms, however, can be found in Rev 9:21; 21:8; 22:15. The term is the source of our words such as *pharmacy;* drugs were frequently employed in occult practices in the ancient world.

The term was also used in connection with concocting drugs for the sake of poisoning, which was considered a form of "sorcery."

In any case, the prohibition of sorcery stands in line with Torah's various condemnations of occult practices. This is not a matter *less* serious now (because after all, believers are not under Torah), but—if anything—*more,* since the true eschatological Healer and Prophet has come in the person of the Messiah.

We have now arrived at the heart of Paul's enumeration. In this next section of the list, the focus is upon "social sins" which could be and probably were rife in the assembly: ***hostilities, strife*** (or ***strifes***), ***zealotry*** (or jealousies), ***wraths, rivalries, divisions, factions***. These sins, in particular, are mirrored by their opposites in the list of the fruit of the Spirit which immediately follows.

Hostilities (ἔχθραι) is found elsewhere in the NT at Lk 23:12; Rom 8:7; Eph 2:14, 16; Jam 4:4. The term is sometimes translated *enmity*, and describes an active state that contrasts to friendship.

On the significance of the plural here, see especially Witherington 400: "In the singular the word refers to enmity or hatred but it is possible that in the plural abstract nouns like this refer to repeated demonstrations or manifestations of this quality. Abstract nouns could be made concrete by using them in the plural, called the *pluralis poeticus*." Thus the point would be that hostility here moves beyond an attitude into the realm of action.

Strife[s] evince a difference between the BNT and Byzantine texts (ἔρις [BNT] / ἔρεις [Byz]), although there is probably little significant difference in the sense. Elsewhere in the NT, the term appears in Rom 1:29; 13:13; 1 Cor 1:11; 3:3; 2 Cor 12:20; Phil 1:15; 1 Tim 6:4; Tit 3:9. What is in view are fights and quarrels. All too often, these arise between believers over petty follies, but the strife itself is by no means petty. The peace of entire congregations has been rent asunder due to microscopic pettiness.

Again with *zealotry* or *jealousy* (ζῆλος / ζῆλοι), there is a difference between BNT and the Byzantine tradition regarding number. Our words *zeal* and *jealousy* are the same word in Greek, and it is very important here to tie the term in with Paul's earlier account of his life in Judaism (see esp 1:14).

Zeal or *jealousy* can be either positive or negative in the NT. Jesus fulfills prophecy by His zeal for God's house (Jn 2:17), and 2 Cor 7:7, 11; 9:2 speak of the Corinthians' zeal for good things. Paul has a divine zeal or jealousy for the purity of the Church as the Messiah's betrothed virgin (2 Cor 11:2). Moreover, God Himself has a zealous fire that will consume His adversaries (Heb 10:27).

On the negative side, various religious leaders are said to be jealous of the apostles (e.g. Acts 5:17; 13:45), and of course, Paul's own zeal had taken the form of persecuting the Messiah's Church (Phil 3:6). Other occurrences can be found in Rom 13:13; 1 Cor 3:3; 2 Cor 12:20; Jam 3:14, 16.

In one instance, the term appears to be nearly neutral; in Rom 10:2, unbelieving Israel has a zeal for God, but not according to knowledge. But this probably is similar to Paul's preconversion zeal, which seemed good at the time, but nonetheless caused him to wage war against the Messiah Himself.

It can scarcely be doubted that Paul sees a fixation with Torah as leading to the same sort of opposition to the Messiah's true people. The actions of the teachers are *zealotries* similar in destructiveness to the previous havoc he himself had wreaked upon the Church.

But such destructiveness is not unique to the circumcision party of Paul's day; in virtually every faith tradition of modern Christendom, there are those who make it their mission to be constantly on the warpath, self-styled Phinehases, having a zeal for God but nonetheless utterly destructive in their ways. This form of "purity" is in fact a *work of the flesh.*

Wraths (θυμοί) is found elsewhere in the NT at Lk 4:28; Acts 19:28; Rom 2:8 (where it refers to divine wrath); 2 Cor 12:20; Eph 4:31; Col 3:8; Heb 11:27; Rev 12:12; 14:8, 10, 19; 15:1, 7; 16:1, 19; 18:3; 19:15. In Rev, the term describes both God's wrath as well as the wrath of the devil because he knows the shortness of his time.

Garlington 251 suggests that the term here refers to the "abandonment of restraint" with regard to zeal. There is now no holding back, similar again to Paul's own past, when he was snorting out threats and murder against the Messiah's disciples (Acts 9:1). While there is a legitimate divine wrath, as a work of the flesh, what is in view is an ungoverned anger toward others.

Rivalries (ἐριθεῖαι) is found elsewhere in the NT at Rom 2:8; 2 Cor 12:20; Phil 1:17; 2:3; Jam 3:14, 16. Those given to rivalries have unholy competitiveness stemming from pride and conceit.

Divisions (διχοστασίαι) is found elsewhere in the NT only in Rom 16:17 (watch out for those who cause *divisions* and create stumbling stones contrary to the teaching you have been taught). While most of the other terms relating to social strife here do not have a particular teaching at the forefront, the parallel with Romans suggests that the *divisions* Paul particularly has in mind are likely those that arise due to the infiltration of a teaching incompatible to the received gospel, which tears at the fabric of the community.

Factions (αἱρέσεις) is the word from where we get the term *heresy*, although at the fore is not so much variation in doctrine (although that element is not absent) as the creation of factions which tear at the unity of the Church. Elsewhere in the NT, the term is found in Acts 5:17; 15:5; 24:5; 24:14; 26:5; 28:22; 1 Cor 11:19; 2 Pet 2:1. In Acts, it is a term employed to describe various sects or parties; e.g. the Sadducees (5:17) or Pharisees (15:5; 26:5); the believers are called by Tertullus "the *sect* of the Nazarenes" (24:5; cf 24:14; 28:22).

Witherington 401 notes that this is almost always a political term, even in Jewish writings. Thus the use of the term "politics" to churchly disputes has precedent in Paul himself.

This array of terms at the heart of Paul's vice list covers all the bases, so far as laying a finger on broken communion within the churches is concerned. Whether it is self-appointed, misplaced zeal, or vanities that exalt one group over another, or novel teachings that strike at the authority of the gospel of the Messiah, or any other sort of divisiveness or factiousness, Paul warns: these are all *the works of the flesh,* manifestations of the old *kosmos* under judgment. Those who sow such works will reap the destruction they are sowing (cf 6:8).

5:21 *Envies, [Byz murders], drunkennesses, carousing, and things similar to these; which things I forewarn you, just as I did forewarn you, that the ones doing such things will not inherit the kingdom of God.*

After mentioning ***envies*** (which may better belong to the central section), Paul closes out his list by shifting back to sins more general among the wider populace: (***murders***), ***drunkennesses, carousing***.

Envies (φθόνοι) is wonderfully described by Bruce as "[t]he grudging spirit that cannot bear to contemplate someone else's prosperity." The verbal form is used in v 26: "Let us not become conceited, provoking one another, *envying* one another." In Mt 27:18 (= Mk 15:10), it is because of *envy* that the Jewish leaders have delivered Jesus up. Similarly, some preach the Messiah out of envy and rivalry (Phil 1:15). The term is used frequently in NT "vice lists" (Rom 1:29; 1 Tim 6:4, Tit 3:3; 1 Pet 2:1).

Murders appears only in the Byz/MT tradition, and requires little comment.

Drunkennesses (μέθαι)—in both Lk 21:34 and Rom 13:13, the term is associated with night, and set in contrast to wakefulness or watchfulness. In Romans, Paul sets it within an eschatological cast: believers belong to the new age, where light has begun to dawn (see Rom 13:11–12). Thus drunkenness is related not only to spiritual carelessness, slumber, dissipation, unalertness, but to a sort of stupor that holds one back from the emerging light provided by the new creation. Garlington 252 suggests that the plural form used here refers to the drinking bouts ("symposiums") that were common in that day, especially in connection with pagan feasts.

Carousing (κῶμοι) is frequently translated *orgies*. It is found elsewhere in the NT at Rom 13:13 (see above on *drunkenness*) and 1 Pet 4:3. Peter summarizes the latter verse in 4:4 as "debauchery." Dunn 306 notes that this term "originally denoted a festal procession in honour of Dionysus, hence the overtone of uninhibited revelry to excess...." It is thus not unlike ἀσέλγεια, although apparently without the necessity of sexual denotation.

Paul adds ***and things similar to these***, reflecting the fact that his enumeration is representative rather than exhaustive. The list as given has served his rhetorical purpose. As always, it is important to keep in mind that the letter is occasional, and does not intend to provide a comprehensive or systematic discussion of sin or anything else.

Paul adds, ***which things I forewarn you, just as I did forewarn you***; on his first missionary journey, he had traveled through South Galatia and then doubled back again. He thus had considerable opportunity for more comprehensive teaching on Christian living and for providing warnings regarding wicked conduct.

Exegetes frequently suggest that one of the "pulls" the Galatians would have felt toward Torah was that it appeared to have much more detailed practical prescriptions than that provided by Paul's Torah-free gospel.[10] While it is true that the Mosaic law is far more detailed than Paul's instructions here, however, we nonetheless see that he had already imparted to the Galatians much more than we will ever know. If there was such a pull, it would at any rate have been primarily at the level of public boundary markers such as calendrical observances (cf 4:9–10).

Unlike certain strands of modern preachers and theologians, Paul was not averse to *warning* believers ***that the ones doing such things will not inherit the kingdom of God.*** The fact that this is, by Paul's own insistence, a *warning* indicates that what is in view is not merely an abstract impersonal observation. The implication is: if *you* do such things, *you* will not inherit the kingdom of God.

The *ones doing* (present participle of πράσσω) refers to those characterized by a practice. One may say that those who are led by the flesh rather than by the Spirit (cf v 18) are those who do such things. These ones are not the righteous, but *the unrighteous who will not inherit the kingdom of God* (1 Cor 6:9–10).

At the same time, this is about *inheriting* the kingdom of God. This warning, and its focus on doing or not doing, must not detract from the fact that the kingdom of God is an *inheritance,* and throughout chapters 3–4, Paul has built up a case for the fact that those in the Messiah are heirs (3:18, 29; 4:1). The point in view is not that one earns the kingdom (inheritance is always a gift), but that repudiation of the family and its future will nonetheless result in disinheritance.

Calvin 104–105 provides appropriate comfort to those who are weak:

> Paul does not threaten that there shall be excluded from the Kingdom of God all who have sinned, but all who remain impenitent. The saints themselves are sometimes heavily burdened, but they return to the way. Because they do not surrender, they are not included in

10 This is one of the primary claims of Barclay, and he has since been followed by numerous commentators. See in particular *Obeying the Truth,* 70–72, but the theme is pervasive at various points throughout his study.

> this catalogue. All the threatenings of God's judgments call us to repentance, for which pardon is always ready with God; but if we continue obstinate, they will be a testimony against us.

The Fruit of the Spirit (5:22–26)

As with the preceding list, the enumeration of the fruit of the Spirit is not a comprehensive list. It tends rather to focus on countering the foregoing *works of the flesh,* particularly the crucial central section.

In connection with the WWJD ("What Would Jesus Do?") phenomenon of a few years back, whatever the practical (mis)applications that may have been involved on occasion, the Reformed tendency to counter simply with WDJD ("What *Did* Jesus Do?") was at least equally unhelpful. The fruit of the Spirit is a description of the character of the Messiah Himself, and what He *did* do is to ground our own living and walking.

The discussion here is communal in character. Witherington 414 writes,

> The answer to the decaying morals of modern society is not merely to try and rebuild some of the major building blocks of society such as the family (*a la* "Promise Keepers"), but to do a better job of creating a Christian church family in which all such sub-units of society can be nurtured and if they are broken, healed.

He goes on to say (415) that Paul's exhortation here is not merely "to private individual Christians, but to the Galatian assemblies as communities of Christ." The battle against the flesh requires more than the Spirit-filled efforts of individuals; it requires the community, because "the Spirit indwells the community as well as the individuals."

As is the case with v 4, there is strong congruency between this passage and John 15.[11] Even as the earlier verse implicitly contrasts

11 There are in fact a remarkable number of echoes between the Farewell Discourse in John as a whole, and the letter to the Galatians. See Appendix 3, "Galatians and the

severance from the Messiah and remaining in Him (as does Jn 15:6 in context), likewise these verses attribute fruit-bearing to the disciple, as does John 15. The surface approach, however, differs. In these verses in Galatians, the Holy Spirit is at the forefront as the source of fecundity, whereas in John, fruitfulness is attributed to sharing in the Messiah's own life (Jn 14:4–5). The apparent difference, however, dissipates as we study this passage within the context of the whole letter. The Spirit bears fruit in the believer precisely by making him share in the character of Christ. After all, the life now lived in the flesh is lived by the faith of the Son of God (2:20).

The connection to John 15's vine imagery, however, pushes the connections back much further. The OT is replete with rich imagery regarding Israel as a vineyard (e.g. Ps 80:15; Isa 5; Jer 12:10), which of course Jesus picked up on more than once (besides Jn 15, see e.g. the vineyard parables of Mt 20–21; Mk 12:1–12; Lk 13:6–9; 20:9–18). The Luke 13 parable, in particular, refers to the failure of the vineyard to bear fruit, and in so doing is a recasting of Isa 5.

With this backdrop of the unfruitfulness of Israel-as-vineyard, therefore, the *fruit of the Spirit* language here is itself an implicit critique regarding Torah, which was "weak through the flesh" (cf Rom 8:3). The result of its hegemony was not after all fruitfulness (or, in the language of Isa 5, the yield was "wild grapes" rather than good grapes).

Now, implies Paul (again echoing Jn 15), the vineyard is re-centered in the Messiah, and the eschatological Spirit will through Him and in His faith-people produce the fruit which God seeks.

This, as Barclay 121 notes, is in accordance with the eschatological expectation of Isa 32:15–16; when "the Spirit is poured upon us from on high," the result is fruitfulness even in the wilderness—which raises interesting echoes in terms of Paul's handling of the Abraham-Sarah-Hagar narrative earlier (see esp the interplay with Isa 54:1 in the citation of Gal 4:27, where the word for *desolate* is ἐρήμος, *desert, wilderness*). As with Isaac, the Spirit's work in the believer is an eschatological apocalypse, a divine intervention that transcends human abilities and intervenes with the power of the age to come. In short, the *fruit of the Spirit*

Farewell Discourse."

is embodied new creation.

But the fruit of the Spirit is love, joy, peace, longsuffering, kindness, goodness, faith/faithfulness. 5:22

The ***fruit of the Spirit*** stands in contrast to the foregoing *works of the flesh* (as well as to *works of Torah* earlier in the letter). It is interesting that Paul pits *fruit* against *works,* even though elsewhere he can stress how strenuous one must be in carrying out godly activity (even using the term *good works* in Eph 2); e.g. 1 Cor 9:24ff. The latter fact warns us against a reading that amounts to "let go and let God"; the metaphor itself, on the other hand, reinforces the believer's utter dependence upon the acting power of God Himself through His Spirit. Dependent faith is not opposed to exertion; rather, the life-giving energy of God's Spirit is the *source* of the exertion of the disciple of the Messiah. Paul elsewhere uses the image of disciplined athletic training (see e.g. 1 Cor 9:24–27), which of course well-suits the broader context here (e.g. v 7). Yet he also affirms that even at the height of his labours, it was not ultimately him, after all, "but the grace of God which was with me" (1 Cor 15:10).[12]

On *fruit,* cf Mt 7:17, "every good tree bears good fruit, but a bad tree bears bad fruit." Cf also Jn 15—bearing fruit requires remaining in the vine, Jesus. The Spirit is the Spirit of the Messiah, and the fruit He provides is the life of the Messiah.[13]

On the singular *fruit* (rather than *fruits*), Witherington 408 offers, "the singular here suggests the unity and unifying nature of these qualities as opposed to the divisive effects of the traits listed in the vice list." Moreover, these are not individual traits that can be divided up, but together form one whole and are to be manifest in every Christian life.

The first three terms, ***love, joy, peace***, come up in Jesus' farewell discourse—John 14:27 mentions peace; Jn 15:9–11 deal with love and joy. In

12 It can scarcely be objected that in that particular passage, he had his apostolic ministry in view. While that is certainly true, he laboured in ministry by the same strength with which he laboured in sanctification.

13 James D. G. Dunn helpfully suggests that the list as a whole is a "character sketch" of Christ Himself.

each case, it is first of all *the Messiah's* love, peace, and joy that is in view. These are gifts which Jesus promises in the face of His own impending death—a death which itself embodies these gifts. In love He gave Himself up for us, for the joy that was set before Him, so making peace.

Love (ἀγάπη) is unsurprisingly at the head of the list, both given the key works of the flesh Paul is countering, as well the programmatic mention of *faith working through love* in v 6 and the Torah-fulfilling role ascribed to it in v 14. Love fills up what was not full in Torah; and it is the specific and controlling characteristic which is worked out by *pistis*.

The priority of love does have roots in Torah itself (love your neighbour etc), but takes particular shape in the Messiah (particularly in 2:20's *who loved me and gave Himself up for me*). Thus, love is a "new commandment": "A new commandment I give to you, that you love one another; *as I have loved you,* that you also love one another" (Jn 13:34; cf 2 Jn 5).

Joy (χαρὰ) is perhaps a surprise, not least given our own sentimental view of happiness as something that comes to us unbidden, as it were. But here, it is something implicitly commanded and enjoined. Joy does not merely "happen"; it is a characteristic to which we are called.

Joy is bidden, in part because its genuine presence itself requires keeping the Messiah's commandments. Jesus tells the disciples to keep His commandments and adds (Jn 15:11), "These things I have spoken to you, that My joy may remain in you, and that your joy may be full."

Given the communal character of all the neighbouring characteristics of the Spirit's fruit, it should be clear that what Paul has in mind is not simply an individualized happiness. Joy that is full is atmospheric and creates the possibility of glad community. It is the suitable and thankful response of those who have been made heirs of a kingdom where there is overflowing life.

It is a commonplace that *peace* (εἰρήνη) is the equivalent of the Hebrew *shalom,* which refers not merely to absence of conflict (cf the vice list above, with its rivalries, envies etc), but to wholeness. Peace is therefore not simply a placidity of heart, but an active sharing of full life and wholeness with others.

Moreover, this peace is, as with the other aspects of the fruit of the Spirit, *personal.* At the prospect of His impending departure and consequent sending of the Spirit, the Messiah says that He leaves *His* peace with us, a peace unlike that provided by the world (Jn 14:27). The Messiah is the Prince of Peace, and His peace is first of all His accomplishment of reconciliation between the Father and us, which is then embodied in our mutual relationships with one another. Just as kingdom reconciliation has brought wholeness where there was emptiness in the divine–human relationship, so too it brings wholeness into the community.

Beyond this, however, *peace* stands over against the *troubling* of the churches that had been brought about by the teachers (1:7; 5:10, 12; 6:17).[14] In the Farewell Discourse, Jesus had encouraged faith in Him over against the possibility of troubled hearts (Jn 14:1), and then later set His *peace* which He was leaving with His disciples as the antidote to such troubled hearts (14:27). For Paul, this call to peace therefore is not simply a generic description of character. It is likely also yet another call to stand firm against the false teachers' troubling activities.

Longsuffering (μακροθυμία) is not merely the *suppression* of anger; it is a self-conscious bearing with others—even if ultimately judgment must be meted out (see God's example in Rom 2:4). In Greek literature, the term refers to a "long temper." It is ultimately exemplified in the Messiah's endurance of the malignance of sinners when at His disposal were hosts of angels.

According to BAGD, ***kindness*** (χρηστότης) is the quality of being helpful or beneficial to others, and carries the thought of generosity.

Goodness (ἀγαθωσύνη) is apparently a virtual synonym for χρηστότης. Goodness, similar to *kindness,* is interested in the welfare of others.

The last word in this verse (but not the list) is the richly ambiguous ***faith/faithfulness*** (πίστις), so familiar throughout the letter, and indeed, Paul's writings as a whole.

According to 2:20, we live by the πίστις of the Son of God, who loved us and gave Himself for us. This faithfulness is also a fruit of the

14 Only in 5:12 is the Greek term different; the rest use ταράσσω, as does John 14.

Spirit, and thus πίστις toward the body is an undoing and prevention of the divisions etc listed above as *works of the flesh*. Witherington 410 also thinks the primary referent here is to *faithfulness* rather than to *faith*, although in truth there are cases where it is hard to distinguish between these two meanings.

In any case, once again the cues should be taken from the fact that the *fruit of the Spirit* is the effect of the life of the Messiah communicated to us by the Holy Spirit, and thus *pistis* is not only belief in the Messiah (although that surely is involved here at a fundamental level), but also a giving over of oneself to the cross in the hope of God's vindication. The Messiah endured the cross for the hope that was set before Him, entrusting Himself to the Father's righteous judgment and care, and when those *in the Messiah* participate in that mind (Phil 2:5!), they are, as Paul has enjoined, *in the Spirit, by faith, anticipating the hope of righteousness* (v 5).

Without this sort of faith, which has the strength to leave off self-vindication and reflexive defensiveness, the life of the community will always be in danger of the rivalries and divisions against which Paul has warned in v 20. It is only when one no longer lives out of his own life, but lives by the *pistis* of the Son of God, that he can work out love (cf v 6) in the manner Paul calls for here.

5:23 *Meekness, self-control: against such people there is no Torah.*

The Greek word which I have given as ***Meekness*** (πραΰτης) is frequently translated *gentleness*, and can certainly have that shade, but overall, the idea of *meekness* seems to be more at the forefront. It is through *meekness* rather than "gentleness" that one is to receive the engrafted Word (Jam 1:21). There are thus overtones of *humility* involved; and once again, Jesus is the pattern.

This of course is not to be mistaken for milquetoast mildness; Ps 45:4 (44:5 LXX) pairs this meekness with the *majesty* of the messianic king riding prosperously, whose right hand teaches Him awesome things—the very portrait of not only skill, but potency.

We must continue to drive the context through our present passage.

The social sins so prevalent in an atmosphere driven by zeal for Torah rather than by the Messiah are met head-on with πραΰτης. When one's vindication is anchored in the Messiah and secured outside oneself, it becomes possible to be powerfully meek. What that entails is not a discounting of one's genuine strength—for again, Jesus was meek but certainly did not do that. Genuine meekness begins with meekness before God and His Word, and that receptive submission is incomparably empowering. Jesus went to His death, not as a hapless, passive victim, but as a conqueror whose meekness was subduing the world, judging the *kosmos* and its god (Jn 16:11; cf 2 Cor 4:4).

The final manifestation here of the *fruit of the Spirit* is ***self-control*** (ἐγκράτεια), which stands in contrast to the drinking parties and orgies castigated among the *works of the flesh*.

This virtue fits well with Paul's frequent theme of self-mortification, i.e. mortify your members; I keep my body under etc. But there is even greater consonance with the maturity theme of ch 3–4. A child is one who has not learned self-mastery. Part of maturity is an internalized discipline that does not require the constant correction of an overseer—a child custodian. If one is led by the Spirit, the result is not anarchy, but a mature self-mastery appropriate to the heir who has come into his inheritance.

Against such people there is no Torah is usually translated with *such things*. As Witherington 411 notes, however, the neuter notwithstanding, this clause is an almost word-for-word echo of Aristotle, in a passage (*Pol.* 3.13.1284) where it is virtuous *persons* whose conduct need not be regulated by law that are in view. Such people "live like gods among humans" and thus become their own law, indeed, a standard for others (cf Rom 2:14!). Christians manifesting the fruit of the Spirit do not "live like gods," but like the God-man; and they do so in and by God the Holy Spirit. Thus even Torah (or any other *nomos*, for that matter) cannot stand against them, because they live by the very divine character.

Now those of the Messiah [Jesus] have crucified the flesh with the passions 5:24
and the lusts.

Throughout, Paul has been implicitly depicting those *led by the Spirit* as those who bear the image of Jesus in their character and conduct. This is now made more explicit as he adds, ***Now those of the Messiah [Jesus]***. (*Jesus* is not present in the Byz text tradition.) As always, the genitive has a range of possibilities, and here could be: *those belonging to the Messiah,* or *those characterized by the Messiah*. The latter in particular provides a counterpoint to *those characterized by Torah*—e.g. 3:10—or *those of the flesh*. Witherington 412 suggests that the genitive of 3:29 refers to those *in Christ,* and thus here too.

Due to this connection to the Messiah, therefore, those "of" Him ***have crucified the flesh***. See again the programmatic 2:20: "I am *crucified with the Messiah*." Cf also 6:14: *I am crucified to the world, and the world is crucified to me*. The aorist here could be inceptive (*have crucified* the flesh, and that *crucifying action continues* in the present), but that is not altogether necessary, since for Paul there are senses in which the flesh has been definitively put away.

It would be tempting to think of the believer's co-crucifixion with the Messiah as a wholly passive thing, and it is true that elsewhere that is generally to the fore. Here, however, the subject is not God, but *those of the Messiah,* and the verb is active. Thus there is some necessity in recognizing that in some way, the individual is responsible for his partnership in the Messiah's death. Jesus, and His cross, are to be actively embraced. This is the first step in being *led by the Spirit*.

Moreover, the crucifixion of the flesh is not a minimalist action devoid of consequences; it is nailed to the cross ***with the passions and the longings***. The pairing may have shades of the more passive and active aspects of the inclinations of the flesh, respectively. The *longings* (*lusts*) that characterize the flesh's warfare against the Spirit (v 17) have been crucified.

5:25 *Since we live in the Spirit, let us also walk in the Spirit.*

Since we live in the Spirit employs the first-class condition to affirm that life in the Spirit has indeed already been granted—as Paul has reminded the Galatians earlier, in 3:1–5. Since the flesh and its lusts have been crucified, therefore we live in and by the Spirit who *longs* (desires) against the flesh. Thus *live in the Spirit* is essentially synonymous with 2:20's *the Messiah lives in me.*

Given the new creation life that has been planted in us therefore, Paul says, ***let us also walk in the Spirit.*** Whereas the "movement" metaphor of earlier in the chapter was primarily a *race,* here the explicit thought is that of a *settled path.* By virtue of the fact that we live in and by the Spirit, we are to follow His pathway (cf 5:7, 18; 3:3).

Genuine and permanent stagnation is not possible. The new creation has been inserted within the context of the old *kosmos,* and to *live in the Spirit* implies a mandate to follow the pathway forward, in the Spirit awaiting the hope of righteousness (v 5). To mix the metaphors of motion and fruitbearing as Paul does, remaining in the Messiah and thus bearing fruit (cf Jn 15:1–10) entails moving with Him through the wilderness where the Spirit leads (cf Mt 4:1). It is through being *led by the Spirit* that one keeps pace with the Messiah and remains in union with Him. Notice, in particular, the themes of severance from the Messiah and being impeded in the race in vv 4, 7.

Let us not become conceited, provoking one another, envying one another. 5:26

Paul closes the section by warning, ***Let us not become conceited***—"empty-gloried," boastful in what is vain—***provoking one another, envying one another.*** All of these things evince a failure to live in solidarity with the body, and are therefore betrayals of love, which heads the list of *fruit of the Spirit.*

The term *conceited* breaks out quite literally in more archaic English as *vainglorious* (κενόδοξοι). It corresponds to the empty boasting of 6:13, where the Judaizers want to boast in the Galatians' flesh. That boast literally is in *nothing* (i.e. the *absence* of the foreskin), but more profoundly so, because the *flesh* counts for nothing.

When one embraces the solidarity of the Messiah and those in Him, however, the absurdity of such empty boasting becomes evident. For those who share together in both joy and successes, sufferings and failures, conceit has no coherence.

Provoking one another suggests working one another up to irritation and anger. In contrast, we are to provoke one another to love and good works (Heb 10:24).

As *conceit* wrongly implies that what I have, I have for myself and my own benefit alone, so likewise *envying one another* implies that what *you* have, *you* have for yourself and your own benefit, so that I cannot rejoice in it. Thus conceit and envy are mirrors, and both of them are designed to multiply alienation.

The body's mutual indwelling of the Messiah stands against all of this. All is of God, and when we boast in the Lord, we truly boast together (cf 1 Cor 1:31).

Participation in the New Creation

THE CLOSING SUBSECTION OF THE LETTER contains within it a variety of subjects, which is not surprising. It is very Pauline to look back at his argument, not only to offer a succinct summary (which he in fact does to a great degree in 6:15), but also to offer further implications (vv 1–10), and sundry parting shots (e.g. vv 12–13).

The Law of the Messiah (6:1–5)

For the time being, Paul sets polemics to the side and further develops his portrait of Spirit-led, *in-Christ* living. The chapter break is not a great misfortune—there is a small shift in the narrative—but in some respects 6:1–10 nonetheless is more closely related to the preceding than to vv 11–18.

The first subsection here runs from vv 1–5, and unpacks an implication of 5:23's call to *meekness* as an expression of Spirit-led Christlikeness. Within this fundamental framework, the passage depicts the communal character of life in the new creation. Men are not left to themselves. Induction into the Messiah is an entrance into a mutual partnership with all those belonging to Him. To use the language of the passage itself, we have moved beyond Torah and now find *the law of the Messiah.*

Brothers, if a man is taken in any trespass, you spiritual ones restore such a 6:1
one in the spirit of gentleness, watching yourself, lest you also be tempted.

Paul refers to the situation where ***a man is taken in any trespass***. He has written extensively in Galatians regarding the power of life in the Spirit, and shown that those led by the Spirit will not leave room for the flesh. Yet he is not a naive idealist who is blind to the reality that in fact Christians, too, are subject not only to sin, but to stumbling.

The *taken* language probably echoes the law's distinction between sins done "with a high hand" and sins that arise out of human weakness (בִּשְׁגָגָה, in error or inadvertence, ignorance, frequently translated unintentionally, e.g. Num 15:22ff; Lev 4:2 etc). See esp Cornelis Van Dam, "The Meaning of Bishgagah" (BH Occasional Paper), who argues that the term refers to sins of wandering, weakness or frailty, in contrast to sins "done with the upraised hand in persistent rebellion for which there is no atonement." Numbers 15:22–29 refers to sins of בִּשְׁגָגָה; while 15:30–31 refers to sins done "with a high hand," for which there is no atonement. (Contrary to a modern mantra, in Scripture, all sins most emphatically are not the same.)

Paul calls upon ***you spiritual ones*** to ***restore such a one***. *Contra* the Judaizers, the *spiritual*—the *of-the-Spirit ones*—are defined, not by who is circumcised, but by who bears the burdens of others according to the law of the Messiah.

The goal is *restoration, mending* the person who has stumbled. This is similar to Matthew 18, where Jesus speaks of the pursuit of one sheep—a pattern which He Himself carved out in His own life and ministry. Just as Jesus' mission was to heal and restore "the lost sheep of the house of Israel," at the core of the mission of those *led by the Spirit* is the calling to restore the lost sheep of the heirs of Abraham, as well as to engage the "frontier," the fallen *kosmos*. Unlike Cain, they recognize that they are their brother's keepers.

The manner of this restoration is ***in the spirit of meekness***. Or is it rather ***in the Spirit of meekness?*** This restoration is, after all, the activity of those led by the Spirit and walk in Him.

The instruction here provides explicit application of *the fruit of the Spirit* mentioned above in 5:23.

Beyond the implicit *gentleness* of the Spirit of meekness is the corresponding *humility*. Paul says that you who are led by the Spirit of meekness are to carry out restoration, ***watching yourself, lest you also be tempted***. In the context following, the false teachers are depicted as those who wish to *boast in your flesh* (v 13). Over against that empty boasting, the truly spiritual correct others with gentleness and meekness.

Bear the burdens of one another, and thus fulfill the law of the Messiah. 6:2

Paul now generalizes what he has just said in v 1: ***Bear the burdens of one another.*** Entering into a brother's brokenness and restoring him is one form of coming alongside of him and bearing his burden together with him. Note especially the contrast here to Jesus' charge against the scribes and Pharisees, who "bind heavy burdens, hard to carry, and place them upon men's shoulders—but they themselves will not move them with one of their fingers" (Mt 23:4).

Over against that is the pattern of the Messiah, who bore the burden of the cross—a burden which was not His by desert, but undertaken because He was not ashamed to call us brothers (cf Heb 2:11), and in so doing He became His brothers' keeper. Thus, even as the Spirit led Him to the cross, the Spirit in uniting us to Him, leads us also to the cross, in order to bear the burden of others.

It is to be noted that *what* burden that the scribes and Pharisees were binding was Torah, along with man-made ancillary regulations they had wedded to it. It was likewise Torah's judgment which the Messiah bore in order to bring release from Torah (see on 3:13). So the significant burden has already been borne by the Messiah; now those *led by the Spirit* of the Messiah bear the *burdens* (plural) carried by one another in the day to day of Christian existence.

This leading is not reserved to ordained leaders or to those of particular callings. The *of one another* indicates reciprocity; we are all, each of us, to mutually bear one another's burdens.

Paul now offers one of his most astonishing statements. This mutual burden-bearing will ***thus fulfill the law of the Messiah***, which stands in contrast to the other *law*, the burden of Torah's yoke.

The phrase *the law of the Messiah* should not itself be astonishing. The gospel's liberation from Torah does not mean lawlessness, but rather a new center of living, the Messiah Himself. As we have already seen, freedom is not absolute; we are liberated into a vocation of service (see on 5:13). It should therefore not be a shock to us that there is *some* law on the other side of the old creation, just as the emergence of a child from the multitude of rules of childhood does not mean entry into a world without constraints. Not being under a child custodian is not the same thing as not being under government altogether.

What is surprising, rather, is Paul's use of the term *fulfill* (ἀναπληρόω), which as elsewhere implies an incompleteness apart from the fulfilling action. Paul has said earlier that Torah is fulfilled by the love that faith works; implicit in that thought is the notion that Torah was not "full," that it looked forward to the sort of love that only the new creation could bring.

But what could it mean that the *law of the Messiah* needs to be *fulfilled?*

The difficult truth is that *the law of the Messiah* is not filled until it is lived out by His body. It is not merely an abstract standard to measure ourselves against, but rather something really and truly to embody practically. *The law of the Messiah* has to do with the *totus Christus,* the whole Christ, Head and body, and it is not sufficient for the Head to have gone through the burden-bearing of the cross. The body too must enter into Him and take up the calling of burden-bearing. Jesus the Head has accomplished the great burden-bearing which only He could accomplish. But now through His body, He carries on the task of burden-bearing, and without that, His work is incomplete in history.

The law of the Messiah is just that—*law.* It is not optional. At the same time, it is utterly, thoroughly, radically *personal:* it is the law of *the Messiah,* the way of Jesus Himself. To be *in Christ* is to embrace that way, to "fill" the path that He traces by the leading of the Spirit.

This still does not answer exactly what the *law of the Messiah* is. Barclay 143 seems to get at something close to the point: "the requirement of the whole Mosaic law … as it is redefined and refocused through Christ"—a statement that can only be understood in connection with Paul's statement in 5:14 that love fulfills "the whole Torah," along with Jesus' own stated purpose to "fulfill Torah and the prophets" (Mt 5:17). Rescue from Torah does not mean lawlessness; it means connection to the Messiah, who embodies the grace and truth of which Moses spoke (cf Jn 1:17).

Wright's statement is also helpful and necessary, if perhaps incomplete: Paul

> has coined the phrase in a deliberately teasing fashion ... [and] he is alluding yet again to something he says repeatedly: that the entire incarnation, life, death and resurrection of Jesus form not only a standard to be adhered to as an external 'command', not only the locus of clear and sharp moral teaching, but also the inner life which must now shape and direct all Christian living.[1]

This assessment can of course be merged with Barclay's comments above. Through His incarnation, life, death and resurrection, Jesus has indeed fulfilled Torah; and in entering into His teaching, His life-pattern, and His resurrection life, we too participate in that fulfillment.

In this context, we should also refer back to our notes regarding the Messiah as the new covenant (see pp 20–23, "Eschatology and Covenant," the final section of the "Galatians as Hermeneutics" chapter, above). Given that Paul seems to be assuming the Messiah to be the new covenantal administration and administrator, it therefore becomes quite natural for him to say, *fulfill the law of the Messiah.* From one perspective, this is simply another way of saying, *fulfill the new covenant by following the pattern of the Messiah Himself.* He is the new covenant within which you now live and move and have your being; therefore, bear the burdens of others, just as He has done for you.

These observations are a needed corrective to the notion that the leading of the Spirit is a subjective inner voice that simply comes in place of objective written revelation. For Paul, all Scripture is God-breathed and profitable, not simply for abstract doctrine, but in fact for correction and instruction in righteousness (2 Tim 3:16). It is not true that in being released from Torah as *covenant,* he has repudiated Torah as *Scripture* (cf 4:21). He does, however, reinterpret Torah in the light of the Messiah, who has come in the fullness of time to bring it to eschatological fulfillment.

For if anyone thinks himself to be something, being nothing, fools himself. 6:3

1 Wright, *Paul and the Faithfulness of God,* 1111.

True identity is found in the Messiah. There is the possibility of being identified with the Messiah, the true Son and heir, or of emptiness. Paul has indicated what he thinks of his past life outside of the Messiah (cf Phi 3:7–8); he has crucified the flesh (cf 5:24), and his present life is not in fact his own, but the Messiah's (2:20).

In that light, therefore, those who will not follow in the way of the Messiah, which is the way of the cross, of burden-bearing, clearly think they are above that path, that they "are" something. And so Paul writes, ***For if anyone thinks himself to be something***. The singular construction δοκεῖ τις εἶναί τι, which by itself can mean *seems to be something*, is a plural form of the idiom found in 2:6 (τῶν δοκούντων εἶναί τι). It may be that there is a subtle swipe at the normativity of Jerusalem *insofar as they fail to follow the Messiah*. Even the identity of the Jerusalem pillars can only mean something *in the Messiah*. (Again, recall that at this point, Peter has just caused a mess in Antioch, and Paul is genuinely unsure of where the Jerusalem pillars are "at.")

This stands squarely in the context of *burden-bearing*, for as Peter himself acknowledges shortly hereafter at the Jerusalem council, the yoke of Torah was a burden "which neither our fathers nor we were able to bear" (Acts 15:10). The actions of Peter in Antioch have had the effect of placing that burden onto Gentiles both there and in Galatia. And to that extent, he has failed to follow the Messiah and has become ***nothing***.

The issue, however, goes beyond the pillars in Jerusalem. Paul's primary target now is in Galatia. The false teachers are now explicitly imposing a foreign burden upon the Galatians. Perhaps they consider themselves to be of the stature of Peter, James, or John. But the truth is that they are *nothing*.

Whatever level of intended resonance with 2:6, the upshot more generally is that the one who considers himself above entering into the way of the cross only ***fools himself***. Paul uses a related noun in Tit 1:10 to refer to the "empty talkers and *deceivers*, above all those of the circumcision." Here, however, the deceit in view is *self*-deceit. Conceit is empty because it is based upon a false view of oneself. The one who takes a vaunted view of himself outside of the Messiah is lying to himself, because he has rejected the foundation of meaning and value. The one who is too good for the meek service of the new creation is, ironically, *nothing*.

The one too big to serve is too small to image the Messiah. The servant is not above his Master, and the Messiah took the opposite tack. Although He was in the very form of God, He did not grasp at His privileges, but *made Himself nothing*, embracing the likeness of lowly men, and humbling Himself to the point of the shameful death of the cross (Phi 2:5–8). That very "mind" (Phi 2:5) was in fact the pathway of His exaltation (Phi 2:9–11); and so likewise, the one who truly wants to be "something" must forgo rivalry and conceit, and embrace humility and meekness (Phi 2:3).

> *Now let each prove his own work, and then he will have the boast concern-* 6:4
> *ing himself alone, and not concerning the other.*

Having established the fundamental shape of communal responsibility, Paul moves forward and insists that there is no slackening of personal accountability: ***Now let each prove his own work***. That is, while each is *led by the Spirit* to bear the burdens of others, at the same time he is called upon to test his own work.

This in fact is an implication of the watchfulness and humility enjoined in v 1. Meekness in this context means not only being gentle with the fallen; it entails recognizing the possibility of being impeded in the course of following the Spirit (cf 5:7). In view of that, therefore, humility dictates that one *prove his own work*, constantly bring it to the light of the Messiah's character and test it. This need not be taken as a sort of morbid introspection nor as an anxiety of constantly impending failure. But it does imply that the Spirit-led life is not one led by feeling or by assumption. The person of faith continually brings his life before God and seeks renewal after the image of the Messiah.

The consequential explanation which follows appears obscure at initial glance. If one tests his own work, ***then he will have the boast concerning himself alone, and not concerning the other***. This sounds a lot like the *conceit* that has come under such censure in the preceding.

But of course Paul could scarcely have made such a self-contradiction.

Even were he not Spirit-inspired, the closeness of the context would forbid such a view. It must be acknowledged therefore that the problem is not *boasting* in the abstract. The agitators in Galatia boast wrongly, in the flesh (v 13), but there nonetheless remains a licit boasting in the Lord (cf 1 Cor 1:31).

The sense of the verse as a whole does contain what we need to discern the difference between this boasting and the forbidden boasting of conceit. The idea is not that one only boasts about oneself, and ignores everybody else. It seems to me, rather, that the point is that *a legitimate joy and satisfaction in one's own work can and should be had, but not by way of comparison to the supposed inadequacies of others,* i.e. a competitive spirit. By contrast, the point of conceit is to elevate oneself in comparison to others. As with envy, it can only be exalted by tearing others down.

When it is *yet not I* who lives, but *the Messiah who lives in me,* the excellence I delight in is the glory of the Messiah, and the boast I make is boasting in the Lord. That joy and satisfaction is not smug or self-serving, but delights in the goodness found in the Messiah. It is, at heart, an example of the thankfulness that gives due glory to God.

6:5 *For each shall bear his own cargo.*

The brief affirmation of v 5, ***For each shall bear his own cargo***—customarily translated *burden* or *load*—looks no less problematic than the difficulties encountered in the previous verse. For Paul has taught mutual burden-bearing in v 2, and here he appears to be denying that anyone but the individual himself can bear his own load. Various possible resolutions have been offered,[2] but nothing seems wholly decisive.

It is worth noting, however, that both the term and number for *burden* differs in the two verses (plural of βάρος in v 2; singular φορτίον here). While the usage of the latter term and cognates in the Gospels (Mt 11:30; 23:4; Lk 11:46) appears similar to how Paul has used βάρος in v 2, the only other usage in Paul's own speech is a reference to ship's

2 See e.g. Witherington 428–429.

cargo in Acts 27:10.

It is therefore possible that in v 2, what is to the fore are the various burdens which weigh down and overpower men in weakness from time to time, while here the focus is on something more "cargo-like" that the believer is called upon to take with him on the journey led by the Spirit. This, I think, would fit well with the connection between vv 4–5 (*for,* γὰρ). One should not concern himself with comparisons between his own cargo and that of his neighbour. He has been given a particular work in the kingdom (a "cargo" to carry on the pathway), and his concern should be excellence in that obedience, rather than a spirit of envy or conceit.

Barclay 162 suggests the possibility that the future tense here is eschatological, pointing to the final judgment. If so, *cargo* here could be a similar idea to the money mentioned in Jesus' parable of the talents (Mt 25:15–30).

Even if the sense here is more along the lines of *burden,* however, we should not, in any case, miss the forest for the trees. We know well enough from elsewhere that Paul wants us to embrace a sort of dynamic: I am always called upon to serve others, but I am not called upon to judge them for not serving *me.* I am responsible to others, but at the end of the day, I cannot blame others for not taking responsibility for *me.*

The Consequences of Sowing (6:6–10)

In chapter 5, Paul first speaks of running a race (e.g. 5:7), then subtly shifts his movement metaphor to that of a walk (most clearly, 5:25). Similarly, in 6:6–10, he again picks up an earlier metaphor, that of bearing fruit, and subtly shifts it, so that what is now in view is not fruit on the vine (as in 5:22–26), but the sowing and reaping of grain. In both instances, however, the metaphor is agricultural and is concerned with practical life in the Spirit. There is nonetheless a shift. With the vine imagery of 5:22–26, fruit-bearing is a present result of being led by the Spirit; here, the sowing to the Spirit is with a view to an eschatological harvest.

These two themes are complementary. It is the one who bears fruit who is in fact sowing to the Spirit and can expect to reap; conversely, the one who sows to the flesh instead manifests the works of the flesh (5:19–21), and will from the flesh reap corruption (v 8).

6:6 *Now let the one being taught the word be a partner to the one teaching in all good things.*

The foregoing *law of the Messiah* has taught the partnership involved in the Spirit-led walk. Those in Christ are to enter into one another's burdens and partner with them. Paul now builds upon that principle to articulate a principle of *sowing and reaping*. Notice the parallel between vv 6–10 and 1 Cor 9:3–14.

Paul provides instruction to ***the one being taught the Word***. The deciding factor is *the Word*. Paul would not credit, say, the false teachers in Galatia with this right.

But with regard to *faithful* teachers, the one who is taught is to ***be a partner***. The terminology here, as elsewhere in connection with financial support (Rom 12:13; 15:26; 2 Cor 8:4; 9:13; Phi 4:15 [cf Phi 1:5]; 1 Tim 6:18; Heb 13:16; and probably Acts 2:42), is that of *koinonia* (κοινωνία), although in this instance the verbal form is used.

The biblical idea of *koinonia* is much more robust than what we often mean by our modern renderings such as *fellowship* or the vague *communion*. The focus of the root is *commonality*, and the full term carries the idea of *mutual participation*, of being *partners in common*. Thus here, Paul is saying that just as the teacher of the Word participates in my life through teaching, I participate with him in his life and ministry through giving.

Why does giving come up here? We are not told, but it may be that with the arrival of the false teachers, the faithful teachers whom Paul had appointed (cf Acts 14:23) had become devalued in the eyes of the Galatians, and they were not receiving what they ought.

6:7 *Do not be deceived; God is not mocked: for whatever a man sows, this also he shall reap.*

Having provided a specific instance of sowing into the partnership of the new creation, Paul provides a more general principle: ***Do not be deceived; God is not mocked.***

Paul has already been speaking of self-deception in v 3. The one who refuses to enter into the way of the cross and bear the burdens of others, thinking he is something when he is in fact nothing, is fooling himself. Paul warns again of such self-deception here.

In this case, the self-deceit in view involves making light of God, but *God is not mocked,* i.e. with impunity, without consequences. Ultimately, even man's intended mockery will vindicate His glory.

The term *mocked* (μυκτηρίζω) has the idea of turning up or thumbing the nose (Witherington 431). It appears frequently in the LXX with reference to mocking God or the righteous (e.g. Ps 44:13; 80:6; Prov 1:30). The one who mocks is treating the other as inconsequential. If God Himself is ultimately someone who can be mocked, that indicates that He will not administer consequences to one's own actions.

In view of that, therefore, Paul warns, ***whatever a man sows, this also he shall reap***. The one who invests his life in such a way that offers the pretension of not being answerable to God, from that God, who is not mocked, he will reap the harvest of his folly.

The principle is general, but the thought here has probably not left the realm of participating in the kingdom in a material way. That is what Paul has opened this subsection with in the preceding verse, and vv 9–10 indicate he has not finished with the subject. (On tying sowing and reaping to giving, cf also 1 Cor 9:11; 2 Cor 9:6.) Life eternal cannot be bought—but part of sowing is "putting your money where your mouth is."

The upshot: God is not mocked regarding money.

We modern Western Christians are averse to talking about money in connection with Scripture, and the discomfort is only increased when it is in connection with such a strong passage as this, which declares plainly that there are consequences to how we use our resources. It has been said that in certain circles a man can preach on nearly anything, so long as he stays away from the pocketbook.

You know what is worshiped by determining what is untouchable (Mt 6:24).

6:8 *Because the one sowing into his own flesh, from the flesh shall reap corruption, but the one sowing into the Spirit, from the Spirit shall reap life eternal.*

Barclay 164 notes that the focus here is upon the soil into which the seed is sown. ***The one sowing into his own flesh*** would include circumcision, which is an investment in the realm of flesh. Contrary to Witherington 431, however, who suggests that circumcision is primary here, the immediate context is one of giving (vv 6, 9, 10), although of course the overall principle is broader.

Sowing into the flesh in this connection can be compared to Jesus' statements regarding laying up treasure in heaven by selling what one has and distributing among the poor (Lk 18:22). While there was a particular historical context to that, the reappearance of the principle here indicates that there is an extended, continuing application that should not be overlooked. The one who invests heavily in his own welfare while ignoring the needs of others and those of the kingdom is *sowing into his own flesh*.

The flesh belongs to the old *kosmos* under judgment, and therefore the one who sows upon that ground ***from the flesh shall reap corruption***. The one sowing into the flesh will participate in the eschatological judgment that comes upon flesh. The way of the flesh ends in death (Rom 8:13; cf Rom 6:23), and therefore sowing into the flesh leads to a harvest of death. This is, one may say, Paul's way of "eschatologizing" Hos 8:7: he who sows the wind reaps the whirlwind; he who sows the *kosmos* reaps the cataclysmic judgment upon it. Cf also Prov 22:8 (whoever sows injustice will reap calamity).

Just as there is a flesh-sowing, Paul can speak of ***the one sowing into the Spirit***. I.e. in the near context, by giving in a spiritual way, but more generally, by following the lead of the Spirit as in the preceding chapter. How does one give in a spiritual way? Paul has shown us one way in v 6: becoming partner with those who teach the Word faithfully. He will broaden out the application in vv 9–10 to non-teachers. But at issue is the leading of the Spirit in one's resources. The way of the flesh is to hoard for oneself, but the Spirit leads in the pattern of the Messiah, who emptied Himself to enrich others.

The one who thus follows the Spirit's lead in investing in the new creation ***from the Spirit shall reap life eternal.*** The consequences do not derive from some naturalistic self-contained law (Paul is not advocating some impersonal karma), but from the Spirit Himself. We by the Spirit await the hope of righteousness (5:5).

This is, if you will, the Christic version of "paying it forward": investing in the new creation, even though it is not yet fully within our view.

It is to be emphasized that there is here a clear link between *eternal life*—as well as eternal *corruption*—and *doing*, thus disproving the common notion that Paul's critique of Lev 18:5 in 3:11–12 (as well as Rom 10:5) is due to its linkage of *doing* and *living*. On that score, Paul and Leviticus make the same connection very explicitly.

Nor is this consonance unique to Galatians. In Rom 8:13, Paul speaks of *action* (putting to death the deeds of the body) in connection with *life*, and correspondingly, living according to the flesh brings death. Similarly, 2 Cor 5:10: all will stand before the judgment seat of the Messiah "to receive good or evil, according to the deeds done in the body." Or again, Rom 8:5–6:

> For those who are existing according to the flesh mind the things of the flesh, but those existing according to the Spirit, the things of the Spirit. For the mindset of the flesh is *death,* but the mindset of the Spirit is *life* and peace.

In all of these passages, there is a personalism that entails consequences. Living and doing in terms of the flesh will ultimately bring death, and living and doing according to the Spirit will bring life. Witherington 437 comments,

> In a moral universe, even a moral universe gone wrong, it must be the case that there is some sort of final reckoning or else God is indeed an absentee landlord about whom no one ever need worry … sin, however

> pleasurable in the undertaking, always has consequences, bad consequences even in this lifetime.

The point, again, is not a naturalistic "whatever goes around comes around," but that He who "came around" before "will come around again demanding accountability" (437–438).

6:9 *But let us not become discouraged, those doing the good, for in its own time we shall reap if we do not give up.*

Paul employs the metaphor of patient farming to show that doing good requires patience as well: ***But let us not become discouraged, those doing the good.***

Unlike in natural farming, however, here the harvest is guaranteed, since "God is not mocked" (v 7). He is the guarantor of reaping.

Contrary to certain kinds of "worm theology," Paul assumes here and elsewhere that *doing good* is genuinely possible and has eternal significance (cf Rom 2:6, 7, 10). The thought is used in a similar material sense in 2 Cor 9:8 ("abound to every good work").

All long-term commitments are susceptible to "getting old," and financial commitments not the least among them. (On not growing weary of financial giving, cf also 2 Thess 3:13.) So Paul provides encouragement here, not simply by a verbal warning against discouragement, but by the supporting argument, ***for in its own time we shall reap if we do not give up***. Just as a farmer cannot expect to see a crop on the day he starts to sow seed into the ground, so neither should we become discouraged by the waiting which faith requires. The hope of righteousness, and all the things given with it, will come *in its own time,* the time of eschatological harvest.

But we can only partake of that reaping *if we do not give up*. The one who reaps is the one who is led by the Spirit all the way into the new creation.

6:10 *Therefore, as we have occasion, let us do the good to all, but especially to the household members of the faith.*

The sowing to the Spirit is a universal calling, and it is a full-orbed calling. It is not, however, an *impossible* calling, and with reference to material support of others, it is ***as we have occasion***. There is neither means nor opportunity for each of us to provide for everyone, but we can do good within our sphere and resources. Both our context and our resources are divinely entrusted to us to provide an occasion for doing good.

Within those constraints of occasion and resources, the mandate is for us to ***do the good to all***. God Himself sends His rain and sunshine upon the good and evil alike (Mt 5:45), and we are to be "complete" (τέλειός) even as He is complete (Mt 5:48). The *law of the Messiah* was embodied in His own ministry in that He *endured hostility against Himself at the hands of sinners;* and in like manner we are not to be discouraged nor faint in our own living (Heb 12:3).

While doing good to all is a participation in the Messiah's mission to the world, there is a different kind of relationship, an ***especially***, to those who are ***the household members of the faith***. The phrase of course is consonant with the familial metaphor so pervasive earlier in the letter; believers are *sons of God* and *sons of Abraham* by virtue of having been clothed with *the* Son, and therefore together are one household. (Cf the phrase *house of Israel* throughout the OT.)

Commitment to doing good *especially* to this household (as Paul says) is important not only for witness to the world (cf Jn 13:35), but because this is, after all, *your family*. As Calvin puts it, "Our common humanity makes us debtors to all; but we are bound to believers by a closer spiritual kinship, which God hallows among us."

Conclusion (6:11–18)

See, how large a letter/letters I have written to you by my own hand! 6:11

Paul now commences his closing. Whether he is intending ***See**, how large a letter I have written to you by my own hand* (as taken by older translators, e.g. KJV) or ***how large letters I have written***, the overall primary significance would appear to be the same. Paul is underscoring the urgency with which he has approached the situation; even without an amanuensis, he has immediately taken up writing a quite lengthy letter himself. (Even if, on a third view, Paul takes up the pen only *here,* writing the closing words with his own hand, the attention he draws to it would likewise emphasize urgency.)

Witherington 440 mentions two arguments against the referent *letter* rather than the size of the glyphs he wrote: (1) following Lightfoot, a different grammatical form is expected; (2) Paul usually employs ἐπιστολή to refer to epistles, not γράμμα.[3]

6:12 *As many as wish to make a good showing in the flesh, these are compelling you to be circumcised, only in order that for the cross of the Messiah, they may not be persecuted.*

Paul is in his closing section, but he is not done referring to the main point, which is not unusual for him. He refers to the false teachers as those who ***wish to make a good showing in the flesh***.

The term *make a good showing* (εὐπροσωπῆσαι) appears only here in the NT, and is etymologically similar to the English phrase *putting a good face on it.* Perhaps Paul is subtly making an amusing and ironic point regarding putting a good face on the genitals, which are normally private and unseen—another jab at circumcision.

As throughout, there is double entendre with the phrase *in the flesh.* The term refers to Paul's general metaphor for the old creation, but also more specifically to the flesh of the foreskin, picking up on Gen 17 as well as Leviticus. (Cf Leithart, *The Glory of Kings* 63: "In the purity laws of Leviticus 15, 'flesh' refers specifically to the sexual organs, from which defiling issues flow.")

These teachers who are flesh-oriented and respecters of the faces

3 It should be noted, however, that the *to you* (ὑμῖν) is positioned diagrammatically in relationship, not to the verb (thus *I have written to you*) but the noun (thus *a letter to you*), which perhaps seems unnatural on Lightfoot's reading (*oversized letters-to-you?*). Although it may be objected that by Paul's standards, this epistle is not long, it is likely that he usually employed an amanuensis, and so the lengthiness he mentions could be in consideration of the fact that he has written by *my own hand.*

of foreskins[4] are ***compelling you to be circumcised***. Paul has used the language of compulsion (ἀναγκάζω) earlier; by his withdrawal from table fellowship with Gentiles at Antioch, Peter had implicitly compelled them to live as Jews (2:14). In Galatia, of course, the compulsion was more direct.

The teachers' compulsion is not simply out of pure zeal for Torah; it is applied ***in order that they may not be persecuted for the cross of the Messiah***. Paul has quietly implied as much in 5:11 (where Paul asks why he is still being persecuted if he preaches circumcision, and asserts that in that case, the offense of the cross has ceased); here he states so explicitly. It is appropriate to note that this verse again illustrates that the matter at hand is not about a "ladder-climbing" theology.

For neither the ones being circumcised themselves keep the law, but they 6:13
wish you to be circumcised, so that they may boast in your flesh.

Now we learn more about ***the ones circumcised***; they ***do not themselves keep the law***. Here Paul is doubtless alluding back to 5:3, where he has informed the Galatians that if they become circumcised, they will be duty bound to observe the entire Torah. It now becomes apparent that the teachers themselves were only partially Torah-observant. We are not told where their observance ended; it may be that they kept everything short of the "sacrificial" end of the bargain. After all, it does appear indisputable that they were Messiah-believers of sorts (as were the people who caused trouble in Antioch).

I have translated περιτεμνόμενοι (BNT) / περιτετμημένοι (Byz) here as *the ones circumcised*, but some interpreters suggest that the BNT's present passive participle may indicate that the teachers are not themselves native Jews, but Gentiles who have become circumcised.

The Byz perfect participle, however, would not allow that reading, and most commentators do not take that route, either, providing

4 Etymologically, Greek terms with the general meaning of *partiality* quite literally work into English as *receiving a face* or *regarding a face*. In Galatians, see 2:6—*God does not receive the face of a man* (πρόσωπον [ὁ] θεὸς ἀνθρώπου οὐ λαμβάνει).

varying rationales for the present tense.[5]

The assertion that the teachers *do not themselves keep the law* is sometimes taken to mean that they didn't *really* keep the law, but fell short of its spiritual requirements. But such a thought is not appropriate to the context. Given what Paul has just said in v 12, it rather seems to be the case that the teachers were trying to go partway with Torah to appease their fellow Jews. It would have been one thing for the teachers to be nonobservant with reference to various details of Torah—a fact that may have been hidden from their unbelieving kinsmen—but it would have been quite another if they were known to be consorting regularly with uncircumcised Gentiles.

Thus, they put pressure on the Galatian Gentiles to become circumcised, ***so that they may boast in your flesh***. If their pressure succeeded, the teachers could boast to their fellow Jews of their triumph, and the similarity of their own faith to that of other Jews would (they hoped) keep them from being persecuted.

Timothy George 433–434 helpfully points to the Saul–David story of 1 Sam 18: Saul demanded from David the price of 100 Philistine foreskins as the price for giving Michal as wife. Here, the false teachers are ostensibly playing the role of David, collecting foreskins to please their fellow Jews. As earlier with Saul's initial similarity to Esau (see on 1:13), here again there is a role reversal. The new Saul no longer demands foreskins, because he has become the servant of the Greater David.

As in v 12, *in your flesh* carries the overtones both of the flesh of the foreskin directly, and Paul's extended flesh metaphor.

6:14 *But it is impossible for me to boast, except in the cross of our Lord Jesus, the Messiah, through which the world has been crucified to me, and I to the world.*

Over against the boasting of the false teachers stands Paul: ***But it is impossible for me to boast, except in the cross of our Lord Jesus, the***

5 Bruce 270 takes the participle as "middle voice with causative significance," thus referring, not to the teachers' own circumcision, but to their compulsion of the Galatians to be circumcised.

Messiah. This statement is very similar to 1 Cor 2:2, which also comes in the context of a boasting theme (1 Cor 1:29, 31).

The *impossible* is Paul's standard exclamation (frequently translated *God forbid!*), but whereas the construction is generally an interjection, here he incorporates it into a sentence. Although in sentence form, the forcefulness of the interjection should be retained here.

Insightfully, Garlington 285–286 draws attention to Paul's use here of Jer 9:23–24. Not only does this text instruct wise men not to boast in their wisdom or strong men in their strength, but rather to boast in the knowledge of YHWH; what immediately follows is a promise of punishment of "all who are circumcised only in the flesh: Egypt, *Judah,* Edom, Ammon, Moab, and all who live in the desert in distant places. For all these nations are really uncircumcised, and the whole house of Israel is uncircumcised in heart" (Jer 9:25–26; cf Rom 2:25–29).

The Jeremiah allusion teaches us that knowing Yahweh means knowing Jesus, and even more specifically, knowing Jesus as the one who has been crucified. The knowledge of God and boasting in Him is bound up with the ignominious cross. In place of boasting in *sarx,* Paul advocates boasting in the scandal of God (cf the Messiah as stumbling stone and rock of offense).

In the words of Isaac Watts, "Forbid it, Lord, that I should boast, save in the death of Christ, my God."

It is *through the cross*[6] that ***the world has been crucified to me.*** The death of the Messiah is global in its scope and entails the death of the old *kosmos.* However, this death of the old creation for the time being is very specific—it is not simply dead and gone; it is dead *to me.* The *kosmos* still awaits the final judgment when all things will be made new.

This is a broader (and less cryptic) statement correlating to 2:19: *through Torah I died to Torah.* Just as Torah imposed the cross upon the Messiah and thus ironically brought liberation from itself, so the cross as the most cruel instrument of the *kosmos* becomes instead the unwitting agent of the Messiah's liberation from *this present evil age* into the new creation. To further the parallel, 2:20 likewise has the thought of

6 Or perhaps, *through the Messiah;* either is a possible understanding of the Greek masculine pronoun. In any case, one implies the other in this context.

being *crucified with the Messiah.*

Again the link to 4:4–5 is implied: back of being *born under Torah,* the Messiah was *born from a woman* and therefore into the *kosmos.* His redemption is not simply for Jews, granting release from Torah, but for the nations, granting release from τὰ στοιχεῖα τοῦ κόσμου, the *elements of the world* (4:3). Through the cross, the Messiah has brought rescue from bondage to the old *kosmos.*

If as far as Paul is concerned, the world is dead, the feeling is mutual: *the world has been crucified to me,* ***and I to the world.*** In our present religious context with its emphasis on individual salvation, this side of the equation is a bit more familiar. By dying with the Messiah I am dead to *the world.* As in 2:19–20, "I-in-*kosmos*" no longer lives; the Messiah, the One who has been crucified and raised into the new creation, the new *kosmos,* lives in me.

6:15 *For [in the Messiah, Jesus] neither circumcision is [Byz effectual for] anything, nor uncircumcision, but [a] new creation.*

Paul adds, ***[in the Messiah, Jesus] neither circumcision is [effectual for] anything, nor uncircumcision.*** There is a slight difference again here between BNT and Byz texts, but it is not exegetically significant, since what the Byz texts have included is implicit in any case.

The pairing *circumcision* and *uncircumcision* is placed under the heading of *kosmos* by the previous verse; they are Torah-categories, and Torah is part of the *stoicheia* of the *kosmos* (*elements of the world*), according to 4:3ff. As the constitutive elements of a weak age, so weak that for Paul it is dead (cf v 14), they themselves are not strong or effectual.

Note that it is not simply *circumcision* which is insignificant and ineffectual. So is *uncircumcision.* But the circumcision–uncircumcision pairing itself is Torah-determined; it is significant only within the setting of the *kosmos.* Therefore, there is no more ground to remove the marks of an earlier circumcision than there is to get circumcised now (see 1 Cor 7:18).

What *is* significant and powerful is rather a ***new creation.*** Not merely *a new creature,* as some older versions had it, as if Paul's concern were primarily the spiritual renovation of individuals. No, Paul is making a contrast between the old *kosmos* and the new; the scale is *cosmological,* if you will. Thus it is not merely new creatures, but *a whole new creation* which emerges on the other side of the crucifixion of the *kosmos.* Cf 2 Cor 5:17.

Paul's point therefore is that what is powerful ("effectual") is not what is evident to the *kosmos* and those who belong to it—a healthy antidote for believers when they are tempted to look around in despair at the circumstances of the world. The *kosmos* was nailed to the Messiah's cross, and even though it is still visible to our eyes, its rule is merely *de facto* and its days are numbered. The real power is in the new creation, whose Spirit we have received as a down payment.

In 2 Corinthians 4–5, Paul outlines the now-and-not-yet character of the new creation. The outer man is wasting away, but the inner man is being renewed day by day. If anyone is in the Messiah, there is indeed a whole new creation—yet, he is still surrounded by the old creation.

And as many as walk by this rule, peace upon them, and mercy—and upon 6:16
the Israel of God.

Paul offers a benediction upon ***as many as walk by this rule***. The *rule* (κανών) could refer to a *sphere,* thus *as many as walk in this realm,* i.e. *within the new creation,* but at any rate, the reading of *canon* as *rule* has similar implications.[7] The benediction is upon those who follow the Spirit's leading according to the primacy of the new creation rather than that of the old *kosmos.*

The benediction provides a bookend at the end of the letter corresponding to the anathema at the beginning (1:8, 9). The new creation gospel which Paul warns against perverting is the good news of new creation in the Messiah.

The reference to *walk* again picks up on the themes of running, walking and being led which dominated chapter 5; of particular note are 5:18 (*if you are led by the Spirit, you are not under Torah*) and 5:25 (*if*

7 Interestingly, Josephus calls the Torah by the same name in *Ag. Ap.* 2.174 (cited in Garlington 292–293).

we live in the Spirit, let us also walk in the Spirit).

The blessing pronounced is ***peace upon them, and mercy***. Peace is new creation *shalom*, and along with the opening blessing (1:3) is also listed as a characteristic of *the fruit of the Spirit* (5:22). Those who live by the sword will die by it, and those who live by peace will receive the life that peace brings. Here in particular *peace* stands in contrast to the division and schism which the false teachers have been stirring up.

Mercy is apparently equivalent to Heb *chesed:* God's covenant faithfulness and lovingkindness. This is now connected, not to Torah, but to the covenant of the new creation—to the Messiah. On the connection of new creation, peace, and mercy, see especially Isa 54:10 as well as Ps 85, in particular v 10.

The appended recipients of the benediction, ***and upon the Israel of God***, are a matter of considerable exegetical disagreement. The phrase is often taken as epexegetical, essentially standing in for the faithful Church of Jesus Christ, Jew and Gentile.

While Paul frequently ascribes Israel-characteristics to the Church, however, this would be the only instance of him actually calling Gentile Christians *Israel*. Not an impossible objection to overcome, but it may be that Paul is instead putting the stress on *of God* and referring to genuine believing Jews—in particular, those who walk straightly with the truth of the gospel by living in unity with their Gentile brothers. This group then would be defined over against *false brothers* (cf 2:4) such as the teachers. This usage is analogous to Paul's concern for *the poor* in 2:10, which is not likely a general reference to the poor, but to *the poor saints in Judea*.[8] Israel as a whole can no longer be described as the Israel *of God*, but those among Israel who have followed the leading of His Spirit and embraced His Son—and their fellow heirs, the Gentiles *in Christ*—are His.

This distinction fits well with Paul's overall purpose.[9] By this implic-

8 Cf Marius Victorinus (cited in Bruce 274): "not 'on Israel' in the sense of any and every Jew, but 'on the Lord's Israel'; for Israel is truly the Lord's if it follows the Lord, not expecting its salvation from any other source."

9 Against Wright, *Paul and the Faithfulness of God* 1151, who essentially claims that any position not equating *Israel of God* here with the whole of the Jew-Gentile church makes "nonsense of the whole letter." To be sure, a generic benediction upon Jews

it exclusion of the teachers and other Jews like them, he subverts their message, which was based on the supposed necessity of the Galatian Gentiles becoming circumcised in order to become members of Israel. In fact, however, they themselves are not part of the Israel that matters—*God's* Israel.[10]

At any rate, the benedictory structure here is familiar, particularly in several Psalms (125:5 [124:5 LXX]; 128:6 [127:6]: peace upon Israel. In addition, the Eighteen Benedictions say, "May peace ... and mercy ... be upon us and upon all Israel thy people."[11] Following Hubbard, Garlington 294 also points out the contrast between *Israel of God* here and Paul's language elsewhere of *Israel according to the flesh* (see 1 Cor 10:18; Rom 2:28–29; 9:3, 6 etc). There is clearly an implied contrast to the false Israel, the "Israel not-of-God," represented by the false teachers in Galatia.

From now on, let no one cause me trouble: for I myself bear the identifying 6:17
scars of [the Lord] Jesus in my body.

Paul alludes to the trial arising from his deep concern for the churches (cf 2 Cor 11:28) by writing, ***From now on, let no one cause me trouble***. The opening phrase, Τοῦ λοιποῦ, is apparently used adverbially as a reference to time.

In contrast to the false teachers, who compelled circumcision in order to avoid persecution themselves, Paul says, ***I myself bear the identifying scars of*** [Byz ***the Lord***] ***Jesus in my body***. The term I have translated as *identifying scars*[12] can refer to *branding*, indicating ownership. Paul's body bears the marks of the sort of persecution (such as the stoning in Lystra, Acts 14:19) avoided by the false teachers, and thus he shares in the Messiah's own sufferings. Paul has no identity crisis; he is branded with the scars of Jesus. Just as Jesus retains scars in His hands,

would be quite incomprehensible in this context. But to make a pointed reference to *believing Jews who are embracing Paul's vision of new creation* is another matter entirely.

10 For related thoughts on the phrase *the Israel of God*, see the Excursus: Jacob and Paul at the Exposition for 1:13, above.

11 Whether this antedates Paul, however, is open to dispute.

12 Στίγματα, plural form of the Greek word from which we derive *stigma*.

feet and side, so His servant has scars that mark him as one who has borne with the death throes of the old creation, for the sake of the birth of the new.

Wright (*Paul for Everyone* 81) points to the telling contrast to the mark the teachers were focusing on: circumcision. "If it's bodily marks you want, it is the signs of the cross, not of the circumciser's knife, that matter; and the signs of the cross are the marks of persecution, the 'wounds of Jesus.'"

It is surely no accident that Paul uses the language of *bear* (βαστάζω) here. Just as he has called upon those *led by the Spirit* to *bear the burdens of one another, thus fulfilling the law of the Messiah* (v 2), he claims to be *bearing* the burden of the Messiah's suffering. Here, the burden carried is not that of one caught in transgression or the struggles of weakness, but the privilege of being identified with Jesus. (Cf Paul's goal in Phi 3:10, not only to know the Messiah and the power of His resurrection, but also to share His sufferings, becoming like Him in His death.)

This is a badge which the false teachers refuse to carry, and one in which Paul boasts (2 Cor 12:5, 9), over against their boast *in the flesh* (v 13). They boast in a mark in the flesh that will salvage their reputation and secure them from persecution; he boasts in the marks in his flesh that demonstrate he has embraced the shame of the cross.

6:18 *The grace of our Lord Jesus, the Messiah [be] with your spirit, brothers. Amen.*

Paul's common benedictory formula, ***The grace of our Lord Jesus, the Messiah***, carries particular resonance in the context of a letter such as this. It is the grace from which the Galatians have been turning (1:6), and away from which they have been falling (5:4). It is the grace of God which brings righteousness apart from Torah (2:21). It is this grace with which Paul stamps them, and by which he claims them.

Paul's formula here is that this grace ***be with your spirit, brothers***. The address to *your spirit* is relatively rare in his benedictions, but cf 2 Tim 4:22; Phlm 25. Apart from benedictions, Paul indicates that *spirit* is the agency or means of "absent presence," e.g. in Col 2:5, Paul says he is with the Colossians in spirit; in 1 Cor 5:4, he calls for discipline to occur when you are assembled in the name of the Lord Jesus "and my spirit is present."

This is, after all, a letter to *brothers*. The Galatians are not beyond hope, and by the grace he has just pronounced, Paul's faith is that they will walk forward with him, *led by the Spirit* as fellow sons of Abraham.

Amen.

Epilogue

NUMEROUS MODERN SCHOLARS HAVE SUGGESTED that neither Paul's conflict with Peter nor the matter in Galatia were resolved to his satisfaction. The coherence we have seen between Galatians and Acts indicates otherwise.[1] Peter probably echoes Paul's rebuke (Gal 2:16–17) in his speech at the Jerusalem council (Acts 15:10–11), and if my reading is correct, Paul's return with the Jerusalem letter to the churches in Derbe, Lystra, Iconium, and the surrounding area results in the strengthening and growth of those churches (Acts 16:1–5), not rejection or alienation.

There were certainly matters of division in the early churches (see not least, 1 Corinthians). But the recent cynicism that posits an irreconcilable and ultimate rift between Peter and Paul cannot be sustained. While Peter at various times wavered in his practice, he shared Paul's vision; it was his own conviction that God gave Gentiles the Holy Spirit on the same terms and on equal footing as He did to Jews (Acts 11:17; 15:7–9).

Paul and Peter, the confrontation recorded in Galatians 2 notwithstanding, were allies in the larger picture. The same God who entrusted the gospel of the circumcision to the one also entrusted the gospel of the uncircumcision to the other, and together with the other apostles and prophets, they laid the foundation upon which the Messiah's Church has ever stood (cf Eph 2:20).

The epilogue to this letter, however, is still being written by those who read and obey it, as well as by those who misunderstand it or resist its teaching. It is therefore appropriate here to offer a few summary reflections upon the practical import of what we have learned.

It is true that, other than in a few "Messianic Jewish" circles, the central temptations in Galatia are not directly the temptations faced by modern Christendom. Although it is rather trendy among a number of

1 Along with "Galatians as Biography" in the introductory material, see also Appendix 2, "Chronological Table."

Western Christians to observe aspects of Passover, by and large modern Gentile believers are not under the pressure to circumcise and observe Torah that the Galatians were. In this setting, it may be wondered if sticking so closely to the historical context as I have attempted to do can really serve us with anything much usable.

However, beyond the perhaps relatively obvious implications of the parenetic section running from Gal 5:16–26, I think there are a number of crucial principles which Paul expounds in Galatians that are important, not only to the crisis he himself faced, but to our own generation.

The Unity of the Whole Body in the Messiah

Paul's expression of solidarity among those clothed with the Messiah is an attack upon any notion of a hierarchy of privileges; that certain people are granted more closeness to God than others, no matter what their role in life may be.

This principle stands against many temptations which perennially plague the Church, from clericalism (putting the ordained on a pedestal), to racism (a denial that there is neither Greek nor Jew),[2] to classism of various sorts (a bending to the world's notions of what is "cool," for instance).

The first two of these battles are still being fought. However, it is the latter, in particular, which has now become the acceptable form of earlier kinds of discrimination against others. In many regions, it was once thought normal for Caucasians to despise African-Americans (and Africans in general), but for the most part, this is no longer the case. The plague of racism still exists in the West, of course, even in the Church; but it widely receives just condemnation when it openly raises its head. More can and must be done, but we are not where we were just short decades ago.

All too often, however, one form of flesh-based superiority is simply exchanged for another, which shows that the heart of the issue remains.

2 While it may well be objected that Galatians is not about racism as such, but rather about Torah's defining role, it must be noted that elsewhere Paul extends his principle of Gal 3:28 well beyond matters relating to circumcision and Torah; see especially Col 3:11.

Despising people for their financial status, social class, or their inability to be "cool" (as evident by their failure to buy Apple products, their outdated clothing styles, their less-than-hip taste in music, or whatever) may appear to be innocuous in comparison to the old racism that cost a lot of people their lives, families and well-being. But from the viewpoint of the Messiah's new creation, it is *not* innocuous. Rather, it is another form of the divisions wrought by the flesh, governed by the powers and elements of an old *kosmos* under judgment. Under its hegemony countless wounds are administered and suffered in the Church of Jesus Christ. It is high time that the members of the body affirmed their solidarity with one another and put away the fissures and schisms of what amounts to class warfare.

Courage for Communion

Peter had no difficulty being "a Jew to the Jews" (cf 1 Cor 9:20). He had more difficulty living in full fellowship with his fellow believers who were Gentiles in circumstances where other Jews with a different *ethos* were present. He allowed their position, based in error, to trump the full standing of the Messiah's people among the *goyim*.

We are not all that different from Peter. We too find it much easier to be "a member of the white middle class to the white middle class"—or whatever we are by heritage and natural connection—than we do to fully enflesh the gospel beyond our native habitat.

Thus, although Peter's particular temptation is rare, we need to consider parallel situations where modern believers sacrifice full acceptance of fellow Christians due to pressure from others—pressures which should be resisted rather than followed.

This issue is of course similar to the previous one, but in this case, it arises not so much from one's *own* theological errors or prejudices, but from *fear of others*. Friends, for example, may think themselves above other ethnic groups or social classes, and therefore to "hang" with them requires practically repudiating full fellowship with the people they look down upon.

That desire for acceptance from "my" group at the cost of maintaining the unity and integrity of the Messiah's people is again rooted in what Paul terms *flesh,* and today's Christians must learn to fear God rather than men. The biblical example requires that we stand with God's accepted "outsiders" even if it puts full fellowship with "Peter" at risk for the time being.

The New Creation *Ethos*

Paul's analogy between Torah's calendar and the similar forms of living that were common to contemporary idolatries indicates that this is not simply a matter of *substance* (which matters) *versus form* (which does not).

We must be careful here. It is indeed dangerous on the one hand to "spiritualize" Christian faith into the invisible realm, opposing all ritual as "unspiritual" (something which Paul, with his emphasis on baptism, certainly does not do). At the same time, it is likewise dangerous to make the opposite error, supposing that so long as our rituals are ostensibly in the name of Christ, they are fine.

For Paul, life in the old *kosmos* takes a certain shape and is recognized by various definable elements, and it is not an indifferent matter to attempt to make Christianity look just like that old *kosmos* life, only with a different kernel at the core. That radical disjunction between kernel and husk is just as Gnostic as is a "hyper-spiritualizing" tendency.

In Galatians, the Jewish calendar is the occasion for Paul's remarks, and so it is suitable for us to draw attention to modern analogies with the Church calendar (while also observing that there may be many other instances where the same principle should be reflected upon and applied).

While a Christian calendar may be genuinely helpful, one must be wary of the tendency to turn such observances into holy days. They are *not* holy days, and *cannot* be. Living life in the mature new creation should not have the same feel as living life under the governance of a child custodian, no matter how we may baptize the rules in question.

The Breadth & Depth of Being in the Messiah

In view of our findings in Galatians, I believe we need to reflect further upon Paul's *in Christ* language than is usually done. What He accomplished outside of us, in salvation history, is decisive and fundamental to our existence. But for Paul, faith is not the passive affirmation of an onlooker considering something that happened in the past.

Jesus the Messiah is the crucified One, but He is also the risen one, and through the Spirit, the believer has genuine access to the living *pistis* of the Messiah (2:20), from which he is to draw strength to walk in the same pattern the Messiah Himself did.

While it is necessary to avoid subjectivism and hyper-pietism, it is equally necessary to avoid either a merely cerebral view of faith, or an active view that yet discounts the Messiah's ongoing role in the believer's life. The saving faith which Paul describes is not a mere detached affirmation of Christ's past deeds, but a vital leaning upon Him in such a way that one is led by the Spirit and thus produces the fruit of love. Jesus is the vine from which we as branches draw life, and we are connected, not merely judicially to his death, but really and truly to His ongoing resurrection life. Call it covenant, call it mysticism or whatever you like—but live every day of your life in the flesh by the faith of the Son of God, who loved you and gave Himself for you.

Pocketbook Partnership

It is an interesting—and telling—fact that one of the predominant usages of the *koinonia* language in the NT (including in Galatians) is directly about financial partnership, and yet this gets virtually no attention in a great deal of modern discussion about "fellowship." Paul's twin principles of eschatological transition (movement from *this present evil age* to new creation) and of the solidarity of those in the Messiah both contribute to what he writes regarding sowing and reaping in 6:6–10. That entire discussion is triggered and determined by references to sharing materially. Because those in the Messiah have been transferred from the old *kosmos* (1:4), their investments are to be in the new creation; and similarly, because they have been identified with an Abrahamic family which shares its identity in Christ (3:29), their giving is to be conditioned and shaped by the reality of belonging to a common household (cf 6:10).

These principles and mandates are in some ways nearly surreal for us, living as we are within what is surely the most consumerist culture in history. Contrary to *nouveau* liberation theologians, the point is not a "critique of capitalism" (where in fact said critiques are nearly always every bit as based in a materialist worldview as that which is critiqued, if not more so), but rather the new responsibilities that arise from being transplanted from one citizenship to another; responsibilities that bind us to the advancement of the eschatological kingdom and to partnership (especially, but not exclusively) with those who share with us a new identity in the Messiah.

Owning this viewpoint requires that we get beyond the at best heterodox notion that the Christian faith is unearthly, internal and "personal" in a private sort of sense. The cross of the Messiah was a public event, and it calls the people of the Messiah to a public faith, and to a faith that travels by way of events in real time, sharing one another's sufferings and strengthening one another's hands.

Preaching a Multivalent Gospel

Finally, I want to reflect briefly and very tendentiously on the kerygmatic implications of the overturning of the Puritanesque notion of smashing people under the law in order to drive them to Christ for relief, which was based on a very wrong reading of Gal 3:24.

We are emerging from a period in the West where the assumptions even of unbelievers were governed to a great degree by a particular worldview, one which revolved greatly around the notion of legally-defined guilt. This heritage was a mixed blessing. The Bible most emphatically does have a very strong guilt and grace theme near to its heart, and the Western worldview was in some important respects a way of getting at that.

Nonetheless, we should not overlook the fact that the Bible's presentation of the saving work of the Messiah is not merely a story of jurisprudence, and working almost solely within the paradigm of forensic guilt not only distorts the overall biblical message; it contracts the kerygmatic possibilities of the genuine gospel. In other words, focusing exclusively on guilt shrinks the gospel and limits opportunities for the message of Jesus to be applied to the world He confronts.

Lest it be thought this is an exaggeration, we should study, and meditate upon, the apostolic preaching recorded for us in the Book of Acts. In Paul's preaching to the Gentiles, for instance, he never draws them to the law in order to drive them to the gospel. He is able to speak from a different paradigm, but no less decisively. Consider his discourse in Athens: the apostle exposes the folly of Gentile worship; appeals to the creative authority and goodness of God; and announces Jesus as the resurrected King who will judge the world (Acts 17:22–31).[3]

Is there implied guilt in this sermon? Certainly. God is in charge, and His appointed King is going to judge everybody. But there is no appeal to the law; nor is there any effort to force the hearers into some drawn-out Augustinian angst. The message fundamentally amounts to this: "You're worshiping the wrong gods, and serving the wrong king. The God who created all things, including men, has conquered death by the agency of the resurrected Man who will judge the world."

Embedded within this is not a decontextualized rubbing-their-noses-in-their-guilt, but a creational and eschatological call to turn to the true and good God and serve His invincible King who has conquered death itself and therefore has the power of universal judgment. This addresses men in their individual sins, but in doing so it addresses them as political and social beings; the sermon challenges the pretensions of Caesar every bit as much as it challenges the autonomy of the individual.

The point in this exercise is not so much to insist that we study Paul's sermon in Athens and "Go and do likewise"—although that indeed would be much better than we frequently do, and would surely be helpful in reflecting how better to preach the gospel to an unchurched culture.

But my concern rather is to suggest that we need to revisit our assumptions regarding the "proper" controlling metaphors and

3 This sermon is fully consonant with what is recorded of how Paul spoke to Galatian Gentiles. See Acts 14:14–17, although it is probably saying too much to identify this as a "sermon." Even Paul's preaching to Jews, however, is not based on an appeal to law-defined guilt, but rather consists of a salvation-historical message whose goal is to proclaim Jesus as the Messiah (Acts 13:16–41). Even in Peter's sermon in Acts 2, which is quite strongly guilt-oriented, the guilt in view is not failure to live up to the law, but the guilt of rejecting and murdering God's Messiah.

paradigms of the Christian kerygma. The study of Paul's letter to the Galatians teaches us that he can say a great deal about the gospel for long stretches without at every point bringing things back to where we Western Christians generally bring things back to. The redemption of the Messiah is of cosmological breadth and covenantal depth, and the more we come to appreciate that, the more readily we will be fitted for proclaiming His salvation to all men.

APPENDIX 1

The Reverse of Ebal in Gal 3:10–14[1]

IN POPULAR READING, GALATIANS 3:10–13 is essentially to be read this way: "Those who self-righteously lean on their own works are accursed, because they can never be good enough. No one is right with God by works, but by faith. Doing good works for salvation will result in death. But Christ freed us from the curse by becoming a curse for us in His death."

Despite the prevalence of this reading, however, it suffers from a number of flaws.

1. Paul simply never says that he is speaking of those who are self-righteously relying upon their own works. That much cannot be sustained by the actual words of the text, which merely affirms that those who are of works of the law are under a curse. Given that all Israel was to be characterized by Torah obedience, surely the natural reading of the phrase "all those who are of works of the law" is simply: those who are under the Mosaic covenant.[2]
2. Under this reading, a self-conscious integration of verses 10 and 13 would mean that in the latter verse, Paul is saying that Christ's death was for the purpose of redeeming those who were self-righteously relying upon their own works—a point which seems rather odd for Paul to be making, to say the least.
3. The required unstated premise is that no one perfectly fulfills

1 This appendix is an elaboration and further development of work I did on Gal 3:10–14 in *These Are Two Covenants*. See, in particular, 22–26, 61–66. For further discussion, see the relevant section in the Exposition.

2 On *nomos* (law) as a reference to the Mosaic covenant, see e.g. *Two Covenants*, 12–16.

> the requirements of Torah, but so far as the biblical texts to which Paul appeals go, there is no such thought of sinless perfection—a notion which simply does not arise in the law. Moreover, the OT itself indicates that at least at times, the requirements of Torah were kept by real human beings (2 Chron 34:32), in contrast to those who did not keep them (2 Chron 34:21).

The Corporate Alternative

In more recent years, others have attempted to get around these difficulties by arguing that in 3:10, Paul is not speaking of individual condemnation, but of the fact that Israel as a whole still labours under the curse of exile.[3]

This approach has not gained widespread acceptance, and in my judgment it does not fit sufficiently well into Paul's surrounding narrative[4] nor make satisfactory sense of the verse itself.

It is true that the Old Testament prophesies in numerous places that Israel would wander away from Yahweh and suffer judgment, and it is also true that the corporate plight of Israel is in fact a theme that concerns Paul.

In the instance here, however, he is not working along those lines. Rather, Paul cites the covenant formalization ceremony of Mounts Ebal and Gerizim, and both the quoted text (Deut 27:26) and related passages dealing with that ceremony all primarily have to do with the effect of individual disobedience to and apostasy from Torah. It is in the succeeding chapters (Deut 28ff) that the corporate element comes to the fore.

Moreover, the term *all* in Deut 27:26 is not a collective referring to

---

3 This is argued most notably by N. T. Wright; see e.g. *Climax of the Covenant* 142: "It is a matter of the life of the nation as a whole." Cf Wright, *Paul and the Faithfulness of God*, 863–867.

4 While Paul does discuss a corporate plight later in the chapter, that plight is not about exile, but a plight of being under Sin itself, and indeed of being confined under Torah itself. In other words, in this context Paul is not particularly concerned about the consequences of Israel's apostasies, but rather with the shape of her life under Torah.`

"all Israel" (cf Rom 11:26); the LXX's singular pronoun *hos* (ὅς) dictates that *pas* (πᾶς) is to be taken in the sense of "each." "Cursed is *each one* who does not remain in all the things written in the Book of Torah, to do them."

Therefore, the cursing in view here is not simply what Israel would experience from time to time under national judgment, but what comes upon any Israelite at any time who would apostatize from the terms of the Mosaic covenant.

Role Reversal

Recognizing these difficulties, Garlington has suggested that the issue is one of *role reversal.* Over against Abraham and his blessing, the Judaizers "have severed their connections with the patriarch by virtue of their preference for the Mosaic period" (*Galatians* 143). Garlington suggests that Paul, rather ironically, charges the circumcision party with the apostasy warned against in Deut 27:26, the supporting passage which Paul cites. Because Paul's own biography has been "reversed," he recognizes that zeal for the Messiah now comes in place of zeal for Torah. Therefore Deut 27:26 (and the other passages cited in 3:10–13) is being reinterpreted to refer, not to loyalty to Torah, but to apostasy from God through the refusal to follow Christ ("Role Reversal" 86–88).

There is certainly role reversal in Galatians (those previously in covenant with Israel's God are now outside, and *vice versa*). Furthermore, Garlington's analysis showing that Deut 27:26 is fundamentally about apostasy is exactly on target. Moreover, his argument has the apparent benefit of associating the *under a curse* (ὑπὸ κατάραν) phrase of 3:10 with the *let him be accursed* (ἀνάθεμα ἔστω) language of 1:8–9.[5]

While all this is promising, I do not ultimately find Garlington's overall reading convincing, for several reasons.

1. It essentially implies that Paul wholly subverts the biblical passage he is citing for support. While it is not to be assumed that Paul only uses the Hebrew Scriptures in their original

5 Note that the Greek terms differ, unlike the connection between 3:10, 13.

sense and nothing more—he in fact reads the texts in the light of the eschatological revelation of Jesus as the Messiah, and he certainly applies other passages typologically—this particular subversion does not appear to be in character. Compare e.g. to his surface re-reading of Deut 30:12 in Rom 10:6, or indeed his handling of Hab 2:4 here in v 12: a careful look at the original contexts reveals eschatological anticipation. Deut 27, however, is directly and squarely about how to live with Yahweh under Torah, and Paul's use of it is comparable to his use of Lev 18:5 in v 11.

2 Not only is the original context of Deut 27 about Torah on a *conceptual* level. Equally crucially, it is so *verbally* and *rhetorically* as well, and Paul's use of it in fact rubs our noses in Torah and its claims. As it stands, Deut 27:26 LXX, and therefore Gal 3:10, emphasizes that one must "remain in *all* the things in the book of Torah, to do *them*" (πᾶσιν τοῖς γεγραμμένοις ἐν τῷ βιβλίῳ τοῦ νόμου τοῦ ποιῆσαι αὐτά)—features of the text for which Garlington does not sufficiently account.[6] This is reminiscent of Paul's later warning in 5:3 that whoever becomes circumcised will be obligated to keep *the whole Torah* (ὀφειλέτης ἐστὶν ὅλον τὸν νόμον ποιῆσαι). All of which means that if Paul is intending to subvert the original meaning of the verse and reapply it to the Messiah, it appears that he has failed on the rhetorical level. Had he wanted to do what Garlington suggests, the obvious text would surely be Gen 12:3, where God promises to curse those who curse Abraham.

3 If we are to take v 10 as referring to apostasy from God by not clinging to the Messiah, then to be consistent, that reading would need to be followed through to Paul's resolution of the problem of v 10 in v 13. That would then come down to

6 In "Role Reversal" 95–99, Garlington's treatment of Deut 27:26 offers extensive attention to various contextual features as well as the LXX's choice of ἐμμένει as a rendering for the Heb יָקִים but passes over this fundamental aspect of the text. His commentary is likewise silent regarding the significance of the phrase *all the things* and misses the connection to 5:3.

> something like: "Christ has redeemed those of us who apostatized from God by rejecting Christ." This of course will not work, since Paul's claim in v 13 is that the Messiah died specifically under Torah's curse, *as an apostate from the law* in terms of Deut 21:23. Moreover, such a take on 3:13 would sacrifice the apparent parallel to 4:4–5, where the *redemption* is very different, i.e. a liberation from Torah itself.[7]

Along with 4:4–5, there are further features of the Galatians text that cohere better by way of a different reading, as I hope to illustrate below. Among these is the fact that for Paul, a covenant cannot simply be set aside (cf v 15), and he most emphatically views Torah as a covenant (see 4:24). As in Rom 7:1–4, and already alluded to in Gal 2:19, his theology requires a specific mechanism of dying to Torah, and if we explore 3:10–13 in that light, the coherence of the letter's narrative comes to the surface.

Under the Terms of an Oath

A number of years ago, Joseph Braswell offered a different resolution to these difficulties,[8] although I am not aware that any major commentary has borrowed his insights (as I do).

In Braswell's view, "under a curse" is not another way of saying "accursed." It is rather an assertion that the threat of a curse hangs over someone due to an oath. This removes not only the difficulties stated above; it also relieves us from assuming Paul has an unstated premise in verse 10 (i.e. that no one does in fact remain in all things written in the law, or can).

I believe that something like what Braswell argued is necessary

7 Garlington himself ("Role Reversal" 117) recognizes the connection to 4:4–5, but does not appear to recognize that it compromises his reading of 3:10. In my view, Garlington's reading of v 13 is better suited to the proposal for v 10 which I discuss below than to his own.

8 Joseph P. Braswell, "'The Blessing of Abraham' Versus 'The Curse of the Law': Another Look at Gal 3:10–13" (*WTJ*, 53 [1991]), 73–91. It should be noted that I am not attempting to follow Braswell slavishly. His take is slightly more generalized than my own, but the idea is fundamentally similar.

to make good sense of how 3:10–14 fit within Paul's full argument in Galatians, and I wish both to defend his thesis with greater detail than he provided, as well as push through some of the implications for the immediate context. (The implications for the broader context, of course, are largely pursued throughout the course of the commentary.)

Gal 3:10: Under Ebal's Curse

Paul says that as many as who are of Torah are under a curse—subject to the terms of a curse-bearing oath. Although employing different terminology, in Numbers 5:21 (LXX) we find an example of a similar usage. When the priest is attempting to determine whether a suspected woman has committed adultery, he causes her to "enter into the oath of this curse" (ἐν τοῖς ὅρκοις τῆς ἀρᾶς ταύτης). Surely that language, which literally comes out to "in the oath of this curse," is every bit as strong as Paul's ὑπὸ κατάραν, yet it refers, not to someone *accursed*, but to someone subject to an oath which has the possibility of bringing down cursing.

Elsewhere, κατάρα is paired with ὅρκος in a manner in which *curse* and *oath* are parallel (e.g. Dan 9:11 LXX). In those instances (unlike Num 5:21), what is in view is a curse that had become *cursing*. The rhetorical parallel is nonetheless significant for our purposes, illustrating that, at base, to be "under curse" is simply to be "under oath."

This is similar to blessing, as well. The priest was called to place the blessing over and upon the people of Israel. The benediction placed YHWH's name "upon" Israel, and in consequence He promised to bless them (Num 6:27). Yet we know that blessing was not automatic; according to Lev 26, Deut 28, and elsewhere, such blessing came to those who were obedient, who remained faithful to the covenant.

And so likewise, we should understand that just as the blessing was pronounced over all Israel, *so too was the curse*, and it "kicked in"—became operative—when people were unfaithful to the covenant and departed from it.

In this regard, we must draw special attention to the dual blessing and cursing ceremony at Mounts Gerizim and Ebal. The corresponding curses are referred to by the LXX in Deuteronomy 11 (26, 28, 29). The curse was placed upon Mount Ebal, and corresponded to the blessing placed upon Mount Gerizim (Deut 11:29). These two mountains overlooked Shechem, and thus both blessing and curse were "over" Israel, promising life if the nation stayed within the covenant, and cursing if she departed. (Interestingly, *Ebal is taller than Gerizim,* implying that curse towered over blessing.) Half of the tribal representatives were to stand upon Mount Gerizim to bless the people; the other half were to stand on Mount Ebal for the curse—and the Levites (representatives of Torah) were to declare the curses to Israel "in a loud voice" (Deut 27:11ff).

These blessings and curses were to be pronounced from the mountains while "all the men of Israel" stood below (see Deut 27:14). *The implication of this oath ceremony upon Gerizim and Ebal, therefore, is that not only was Israel under a blessing; they were also under a curse.* This is the corporate pronouncement of Torah's sanctions over all Israel.

Moreover, while this is surely the curse to which Paul refers in Gal 3:10, it is important to underscore that none of the blessings of Gerizim refer to "the blessing of Abraham" which Paul refers to in Gal 3:8–9. *Torah offered the curse which Paul has in view, but not the blessing.*

Furthermore, it is significant that the altar made of uncut stones, upon which were to be written "all the words of this law," was to be erected, not upon Gerizim, but upon Ebal (Deut 27:4–8). These are cues that teach us to see the curse-orientation of Torah.

In Deuteronomy, immediately following the instructions for placing the blessing and curse upon Gerizim and Ebal, respectively, YHWH instructs Israel regarding His (singular) chosen place of worship (Deut 12), which ultimately of course turned out to be Jerusalem.

Thus, we can see that back of everything in Paul's letter is a profound insight regarding the Jerusalem-centric, Israel-orientation of Torah. This "Jerusalem below" is "in slavery with her children," because it sits below the curse, bound to slavery by an oath (cf Gal 4:25). This Jerusalem, however, is not the mother of those in the Messiah, who belong to the free "Jerusalem above" (4:26).

The Ebal–Gerizim connection is especially germane to Galatians 3:10, of course, because Paul supports his "under a curse" assertion by appealing to Deut 27:26—one of the chapters devoted to providing for the blessing and cursing event.[9]

In Paul's argumentative context, the curse of Torah pronounced upon Ebal stands in contrast to the blessing of Abraham referred to in verses 7–9. Paul is saying that Torah is a roadblock to the enjoyment of the Abrahamic promise. Those under Torah must live under its Jew–Gentile terms—which are among the *all things* mentioned in Deut 27:26—and those terms introduce an incompatibility with the full integration "in Abraham" promised by the eschatological blessing.[10] But meanwhile, Torah carries a curse-bound oath against those who would turn away from its authority.

Beyond the specifics of Ebal's curses, there is a somewhat more general aspect that this reading affirms: in Paul's view, a covenant (which Torah was; see 4:24) cannot simply be discarded or ignored. We know this is his view, because he says so outright in the section immediately following our passage (v 15). If the Abrahamic covenant could not simply be set aside in favour of Torah, Paul's assumption here would seem to be that neither may Torah simply be set aside in favour of the covenantal revelation of the Messiah.

We are not, however, left to mere inferences to determine that this is Paul's view. He articulates this very position very clearly in Rom 7:1–2, where he writes that just as a woman is bound to her husband so long as he lives, so the one under Torah is subject to Torah as long as he lives. There is no possibility of simple departure, which constitutes apostasy and incurs Torah's curse; something else is necessary.

Gal 3:13: Redeemed from Ebal's Threat

Galatian 3:10, therefore, raises the problem of Torah sealing in its adherents, and of course throughout the context, Paul has been presenting life in the Messiah as incompatible with remaining under Torah.

9 It is also interesting to note that Abram's first place of worship upon entering the land promised to him was at Shechem, under the shadow of Gerizim (Gen 12:6–7; cf Judg 9:7).

10 This implied incompatibility raises the rhetorical question of 3:21: "Is Torah therefore against the promises of God?" While Paul's answer is emphatically negative, the very fact that the question is raised by his form of argument is illuminating.

This apparently raises a rather vicious circle.

Paul, however, answers this conundrum in verse 13.[11] "Christ redeemed us from the curse of Torah, becoming a curse on our behalf, just as it is written: 'Cursed is every one who hangs upon a tree.'"

While this verse is usually taken to mean that Christ bore the wrath of God's curse again sin in general (a proposition that is true enough), that does not arise from Paul's own line of argument here. He is dealing with the difficulty of Israel being bound to Torah, a covenantal arrangement that is incompatible with the fulfillment of the Abrahamic promises.

Moreover, the term for *redemption* which Paul uses here, *exagorazo* (ἐξαγοράζω), is relatively infrequent in his writings. He uses it in this letter also in 4:5; elsewhere, only in Eph 5:16 and Col 4:5. In neither of those latter two cases does it refer to redemption from sin, but to redemption of time.

In 4:5, Paul has been speaking expansively regarding Torah's role as a *paidagogos*, and has said that under Torah, Israel differed nothing from a slave. When "we" were children (minors), he says, we were enslaved under the elements of the *kosmos* (the first world/creation). It is in that context that Paul says, "When the fullness of time had come, God sent His Son, born from a woman, born under Torah, in order that He might *redeem* those under Torah, in order that we may receive the adoption" (4:4–5).

What should be clear from the usage in 4:5 is that it is not sin's penalty that is to the forefront, but rather, the slavery that characterized life under Torah. *Redemption* should be understood in the basic sense of *liberation* (as with the "redemption from Egypt" theme so frequent in the Hebrew Scriptures) rather than in the less common sense of *paying a debt*.

Moreover, *adoption* in this case is not set over against a theme of

11 Galatians 3:10–13 is essentially a thematic chiasm (and to a lesser degree, a verbal chiasm, as well). The theme of Torah's curse is the focus of 10 and 13, while verses 11–12 are focused upon life in terms of the law or faith. This is fundamentally why I have chosen here to treat, first, vv 10 and 13–14, and then vv 11–12. In the main Exposition section of the commentary, I of course handle the verses in sequence.

downright alienation from God, but rather of *childhood*. The metaphors are not drawn straight from real life—or rather, not from what we know as adoption. In Paul's scenario, the one who receives this "adoption" may already have been in the family.

A child differs nothing from a slave until the time set by the father (4:2), but normally, in real-world cases, that "time" would refer to a given year or age. In this case, however, the "time" is not based upon Israel's age or maturity; it is "eschatological time"—the "fullness of time" when God sends His own Son and dramatically intervenes in the course of Israel's history under Torah. Rather than a simple coming of age, in this case, release from the *paidagogos* requires a redemption enacted by the true mature Son.

Thus, in Israel's case, the "adoption" which concerns Paul is not a transfer from utter pagan darkness to what we generally call "sonship." It is rather an event which transfers "us" (believing Israelites; people like Paul who had been under Torah but were now brought to the Messiah) from a status of children unable and unqualified to participate in the eschatological fulfillment of the promises to Abraham, to a position of present inheritance.

My claim is that chapter 4:1–5 should be understood as an exegesis of the cryptic elements of 3:10, 13–14. Because the Messiah was born of a woman, born under Torah as a representative of Israel, His death upon a cross—the penalty against apostates from Torah—serves as the representative release from Torah.

This likewise explains that other cryptic statement earlier in the letter: "For through Torah, I myself died to Torah, so that I might live to God" (2:19). It is through Torah's curse against apostasy which was applied to the Messiah that Paul himself was liberated from Torah's rule. Because he is united to the Messiah, who died under the curse of Torah, the curse of Torah holds no more threat against him, and he is released into the freedom of the new covenant.[12]

---

12 This is not the only time Paul speaks in this way. He says the same thing also in Rom 7:1–6. Torah is binding on someone only as long as he lives, but if he dies, Torah has no more sway. So those who had been under Torah "have died to Torah through the body of the Messiah, so that you may belong to another: the one who was raised

We can now go yet further with the Ebal and Gerizim connection. In that regard, to this point we have explored only the instructions in Deuteronomy for the ceremony. Now, however, we turn to the actual event in Joshua 8 where the task was carried out. That description by itself is not particularly remarkable; it is essentially a straightforward record of the carrying out of what had been commanded earlier (Josh 8:30–34).

What is remarkable about the narrative in Josh 8, however, is the event in the verse immediately preceding (Josh 8:29). There, following the burning of Ai, Joshua (Greek ’Ιησοῦς, *Jesus*) hung the Gentile king of Ai upon a tree (!). At evening, he had him taken down, thrown at the entrance of the city gate, and buried by a stone heap.

Understood in context, this event at the entrance of Canaan is part of the complex of events which sealed Israel into a separate existence from the Gentiles, symbolizing geographically and militarily what the enforcement of Torah's oath accomplished covenantally.

Now, surely we cannot miss the connection between the king hanging upon a tree in Josh 8 and the king hanging upon a tree in Gal 3:13. Whereas the first Joshua-Jesus hung the Gentile king upon a tree as part of Israel's separation from the Gentiles, the new Joshua-Jesus Himself hangs upon a tree, in order to reverse the separation and reintegrate Gentiles and Jews in Himself.

Galatians 3:13 therefore depicts the work of the cross as the means by which Israel died to Torah (cf Gal 2:19), and the events and laws which separated her from the Gentiles were overcome.

Gal 3:14: Abraham's Promise Released

This reading helps further with the transition from 3:13 to 14. Under the traditional reading, Paul's logic is inscrutable. What does verse 13 have to do particularly with Gentiles and Abraham, and how does it relate to the reception of the Spirit?

But recognizing that Paul is talking about how the Messiah's death provides a transition from the rule of the Mosaic covenant into the

---

from the dead, in order that we may bear fruit to God" (Rom 7:4).

reception of the eschatological fulfillment of the promises to Abraham puts the puzzle pieces together. Because the Messiah has brought "Abraham" out from under Torah, the blessing promised Abraham—that is, the promise of Gentiles being fully integrated *into* him, full partners with his own descendants—can come about. Likewise, the Holy Spirit is the eschatological gift, the firstfruits of the new creation. It is precisely because in the Messiah's death there is a shift from Torah—which belonged to the old creation—that the new creation Spirit can be enjoyed.

Note that this directly parallels the immediate movement to mention of the Spirit in verse 6 of chapter 4, as well. The overall structure of thought is the same, but more explicit in Paul's later development of the theme. Again, this similarity reinforces the notion that the *redemption* in 3:13 is the same as in 4:5.

Gal 3:11–12: Torah *vs* "Faith"[13]

It now remains to give brief attention to the significance of Paul's citation of Scripture in the intervening verses, 3:11–12. These quotations are of Lev 18:5 and Hab 2:4.

Paul twice handles Lev 18:5 in a way which contrasts life under Torah with life in the Messiah. We will not treat Rom 10 here, although Paul's statements there are complementary to what he says in Galatians.

In Gal 3:11–12, the Leviticus text is juxtaposed with Hab 2:4. As is true of Rom 10, the fundamental point centers upon a movement from the old covenant period (and thus concern with the things of the law itself) to the new (and thus concern with the eschatological fulfillment of God's righteousness accomplished in the Messiah and the Spirit).

We cannot stress enough that in this very epistle, Paul himself makes a strong connection between *doing* and *life*. He writes in Gal 6:8–9, "Because he who sows unto his flesh, from the flesh will reap corruption; but he who sows unto the Spirit, from the Spirit will reap *life everlasting*. Now as those *doing good*, let us not become disheartened, for in the proper time, we will reap if we do not give up." The apostle thus is unafraid to say for his own gospel that *the one who continues in doing*

13 What follows is adapted from *Two Covenants*, 61–66.

good will live. A stronger analogy to Lev 18:5 could scarcely be sought.

It is my view that in Gal 3:11–12, the contrast Paul sets forth is between faith as eschatological, on the one hand, and life in Torah as immanent and therefore temporary and pre-eschatological, on the other. It is from here, to be sure, that the prevalent "believing" versus "doing" notions usually derive, since Paul says, "but the law is not from faith, but 'the one doing them shall live in them'" (Gal 3:12).

With regard to the citation of Hab 2:4, we must note that Paul is again appealing to a text that was written during the period of the Mosaic covenant. A reading that suggests that Lev 18 requires salvation by works, while Hab 2 calls for salvation by faith, is simply untenable. In Paul's redemptive-historical scheme, both texts fall within the same overarching period. Habakkuk himself was "under the law."

Even further, Hab 2:4 and Lev 18:5 stand in a great deal more continuity than is often appreciated. While Habakkuk is not as close to Lev 18:5 as is Deut 30, the fundamental meaning is certainly not in direct antithesis. The word for "faith" in Hab 2:4 derives from the Hebrew word *'emunah,* which means *steadfastness* or *faithfulness.* (The Greek rendering *pistis* can be read either as *faith* or as *faithfulness;* the Hebrew concepts tend to shade over into one another.)[14] How does Paul's appropriation of this text relate to its original meaning?

The little prophetic book of Habakkuk, written on an occasion when God's people are being judged by nations much more wicked than themselves, is a meditation upon the problem of evil. How to justify God, not so much because He is judging Israel (which is deserved), but because He does so by the instrumentality of those who are even worse? The overall answer is that God's righteous one must live by faith that God will ultimately vindicate Himself and His faithful people; the faithful must remain steadfast in the face of a situation that cannot be comprehended.

Thus the faith in question in Hab 2:4 has to do with the horizon; we may even say that it is *eschatological* (notice the eschatological overtones

14 In fact, in Qumran, Hab 2:4 was interpreted as referring to faithful Torah-observance (*1 QpHab* 7:10–11; 8:1–3). See Dunn, *Theology of the Apostle Paul*, pp. 373–374.

of 2:14—the earth will be filled with the knowledge of the glory of Yahweh, even as the waters cover the sea). This fits with Paul's strange language in Gal 3:23–24, which speaks of "the faith" coming, with the Messiah. Perhaps the apostle is even calling the Messiah Himself "the faith" (or referring to the *faithfulness* of God, revealed in the Messiah), but more likely he is primarily referring to the faith, or faithfulness, *of* the Messiah (taking the recurring phrase *pistis Christou* as a subjective genitive).

Paul introduces the Habakkuk quotation with the statement: "that no one is justified by [or *in*][15] the law is evident." This reading suggests again that the justification which concerns Paul is not "immanent" within Torah; its advent comes through the Messiah, Torah's goal as God's righteousness.[16]

Stepping back to 3:11–12, then, it appears that the most satisfactory solution to this text is that Paul is once again focusing upon the "by/in *them*" of Lev 18:5. He has, after all, just warned that all those who are "of the works of the law" (by which I take him to mean, all those who are in the Torah covenant) are under a curse to uphold *all things* written in the book of the law (3:10). In that case, 3:11–12 is a reminder of the critical choice that is faced: life in the law—or life in the Messiah who has been now revealed to faith.

This reading is supported, I believe, by Paul's two phrases, "of the works of the law" (Greek *ex ergôn nomou*) and "of faith" (*ek pisteôs*). If I am correct that the former refers to those who are enrolled under the Torah covenant,[17] it is natural to take the latter as covenantal membership in the Messiah, given the terminology of 3:23–24, which

15 The Greek word usually translated *by* is *en;* the most usual meaning of this word is locative/spatial (thus *in*). How much this locative idea enters into Paul's argument is a matter for consideration.

16 We can look at this matter of justification and Torah in two ways: (1) people under Torah were justified (counted righteous and forgiven), but the source of their justification was God's consideration of the future coming of the Messiah as a propitiation for sins (see Rom 3:24–26); (2) in the Messiah an *eschatological* justification has arrived which was not available under the time of "flesh"; it is this great salvation-historical act which could not therefore be obtained under Torah. See the main Exposition of this commentary, particularly on 2:16.

17 See above on 3:10, as well as *Two Covenants*, 20–30.

identifies the Messiah's advent as the coming of "faith." Since Paul can hardly mean that the subjective human disposition or activity of faith only arrived with the Messiah (he has, after all, just spoken of the faith of Abraham in 3:6–9), we are surely justified in seeing "faith" here as referring to the Messiah's own faith.[18]

The primary accent for Paul here, then, is not, "*Do* this and live" (*doing* is bad, or even *doing* is bad if connected with *living*), but rather, "Do *this* and live" (the time of living in Torah is over).

That this is the correct focus is confirmed by Paul's emendation of the structure (but not the meaning) of the Leviticus text. Whereas both the Hebrew and the LXX have "if a man does/will do," Paul creates the participle, "the doing one." The result is a parallelism with the Habakkuk text which works as follows:

Ὁ δίκαιος	*ἐκ πίστεως*	*ζήσεται*	
Ὁ ποιήσας	*αὐτὰ*	*ζήσεται*	*ἐν αὐτοῖς*

Thus, in English:

the righteous one	*from faith*	*shall live*	
the doing one	*these things*	*shall live*	*by/in them*

Above, the first line is Gal 3:11 (citing Hab 2:4); the second is 3:12 (citing Lev 18:5). It is readily seen that this structure is apparently *intentional*—and ill-suited for placing the contrast between "doing" and "faith." The participle "the doing one" corresponds, not to "from faith," but to the substantive "the righteous one." Instead, "from faith" corresponds to "these things," which refer to the commandments of Torah. The extra phrase of the second quotation, "by/in them," referring again to Torah's commandments, only doubles the effect. The contrast is not between

18 As noted above, this "faith" (*pistis*) likely refers to the Messiah's own faithfulness; He is the very embodiment of *pistis* who has now come. Cf. esp. Gal 2:20: Paul lives by the faith(fulness) of the Son of God, "who loved me and gave Himself for me." On the proper translation of the Greek phrase *pistis Christou* (and related phrases), see especially Richard Hays, *The Faith of Jesus Christ*.

generalized "doing" and generalized "faith," but between *Torah's commandments and eschatological faith*—in short, between Torah and the Messiah, between old covenant and new.[19]

While this reading can doubtless benefit from further nuance for the sake of clarity, it seems to me that something like it is necessary if we are to explain a number of biblical features, not least Paul's own connection between *doing* and *life* (e.g. Rom 8:13; Gal 6:8–9). The one who is within the Torah covenant must do the things of Torah; the one who is within the new covenant (that is, in the Messiah) must do the things of the Messiah: he must put to death the things of the flesh and live by the new creation Spirit.[20]

The antithesis between Paul's gospel and Lev 18:5 is therefore not fundamentally governed by an antithesis between grace and legalism. That antithesis certainly can be deduced from Paul, as elsewhere he makes manifestly clear that justification and life are a gift of grace which cannot be earned (Rom 4:4–8; 6:23). But while such an antithesis is necessary, it is simply not the issue which concerns Paul in connection with Lev 18:5.

Rather, the apostle is claiming two related things:

(1) It is not possible for "flesh" to bring in the new creation; that is something that only God Himself can do—and has in fact done in the Messiah.

(2) New creation life is governed by the Messiah, rather than Torah, which belongs to the old creation epoch.

The first of these points is a reminder that only the God who "makes

19 Cf. James D. G. Dunn, *Theology of Paul the Apostle:* "What is in view [in Lev 18:5] is the way life is lived within and by the community of Israel, the covenant people.... keeping the law is thought of primarily as the way of living appropriate to the covenant and its continuance" (p. 152). Note also Ezek 20:5–26, which Dunn rightly points to as a prophetic application of Lev 18:5.

20 This mandate is a recapitulation of the experience of the Messiah, to whom the believer is united. Christ died in the flesh, and thus was raised to life by the Spirit. Since the believer participates in this reality, he is to work out that reality practically in his members. This is Paul's logic in his movement from Rom 8:1–4 to 8:5–17. He who, by virtue of being joined to the crucified and risen Messiah, is no longer in the flesh but in the Spirit (8:9), must now put his mind on the things of the Spirit (i.e. the new creation) and put to death the deeds of the flesh (i.e. the old creation).

the dead live and calls into being the things which do not exist" (Rom 4:17) can bring about the resurrection life of the new creation; the second is a reminder that those who participate in that resurrection life must live and walk in its terms (cf. Gal 5:25).

The reader will have noticed that in the foregoing, I have provided alternative ways of reading the preposition in Lev 18:5: "He who does them shall live *in* them," or "He who does them shall live *by* them."[21] The underlying term, both in Hebrew and in Greek,[22] may rightly be understood locatively (*in*) or instrumentally (*by*), and I have not attempted to answer definitively which is to the fore. The coordinate points of Paul's interest in the Leviticus text suggest that there may be a "both/and" in view. Torah is not the *instrument* of bringing about the new creation, and thus one does not arrive at life *by* works of Torah. But likewise, Torah is not the *sphere* of the new creation, and thus one who is in the Messiah does not live *in* works of Torah.

Returning to 3:11, we can see the nature of the transition between v 10 and v 11 (δὲ). On the one hand, Paul says, all who are under Torah are subject to its curse against apostasy. But remaining under Torah is not an option, since it is not in Torah where eschatological justification will occur, because after all, the righteous one will live from (an eschatological) faith—one which is not compatible with life under Torah. Thus vv 11–12 compound the tension posed by the problem raised in v 10. Verse 13 deals directly with the problem of v 10, as we have seen, preparing the way for the rest of the chapter to deal more thoroughly with the issues at play in vv 11–12.

Summary

To sum up, taking ὑπὸ κατάραν in the sense of *under a curse-bearing oath* is preferable to taking it in the sense of *accursed*, for at least the following reasons:

1 Not all those under Torah were *accursed*, but all *were*

21 So too with Paul's negative statement in Galatians 3:11: "Now *by/in* Torah no one will be justified before God."

22 The Hebrew preposition is *b*ᵉ; the Greek is *en*.

subject to the curse-bearing oath pronounced upon Mt Ebal. Moreover, it is simply not true that in its own terms, it was impossible to keep the law, as is made evident by Scripture itself (see especially 2 Chron 34:32 in connection with v 21 of the same chapter; cf also Lk 1:6, where Zacharias and Elizabeth are both said to be *blameless* in connection with "all the commandments and ordinances of the Lord").

2 In the strongly parallel statements in 4:3–5, Paul is not referring to the impossibility of Torah-keeping, but to the matter of being released from the rule of a *paidagogos,* so that those under Torah can enter into the inheritance of mature sons.

3 In the following context of 3:15–18, Paul builds directly on the principle that a covenant cannot simply be altered or amended, the very presupposition underlying 3:10, 13—necessitating the death of the Messiah in order to liberate Israel from Torah.

In thus taking ὑπὸ κατάραν in Gal 3:10 to refer to Torah's curse against apostasy (departure from Torah), we now have the elements to piece together a coherent reading of 3:10–14 within the context of the letter. (For more on the preceding and succeeding context, of course, see the Exposition.)

Paul has just reminded the Galatians that God had promised to Abraham blessing for the Gentiles *in* himself, something inconceivable in terms of Torah. Meanwhile, all those under Torah were oath-bound to remain there and live by its terms rather than the terms of the coming eschatological faith. Departure would mean incurring a curse. Given that Torah represented a wall between Jews and Gentiles, how then could the promise of an Israelite-Gentile people united in Abraham come about?

The Messiah has provided the resolution; He has borne the curse of apostasy Himself, so that those in Him are enabled to move out from under the shadow of Mount Ebal. As sharers in the Messiah's death, they too have died, and are freed from the rule of Torah. They therefore can now live in the eschatological blessing, where Jew and Gentile share freely and equally together in the Messiah and the Spirit of the new creation.

Building on what he has just presupposed—that a covenant cannot simply be annulled or amended once it is in force[23]—Paul argues that just as Torah could not be amended, neither could the even earlier covenant promise made to Abraham (3:15–18). Torah is thus not a codicil that refines the Abrahamic covenant; it is a temporary measure until the seed of promise should arrive to introduce a new order of things (3:19–25). With His arrival, the Levitical hierarchy of persons, places, and times is no more: all those baptized into the Messiah have been clothed with Him, so that just as He is the true heir, so are they (3:26–29).

23 This is unstated, but undergirds Paul's argument in 3:10–13. Rather than simply change some rules in Torah to fit with the new covenant context, God redeems those under Torah—liberates them and places them into a different covenant.

APPENDIX 2

Chronological Table

*I*N MY VIEW, THERE IS A CLEAR SEQUENCE OF EVENTS IN PAUL'S LIFE between his conversion and the Jerusalem Council. This sequence can be established *via* a careful comparison of Galatians and Acts.

While critical scholars tend to take delight in criticizing Luke's factuality (never mind his chronology), in my view presupposing his unreliability is taking the easy way out—just as scholars who posit incoherence and self-contradiction in Paul thereby avoid grappling with the hard questions in his letters.

Frequently, conservative scholars too have difficulty establishing this chronology. I suggest that much of the reason for this is bound to wrong assumptions: in particular, the view that the meeting described in Gal 2 *must* correspond to the Jerusalem Council of Acts 15.

In addition, some scholars commit themselves to the view that the letter must be written to ethnic Galatians, and of course this rules out the possibility of harmonizing very much with Acts, since Luke provides no record of the apostle ever preaching in North Galatia.

I have dealt with these latter two assumptions, in particular, in the introductory material (see "Galatians as Biography"). As far as suppositions regarding the supposed unreliability of Luke go, clearly much rests upon one's view of Scripture. Nonetheless, one need not believe in inerrancy in order to embrace a chronology that has demonstrable coherence. One needs only to refuse to be committed to believing that Luke simply *must* have got things wrong.

For details regarding the chronology in the table on the reverse, I again refer the reader to the introductory matter. I have provided this appendix on the assumption that more visual readers may appreciate a more visual representation of the sequence of events.

Conversion to Council: A Pauline Chronological Table

Location	*Event*	*References*
DAMASCUS	Conversion & call.	ACTS 9:1–19 / GAL 1:15–16
DAMASCUS & ARABIA	Post-conversion activity.	ACTS 9:20–25 / GAL 1:17
JERUSALEM	**First Jerusalem visit.** *(3 years after conversion)*	ACTS 9:26–30 / GAL 1:18–20
TARSUS (CILICIA) & ANTIOCH (SYRIA)	Return to home area; helping with establishment of church in Antioch.	ACTS 9:30; 11:25–26 / GAL 1:21
JERUSALEM	**Second Jerusalem visit.** *(famine relief; 14 years after conversion)*	ACTS 11:27–30; 12:25 / GAL 2:1–10
ANTIOCH	Return to Antioch; call to First Missionary Journey.	ACTS 12:25–13:3
CYPRUS, PAMPHYLIA, GALATIA	First Missionary Journey; Paul plants Galatian churches.	ACTS 13:4–14:25
ANTIOCH (SYRIA)	(Extended furlough) Peter visits Antioch. Circumcision party in Antioch—Peter breaks off table fellowship with Gentiles. Paul rebukes Peter. Judaizers enter Galatia. Paul writes Galatians.	ACTS 14:26–28 GAL 2:11 ACTS 15:1–2 / GAL 2:12 GAL 2:14–21
JERUSALEM	**Third Jerusalem visit**: Jerusalem Council.	ACTS 15:3–29

APPENDIX 3

Galatians and the Farewell Discourse

THERE ARE A REMARKABLE NUMBER OF ECHOES between Galatians and Jesus' Farewell Discourse recorded in the Gospel of John. The resonance is at its strongest in Galatians 5, but is also noticeable elsewhere in the letter. The chapter, and more broadly, the letter, in many respects resembles an exposition of relevant aspects of the Discourse.

This of course sounds unlikely on the face of it, given the current dominant scholarly assumptions regarding both the Gospel tradition as well as Paul's knowledge of Jesus' life and teaching. The acid test, however, is in comparison of the actual texts. What follows is a list of resemblances, most of which include not only similar general concepts but verbal parallels.

1 John 15:1–8, 16 treats an extended metaphor of *fruit-bearing via* remaining in the vine, Jesus; and much of the surrounding material regards Jesus' promise to send the *Spirit* in His own place as the one who will communicate the things of Jesus to His disciples (e.g. Jn 14:26; 15:26–27; 16:5–15). Meanwhile, the virtue list of Gal 5 is about bearing *the fruit of the Spirit* (Gal 5:22).
2 In John 15:6, Jesus warns that whoever does not remain "in Me" will be thrown away as a branch and cast into the fire; Gal 5:4 warns that those who seeking to be justified by Torah have been *severed* from Christ.
3 John 15:12–17 highlights the commandment of *love* for one another (cf also Jn 13:34–35), while Gal 5:13–14 highlights serving one another through *love*, which fulfills Torah.
4 In John 14:27, Christ's *peace* stands in contrast to that of the *kosmos*. Jesus says He leaves His peace with them, just after saying that He will send the *Spirit* to them (Jn 14:26). Then Jn

15:9–11 deals with *love* and *joy*. Meanwhile, Gal 5:22 lists *love, joy* and *peace* as the first three aspects of the fruit of the *Spirit*.

5 The aforementioned peace which Jesus gives is in connection with a repeated encouragement that the disciples not be *troubled* in heart (μὴ ταρασσέσθω ὑμῶν ἡ καρδία; 14:1, 27). The opponents in Galatia are repeatedly styled as *troublers* (Gal 1:7; 5:10, 12; cf 6:17, although 5:12 employs a different Greek term).

6 There is a repeated metaphor of *following/way/going* in both passages (Jn 13:36–37; 14:4–6; Gal 5:7, 16, 18, 25).

7 Jesus in Jn 16:11 says that the Holy Spirit will convict the world of judgment, because the ruler of this world is judged; Gal 6:14 says that the world itself has been crucified.

8 Jesus speaks of the *travail* of birthpangs in Jn 16:21; Paul says he himself is having that *travail* for the Galatians in Gal 4:19.

9 There is a fairly strong theme of persecution in both passages (Jn 15:18ff; Gal 1:13, 23; 4:29; 5:11; 6:12).

10 Jesus promises, "Because I live, you shall live also" (ὅτι ἐγὼ ζῶ καὶ ὑμεῖς ζήσετε, Jn 14:19), adding that whoever keeps His commandments and loves Him will be loved by Jesus and the Father, and even further that the Father, Jesus, and the disciples will indwell one another ("I am in My Father, and you in me, and I in you"); Paul in turn says, "With the Messiah I have been crucified; now I live no longer, but the Messiah lives in me: But what life I now live in the flesh, I live in faith—the faith of the Son of God Himself (ζῶ δὲ οὐκέτι ἐγώ, ζῇ δὲ ἐν ἐμοὶ Χριστός· ὃ δὲ νῦν ζῶ ἐν σαρκί, ἐν πίστει ζῶ τῇ τοῦ υἱοῦ τοῦ θεοῦ), who loved me and gave Himself for me" (Gal 2:20).

11 It is in the Farewell Discourse that Jesus elevates the disciples' status from slaves to friends (Jn 15:15), and also speaks in the context of privileges of sonship (e.g. Jn 14:18, 21; 16:26–28). Galatians, in particular 3:23–4:10, depicts Israel's role as possessing a status differing nothing from slavery (οὐδὲν διαφέρει δούλου, 4:1) due to subjection to the *paidagogos* and the elements of the world, a status altered in the Messiah to one of inheritance as mature sons.

12 In His high priestly prayer concluding the Discourse, Jesus prays that His disciples "may *all* be *one*" (πάντες ἓν ὦσιν)by virtue of being "in Us" (Jn 17:21); Paul says in Gal 3:26–28 that all (πάντες) who are in the Messiah Jesus are thereby one in Him (εἷς ἐστε ἐν Χριστῷ Ἰησοῦ). In Jn 17:21, Jesus adds that this is so the world may believe that the Father has *sent* Him. In Gal 4:4, God (described in vv 2, 6 as Father) *sent* His Son.

Beyond these relatively clear correspondences, there are further relationships which could perhaps have been in the back of Paul's mind. For example, does Peter's departure from table fellowship with Gentiles (Gal 2:11ff) make Paul think of Jn 13:18, where Jesus cites Ps 41:9, "He who eats My bread has lifted up his heel against Me"? Interestingly, provision for the poor comes up in both close contexts (Jn 15:29–30; Gal 2:10), although admittedly, in John it is incidental, based on a false supposition.

We must always beware of undue "parallelomania,"[1] but the sheer number and clarity of the correspondences between the Farewell Discourse in John and the letter to the Galatians surely suggests something beyond accidental resemblance. This raises interesting questions regarding general scholarly assumptions concerning the supposed lateness of John's Gospel as well as how well-acquainted Paul really was with the words and deeds of Jesus.

1 Cf Samuel Sandmel, "Parallelomania," *Journal of Biblical Literature* 81 (1962):1–13.

Select Bibliography

Note: This bibliography is not intended to be exhaustive. I have limited the works mentioned here to materials cited in the commentary or that otherwise made some significant contribution to my study.

Barclay, John M. G. *Obeying the Truth: Paul's Ethics in Galatians.* Vancouver: Regent College, 2005 (1988).

Belleville, Linda L. "'Under Law': Structural Analysis and the Pauline Concept of Law in Galatians 3.21–4.11," *Journal for the Study of the New Testament* 26 (1986), 53–78.

Betz, Hans Dieter. *Galatians: A Commentary on Paul's Letter to the Churches in Galatia. Hermeneia—A Critical and Historical Commentary on the Bible,* Helmut Koester *et al,* ed board. Philadelphia: Fortress, 1979.

Braswell, Joseph P. "'The Blessing of Abraham' versus 'The Curse of the Law': Another Look at Gal 3:10–13," *Westminster Theological Journal* 53 (1991), 73–91.

Bruce, F. F. *The Epistle to the Galatians: A Commentary on the Greek Text. The New International Greek Testament Commentary,* I. Howard Marshall and W. Ward Gasque, gen. eds. Grand Rapids: Eerdmans, 1982.

Burton, Ernest De Witt. *A Critical and Exegetical Commentary on the Epistle to the Galatians. International Critical Commentary*. Edinburgh: T & T Clark, 1988 (1920).

Calvin, John. *The Epistle to the Galatians. Calvin's New Testament Commentaries,* Vol 11. T. H. L. Parker, trans. David W. Torrance and Thomas F. Torrance, eds. Grand Rapids: Eerdmans, 1965.

Collins, C. John. "The Eucharist as Christian Sacrifice: How Patristic Authors Can Help Us Read the Bible," *Westminster Theological Journal* 66 (2004), 1–23.

Dunn, James D. G. *The Epistle to the Galatians. Black's New Testament Commentary,* Henry Chadwick, gen. ed. Peabody, MA: Hendrickson, 1993.

———. *The Theology of Paul the Apostle*. Grand Rapids: Eerdmans, 1998.

Fee, Gordon D. *God's Empowering Presence: The Holy Spirit in the Letters of Paul.* Peabody, MA: Hendrickson, 1994.

Fredriksen, Paula. "Judaism, the Circumcision of Gentiles, and Apocalyptic Hope: Another Look at Galatians 1 and 2," *Journal of Theological Studies* 42 (1991), 532–564.

Fung, Ronald Y. K. *The Epistle to the Galatians. The New International Commentary on the New Testament,* Gordon Fee, gen. ed. Grand Rapids: Eerdmans, 1988.

Gallant, Tim. "Abraham's One True Heir? Galatians 3.16 and 'Identity Interchange." Available online at: http://biblicalstudiescenter.org/interpretation/gal3_16.htm

———. *Feed My Lambs: Why the Lord's Table Should Be Restored to Covenant Children.* Grande Prairie, AB: Pactum Reformanda, 2002.

———. *Sermons on Galatians.* Grande Prairie, AB: Pactum Reformanda, 2012.

———. *These Are Two Covenants: Reconsidering Paul on the Mosaic Law.* Grande Prairie, AB: Pactum Reformanda, 2012.

Garlington, Don. *An Exposition of Galatians: A New Perspective/Reformational Reading.* Eugene, OR: Wipf & Stock, 2003.

———. "Role Reversal and Paul's Use of Scripture in Galatians 3.10–13," *Journal for the Study of the New Testament* 19 (1997), 85–121.

George, Timothy. *Galatians. The New American Commentary: An Exegetical and Theological Exposition of the Holy Scripture NIV Text,* E. Ray Clendenen, gen. ed. Broadman & Holman, 1994.

Gordon, T. David. "A Note on Παιδαγωγος in Galatians 3.24–25," *New Testament Studies* 35/1 (1989), 150–154.

———. "The Problem at Galatia," *Interpretation* 41/1 (1987), 32–43.

Hays, Richard B. *Echoes of Scripture in the Letters of Paul.* New Haven: Yale University Press, 1989.

———. *The Faith of Jesus Christ: The Narrative Substructure of Galatians 3:1–4:11,* Second Ed. Grand Rapids: Eerdmans, 2002 (1983).

———. *The Letter to the Galatians: Introduction, Commentary, and Reflections,* in *The New Interpreter's Bible,* Vol XI. Leander Keck et al, eds. Nashville: Abingdon, 2000.

Jordan, James B. "Call Me Ishmael," Parts 1 & 2, *Biblical Horizons Newsletter* Nos. 117–118 (Niceville, FL: Biblical Horizons, 1999). Available online at http://www.biblicalhorizons.com/biblical-horizons/no-117-call-me-ishmael-part-1/ and http://www.biblicalhorizons.com/biblical-horizons/no-118-call-me-ishmael-part-2/

———. "The Meaning of Clean and Unclean," *Studies in Food and Faith 10*. Niceville, FL: Biblical Horizons, 1990.

———. "The Third Word." *Rite Reasons Newsletter*, No. 60. Niceville, FL, 1988. Available online at: http://www.biblicalhorizons.com/1998/11/

———. *Through New Eyes*. Brentwood, TN: Wolgemuth & Hyatt, 1988.

Leithart, Peter J. *The Baptized Body*. Moscow, ID: Canon Press, 2007.

———. "Mother Paul and the Children of Promise (Gal. 4:19–31)," pp 205–220 in *Obedient Faith: A Festschrift for Norman Shepherd*, P. Andrew Sandlin and John Barach, eds. Mount Hermon, CA: Kerygma, 2012.

Lightfoot, J. B. *St. Paul's Epistle to the Galatians: A Revised Text with Introduction, Notes and Dissertations*. Peabody, MA: Hendrickson, 1999 (1865).

Longenecker, Richard N. Galatians. *Word Biblical Commentary*, Vol 41, Bruce M. Metzger, gen. ed. Ralph P. Martin and Lynn Allan Losie, NT eds. Dallas: Word, 1990.

Martyn, J. Louis. *Galatians: A New Translation with Introduction and Commentary, The Anchor Bible*, Vol 33A. New York: Doubleday, 1997.

McKnight, Scot. *Galatians. The NIV Application Commentary*, Terry Muck, gen. ed. Grand Rapids: Eerdmans, 1995.

Moo, Douglas J. "'Law,' 'Works of the Law,' and Legalism in Paul," *Westminster Theological Journal* 45 (1983), 73–100.

Porter, Stanley E. *Idioms of the Greek New Testament, Second Edition*. Sheffield, England: Sheffield Academic Press, 1994 (1992).

Sanders, E. P. *Paul and Palestinian Judaism: A Comparison of Patterns of Religion*. Minneapolis: Fortress, 1977.

Thielman, Frank. *Paul and the Law: A Contextual Approach*. Downers Grove, IL: Inter-Varsity, 1994.

Westerholm, Stephen. *Israel's Law and the Church's Faith: Paul and His Recent Interpreters*. Eugene, OR: Wipf & Stock, 1999 (1988).

Witherington, Ben III. *Grace in Galatia: A Commentary on St. Paul's Letter to the Galatians*. Grand Rapids: Eerdmans, 1998.

Wright, N. T. "4QMMT and Paul: Justification, 'Works,' and Eschatology," pp 104–132 in *History and Exegesis: New Testament Essays in Honor of Dr E.*

Earle Ellis for His 80th Birthday, ed. Aang-Won (Aaron) Son. New York and London: T & T Clark, 2006.

———. *The Climax of the Covenant: Christ and the Law in Pauline Theology* (Minneapolis: Fortress, 1991).

———. *Justification: God's Plan and Paul's Vision*. Downers Grove, IL: IVP Academic, 2009.

———. "Paul and Qumran," *Bible Review* 14 (Oct 1998), 18, 54.

———. *Paul and the Faithfulness of God* (Minneapolis: Fortress, 2013).

———. *Paul for Everyone: Galatians and Thessalonians* (London: SPCK, 2004).

———. "Paul, Arabia, and Elijah (Galatians 1:17)," *Journal of Biblical Literature* 115/4 (1996), 683–692.

Young, Norman H. "*Paidagogos*: The Social Setting of a Pauline Metaphor," *Novum Testamentum* XXIX/2 (1987), 150–176.

Author & Literature Index

Scripture Index

www.ingramcontent.com/pod-product-compliance
Lightning Source LLC
LaVergne TN
LVHW010541100826
845148LV00001B/258

* 9 7 8 0 9 7 3 0 1 1 9 7 5 *